ENCYCLOPEDIA of

FACTS

ENCYCLOPEDIA of

AMAZING BUT TRUE ℞© FACTS

DOUG STORER

Sterling Publishing Co., Inc. New York
Oak Tree Press Co., Ltd. London & Sydney

To my wife, Hazel . . . *for all her help*
in making this book possible.

Photo lab work by Fulmer of Clearwater, Florida

Contents

Introduction

I am often asked who I think is the most AMAZING BUT TRUE person I have ever found during my long years of traveling the world to collect the unusual, the strange, the unbelievable.

Well, that is a question I can't answer because I haven't yet found the one and only. No matter how fantastic anything is, there is always the promise of something down the road that may be even stranger. I may find it tomorrow, or next year—or never. But I know it's out there somewhere, and I'm still searching for it.

However, among the thousands of AMAZING BUT TRUE people I have known, there are a few who were the most unusual of their kind; no one else in the world ever matched their unique records.

Kuda Bux, a holy man from India, walked on fire in the heart of New York City, on a bed of hot coals registering 1400 degrees F. I know, because I supervised the building of the long fire pit he walked through. When the mystic completed his walk—not once but twice—three doctors examined his feet. They were not even warm.

Poon Lim, a Chinese sailor, was blown into the sea when his ship was torpedoed and sunk with all hands, off the coast of Africa in World War II. He found a life raft, pulled himself aboard and then, miraculously, kept himself alive while he floated clear across the Atlantic to the coast of Brazil. The voyage, on a small raft and without provisions, took 133 days, a record of survival never matched. When I asked Poon Lim how he managed this he answered: "The Devil didn't want me."

Those are just two of the AMAZING BUT TRUE people I've known. But in this book you'll find more such fascinating people—many more!

DOUG STORER

Camels in America? At one time 79 camels were brought to the United States because Jefferson Davis, then Secretary of War, thought they could carry military freight across the Southwest desert better than horses and mules. This dromedary mama with baby is one of the camels that carry freight, but it lives in Saudi Arabia.

Accidents

<u>IMPALED ON A FENCE POST</u>

Many of the people who pass us on the street each day simply have no right to be alive. They are the people who have incredibly survived accidents that by all the laws of nature should have killed them instantly.

A 23-year-old man from New York was driving fast along the Connecticut Turnpike when his car swerved suddenly off the road and into a chain link fence bordering the highway. As his car hit and buckled the fence, it uprooted a heavy, eight-foot steel fence post and sent it, like a giant lance, through the left windshield and then straight through the chest of the driver, piercing the man so thoroughly that the end of the pole protruded through the righthand window.

For one agonizing hour, the victim, fully conscious, remained in his car impaled on the fence post while police and firemen worked a handsaw with painstaking care to free him. No automatic cutting tool could be used, as the vibration would have caused profuse bleeding and death.

When the driver was finally removed from his car and taken to the hospital for surgery, he still had a 12-inch length of pipe through his chest.

After a long and delicate operation, the pipe was safely removed from the man's chest . . . and he lived.

RUN OVER BY A TRAIN

A few years ago, a Denver, Colorado, man was involved in a two-car, head-on crash which hurled him with savage force through the roof of his car and catapulted him 100 feet through the air.

With a sickening thud, the man landed directly in the center of a nearby railroad track and just in front of an onrushing train that was highballing through.

Startled by seeing a man fall onto the track before him, the engineer frantically tried to brake the train. But it was going too fast and he could not even diminish its speed before the train passed over the helpless man who lay stretched out on the roadbed.

Finally, the locomotive ground to a halt. The horror-stricken engineer jumped down from his cab and walked back, already weak with fear at what he would find when he reached the spot where the man had been lying.

But he need not have worried. What he found there was not a dead body but a very lively one.

By an amazing chance, the man had escaped destruction beneath the flying wheels of the train by landing in a shallow depression in the middle of the track. Now, badly shaken, he was complaining loudly about a pain in his left leg. It had been broken in the original car crash, and this was his only injury.

THE SANDHOG

The men who build the tunnels we use so frequently have one of the most dangerous of all jobs, and the greatest danger is the terrifying cave-in.

Dick Creedon, a sandhog, was working on a tunnel under New York's East River, when a leak developed in the "shield," the heavy metal wall that protects the sandhogs as they dig. The men were working far beneath the river-bed and under very heavy air pressure when suddenly the small leak ballooned into a giant cave-in.

There was an explosion and Creedon was sucked immediately into the wall of the tunnel as the high-pressure air sought to escape. Carried by the massive bubble, the terrified workman was pushed up through 30 feet of slime and sand to the river-bed. Then he was blown another 30 feet up through the water and hurled 50 feet up into the air. From this great height, Creedon fell heavily back into the river where he was picked up by a passing boat.

Unhurt, he was back at work the next day, repairing the cave-in. When he was asked later how he'd felt during his "ride," through which he had remained conscious, he said: "Like a human geyser."

BOYS AND ACCIDENTS

Small boys and hard falls go together, like football and scuffed knees.

The greatest fall of its kind was experienced by a 10-year-old California lad who crashed down the face of a towering cliff at Lake Arrowhead.

Edging too close for a "real good look," the youngster slipped over the edge of the cliff and plunged downward.

He fell straight down for 200 feet, then hit an almost vertical rockfall. On that, he bounced swiftly down another 1,000 feet to where the cliff dropped off again into a sheer 300-foot wall.

Dropping like a stone, the boy finally landed at the bottom where he lay dazed until he was found by his terrified parents. Despite his incredible fall of 1,500 feet, the boy had no serious injury and not a single broken bone.

For sheer unbelievability, there is only one other "small boy" accident to match this fall.

In 1951, Stanley Willoughby, an inquisitive 8-year-old living in Portland, Oregon, stood entranced at the sight of a 3-ton steamroller busy repairing a street.

Edging up closer and closer to the heavy iron monster, little Stanley was finally walking directly behind it when the driver, not seeing the boy, suddenly backed up.

Down and under went the screaming, terrified youngster, the roller passing completely over his legs. But when the shaken driver jumped down he found not a dead child as he had expected but a little boy comfortably pressed into a soft, very deep bed of warm asphalt—and completely unhurt.

Africa

THE DUCK-BILL TRIBE

Bodily disfigurement is rapidly dying out among the tribes in Africa. Here an older member of the Ubangi (Duck-Bill) tribe calmly puffs his pipe and strikes a pensive pose. Much to the relief of the younger members of the tribe, this type of tribal identification is passé.

Aircraft

<u>FIFTEEN-YEAR-OLD PILOT</u>

During World War II, a young man entered an enlistment center and eagerly asked to join the service. He said his name was Kincaid, he was 21 years old, and he wanted to become a flyer.

He was accepted into the Air Force and after training in the United States he was assigned to a bomber squadron at the Benghazi air base in North Africa.

As a gunner on a B-24 bomber, Kincaid soon ran up a terrific record, was decorated and made a sergeant.

Then one day his buddy was killed, and so deeply did his friend's death affect the young airman that he asked for a transfer.

The transfer was granted. The flyer returned to the United States and immediately went to see his commanding officer. His name, he told the astonished officer, was not Kincaid—it was Fletcher, and he was not 21 years old, as his military record stated, but only 16. He had been only 15 when he had enlisted the year before, and he had lied then about both his name and his age.

Tom Fletcher was the youngest combat flyer in World War II. At the age of 16 he was already a veteran. He had completed 35 combat missions, had flown 300 combat flying hours, had won the Distinguished Flying Cross, and had been given the Air Medal with one silver cluster and 5 bronze clusters.

FALLING OUT OF A PLANE

Some of the wildest stories of survival stem from flying.

Victor Woodrick, a young English aviation cadet, was taking special training in an old open-cockpit, two-seater plane that had dual controls.

Woodrick sat behind the pilot and when they were well up in the air, the pilot had him take over.

Woodrick was handling the controls very well when the pilot gave him further instructions through the speaking tube. The young cadet couldn't hear what was being said to him so he leaned forward to adjust the faulty tube. At that very moment, the plane flew into a down draft. At the same time, Woodrick's safety snapped open.

That did it! The next thing the startled flyer knew, he was plunging down to earth on his back, spiraling round and round, and unable to open his parachute.

Suddenly, something came up behind him and scooped him up with a hard bump. Opening his eyes, Woodrick found himself straddling the tail of the plane from which he had just bounced out.

The pilot, a seasoned and daring flyer, had acted quickly to save the life of his student. Then, with the tail heavily loaded by Woodrick's weight, the pilot landed the plane under full power.

The plane hit the ground hard but safely, with no damage to itself, the pilot, or the "flying cowboy" still wildly riding its tail!

OLD AND NEW

IA/C/62 IMPERIAL AIRWAYS 14 SEATER PASSENGER AEROPLANE

The 1926 English Imperial Airways' first "deluxe" service between London and Paris used a biplane with the pilot sitting on the nose, out in the open. The wings were held together by thin wire. Only 14 passengers could be carried (I was one) and, to keep the weight down, wicker chairs were used. If you needed air, you could open a window. It took 2½ hours at 75 m.p.h. to make the trip.

INTERIOR OF IMPERIAL AIRWAYS AEROPLANE CITY CLASS

THE WRIGHT BROTHERS
WOULDN'T BELIEVE IT

A huge Air Force transport plane sits next to the replica of a Wright Brothers plane at Wright-Patterson Air Force Base, Dayton, Ohio. Volunteer workers who have been building a flyable replica of the 1911 Wright Brothers Model B Flyer biplane rolled it out on the ramp for comparison with an Air Force Lockheed C-5 Galaxy transport, the largest plane in the Air Force. One comparison that showed the progress of aviation in the intervening years: The Wrights' first flight, back in 1903, covered 120 feet, a shorter distance than the 121-foot-long cargo compartment of the four-engine C-5. The C-5 is 247 feet, 10 inches long, and has a wingspan of 222 feet, 8 inches.

Alligators

<u>WRESTLING ALLIGATORS</u>

Ross Allen of Silver Springs, Florida, goes underwater to teach his sons how to capture a live alligator. Wrestling alligators is a dangerous sport. One of his sons, Tom Allen, is pictured on the front cover wrestling an 18-foot-long anaconda under water. (More on alligators on pages 108–110.)

Animals

AN ODD ASSORTMENT

The long enmity between cat and rat has come to a peaceful conclusion for Puss, a black half-Persian, and the baby rat she adopted and now suckles along with her own recent litter.

Puss belongs to Wally Hawryluk, a poultry farmer of Thomastown, Australia. No one knows where Puss picked up the little waif rat: she just appeared with it in her mouth one day and set it down to feed among her own kittens. Since then, it's been one happy family with Puss a model, affectionate mother showing no partiality. When she isn't busy feeding her little rat, Puss nuzzles and cleans it, or plays with it, just as she does with the kittens.

What will happen when weaning takes place is anybody's guess, but in most cases where the female of one species adopts and suckles the infant of another, the alien animal is accepted as a member of the family from that time forward.

Cat loves rat.

Cats really love rats.

There is a great deal of strange togetherness in the animal world, much of it difficult to explain, as many of the animals are natural enemies.

In England, a dog named Titchy has taken under his protection a little rabbit for whom he shows the deepest affection, even to sleeping with it tucked under his paw. The only rift in this odd relationship comes each evening when Titchy has to leave his little friend and go to work. Titchy is a professional

Mouse dances for cat.

greyhound and spends his nights furiously chasing a mechanical rabbit which, if he overtook it, he would immediately tear to pieces.

Sometimes two extremely timid creatures are drawn together. The little koala is a strange teddy-bear-like marsupial whose paws rarely touch the ground during his entire lifetime. He lives in the forks of trees, eats nothing but eucalyptus leaves, drinks no water, and is easily frightened. Yet on a game reserve in Australia one of these wild, gentle creatures came down from his safe treetop to strike up a curious friendship with an equally shy baby wallaby (a species of miniature kangaroo) after her mother wallaby had been killed by a car.

Mutual aid accounts for many animal friendships, such as the one struck up between a monkey named Bashful and a hippo named Hippy at the Mesker Zoo in Indiana. Somehow, Bashful found out that whenever a giant like Hippy eats, he's bound to be sloppy and leave a lot of unchewed odds and ends tucked away in the far corners of his cavernous mouth. Bashful decided to tidy up this situation and, in some mysterious way, wangled Hippy's consent. Now, every day after Hippy downs his colossal meal of grain and fruit, he swims over to the side of his tank where Bashful is waiting for him, opens his enormous mouth and patiently lets the agile little monkey explore around for leftovers. This provides Bashful with a feast, and Hippy gets a painless oral hygiene treatment.

Cat loves rabbit.

It's welcome, whatever it is.

Cat and skunk feed together.

(Opposite page) It's chipmunk's turn.

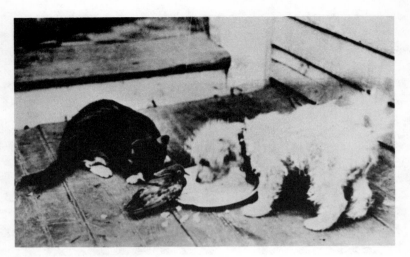

Cat, dog and bird—all friends.

"The baby leopard is drinking out of my glass!"

Circus dog loves
canaries.

Full house—dog, monkey, cat and parakeet.

ANIMALS AND MAN

Ever since man stood upright, the lesser animals have served him. At first, man used animals simply to provide nourishing flesh and warming fur; later the uses became more varied, even bizarre.

The lowly louse, for instance, was once used to elect the mayors of Hurdenburg, in Sweden. In the Middle Ages, the eligible men of the town sat around a table with their heads lowered and their beards spread out before them. A louse was set down in the center of the table, and the owner of the beard into which the louse crawled was made mayor for the following year.

The aborigines of Australia had a unique method of getting fresh honey. They captured a bee, stuck a little feather on it and then, using the marked bee as a guide, followed it to the hive.

The Indians of southeast Alaska long ago discovered that the eulachon, a smeltlike, fatty fish, makes a perfect candle after it has been dried and threaded with a wick. The smell is evil but the light is fine.

Today, 20th-century man, turning to Nature to help him improve the functioning of his intricate mechanical and electronic systems, has created a new science called "bionics" (meaning "life-resembling"). Research in this field calls for the study and use of animals for such sophisticated purposes that had anyone even whispered of these three centuries ago he would have been charged with witchcraft and silenced at the stake.

The bat and the porpoise, both of which perfected their efficient radar and sonar systems millions of years ago, and who guide themselves by bouncing sounds off objects ahead, are now studied by man in an effort to perfect his own echo-location devices. The porpoise, it is found, swims even better when he is blindfolded; the bat, in a pitch-black room crisscrossed at different levels with dozens of fine wires, can dart swiftly about and not collide with a single strand.

The bat is also contributing to our knowledge of longevity.

With an extraordinary life span of 20 years, the bat lives longer for his size than any other animal. The secret of the bat's long life may lie in his ability to go so quickly into the deep sleep of hibernation. He can, almost at once, slow his heart from 180 beats a minute to a near-death *three,* and his respiration from 8 breaths a second to only one every 8 minutes. Asleep, he is kept refrigerated without damage.

Animal behavior, skills and attitudes also help man to understand himself better. The Air Force, doing research on the eye of the octopus because it most nearly resembles the human eye, has taught this tentacled creature of the deep to "read" by distinguishing letter-like shapes.

A study of wolves shows that they are as status-conscious as man, and have a rigid caste system which is observed in the way teeth are bared or tails held. A low-caste she-wolf must keep her tail abjectly curled between her legs in the presence of the "leader," who has secured his position by fang and claw. If the she-wolf forgets and lets her tail hang in the normal position, she is often killed for her transgression.

The rattlesnake and other pit vipers, so called because of deep depressions on either sides of their heads, have a sense organ connected with these pits which enable them to detect a change in temperature as small as 1/1000 of a degree. Knowledge of this acute sense is needed to help man perfect his heat-seeking, anti-missile weapons.

And the common housefly, whose principle of stabilized flight helped develop the first gyroscope, is now being studied for its ability to walk upside down on the ceiling, a skill which man needed for that greatest of all adventures, walking on the moon.

PEACEFUL CO-EXISTENCE

The peak of co-existence—in the animal world, at least—was reached in an amazing three-way relationship among a goat, a sheep, and a lion, all of them living happily together in the same cage at the Osaka Zoo in Japan.

The lion, rejected by his mother at birth, was brought up as a cub on milk and vegetables, and these unlionlike foods continued to form the major part of his adult diet, which included very little meat.

From the beginning, the young lion was a great favorite with the zoo staff, who taught him to walk on a lead and respond to commands. They also soon discovered that he was unusually gentle for a big cat.

Because of this, the director of the zoo decided to make a daring experiment with the lion's tractable temperament by introducing into the big cat's cage first a goat and then a sheep.

Almost from the beginning, the animals shared their common cage in harmony. Nor was this a wary truce in which each animal kept aloof, bristling with suspicion toward the others.

To the contrary. Each day, the happy but nervous zookeepers were able to watch with astonishment as these natural enemies ate, slept, and even played together with mutual trust and pleasure. Often, the spry goat would start a romp by butting the drowsing lion into action, with the sheep soon joining in.

ANIMALS DO THE DARNDEST THINGS!

A woman bird-lover in North Carolina was pleased to see flickers nest near her house and eat the insects in its cedar siding. But as the number of birds increased rapidly and their attack on her house mounted, the woman grew concerned. The steady drumming of hundreds of busy beaks made sleep impossible after dawn, and holes as large as three inches in diameter began to appear in the walls.

So it was decided that the birds had to go. But that proved easier said than done. Tactic after tactic was used to get rid of the house-wrecking flickers, but nothing worked. The flickers stayed on despite special sprays, shotgun blasts (some in earnest) and placing threatening toy animal figures in all the windows. At last report they were still there, pecking away.

"The house now looks like a piece of Swiss cheese," said the former bird-lover sadly.

Pigs certainly seem harmless enough, but a pig in Lüneburg, Germany—acting undoubtedly in self-defense—shot a butcher who was just about to dispatch the animal with a pistol. The man, kneeling beside the pig to load his gun, suddenly found himself the victim of his own bullet when a porcine hoof kicked up and hit the trigger.

A dog riding through Denver on his master's truck grew bored with the slow pace of the city traffic, jumped down from his seat beside the driver and planted a large paw squarely on the accelerator. The result: a car out of control, a crash and four people injured. Fido was not hurt, but from that time on he was known as the stay-at-home dog.

A Michigan man, fishing through ice on a lake at Edwardsburg, was congratulating himself on the success of his catch when he suddenly changed his tune and let out a roar of surprise and pain. He had brought up a four-pound mackerel and had no sooner removed the hook from its mouth than the fish leaped up from the ice and fastened itself on the fisherman's leg. It took two men to pry the determined fish loose and a doctor to treat the injury.

In Marinette, Wisconsin, a frantic call to the police sent the emergency squad on the double to revive two dogs who were found overcome by gas after they had turned on the kitchen stove.

After they were revived, the owner said: "It couldn't have been a suicide pact. They are really very happy dogs."

A couple in Albuquerque, New Mexico, found a small stray monkey on their doorstep and invited him in.

The visitor completely charmed his hosts until he spotted some bottles containing hand lotion and eye wash. He drank these on sight and promptly went off on a simian spree.

He threw pots and pans at the dodging couple, yanked their television wire from the wall, flooded the washing machine, got in a few nips (the real kind) and paused in his monkeyshines only long enough to eat a bowl of plastic fruit.

By the time the police arrived, the monkey was holding his aching head and had worn out his welcome.

An Akron, Ohio, man opened the hood of his car one day, looked down at his engine and found that a small opossum had decided to move in and set up housekeeping in that unlikely place. Among the pipes and pistons, he had built himself a secure nest. He was not troubled by motion sickness.

Being a night creature, the opossum foraged for food after dark and then crawled back up beneath the car to snooze away the daylight hours in his cozy nest.

A sharp pain in his right hand awakened a Baltimore man from a deep sleep one summer night. In the moonlight that filtered through the window, the man saw at once that he had been shot. At the same time, he also saw his attacker. Staring down the sights of the man's hunting rifle, which he had left on a chair near his bed, was the family's pet rabbit.

In Hialeah, Florida, a woman was admitted to the local hospital for abdominal pains. After coming up with baffling results to all their standard diagnostic tests, the doctors finally found that the patient was infested with termites.

This is the only known case of its kind.

This small tabby, Minny, is the world's only feline corn-eater. Naturally, she comes from Iowa.

This chicken is a tightrope walker.

Ants

USEFUL FOR SUTURES

In many parts of the world, the most feared of all living creatures is the lowly ant.

At best, ants can be a nuisance, but large-bodied ants gathered in force, living in huge nests, or traveling in armies of uncounted millions can be a terrifying sight.

On the march, the insects become very dangerous. Looking like a big unbroken cable snaking across the earth, the moving ants will eat everything that gets in their way. They overcome small animals easily, and even attack men. And the sound of their clicking jaws can be heard some distance away.

Only fire will halt these relentless hordes of insects, and travelers who must sleep out in the open often build fire trenches around their camps at night to protect themselves against any surprise invasion.

The big ants do have one useful function, though. For centuries the Indians of South America have used the powerful jaws of the insect for suturing wounds. To do this, the torn skin is held tightly together and a big ant is placed on the wound. Instinctively, the insect bites, embedding its sharp mandibles in the flesh. Then the ant's body is cut off, leaving only his sharp pincers to act as a healing "stitch."

THAT ANT IS DRUNK!

Several insects have been known to drink. The stag beetle, his head equipped with sharp "antlers," is notorious for getting high on the fermented sap of certain bushes. Unfortunately, he is a barroom brawler who, after a drop too many, duels to the death with any other beetle who scuttles into his way.

But the most interesting imbibers in the animal world are found among the ants. Most ants are teetotalers, but there are those who enjoy getting stoned on a nectar which they lap from the bodies of certain beetles.

As everyone knows, ants are no-nonsense insects, always running around on their household errands and very community-minded. When, therefore, an ant gets drunk, the whole nest is involved.

When intoxicated, the problem nipper in the nest acts just as all other creatures do; that is, he will fall down and refuse to move further.

But the sober ants don't let him just lie there. They crowd around, stroke his body in an effort to rouse him and even attempt to nudge him to his six little feet.

When this treatment fails, the ants often carry their happily inert comrade back to the nest, presumably to have him sleep it off in safety.

And one naturalist has reported that, while he was watching a nest, he saw an ant bring up another that was obviously under the weather. They were met at the mouth of the nest by two working ants who refused to let the drunken ant enter. Instead, they grabbed the unprotesting boozer, carried him across the path and threw him into a pond.

The dunking, as it always does in such cases, had a sobering effect.

Lieutenant Colonel Kalisch (left) accepts capitulation from jovial Major General Elster and his staff.

Army

GERMANS SURRENDER TO PHOTOGRAPHER

In September 1944, Lieutenant Colonel Bertram Kalisch, an American pictorial officer stationed in Paris, received word from the public relations officer for the Ninth Army, that something significant was about to happen in the vicinity of Romorantin, France. Kalisch picked up a film and sound crew and headed south to the area.

Kalisch learned that a Lieutenant Magill had made contact with German Major General Erich Elster and had bluffed him into believing that the Americans had a much larger force than they did. Magill's bluff worked well enough to have Elster consider surrender. An armed truce was set up while the Germans pondered the situation.

Kalisch took his film crew to Magill's headquarters, where they found a strange situation: this young American lieutenant was keeping a headquarters behind German lines with German orderlies. Kalisch, through a German staff officer, suggested to General Elster that, since he was considering surrender, he let Kalisch photograph a model German headquarters. Elster agreed. When the American photographer and the German general got together they discovered that Field Marshal Rommel, General Elster's commanding officer, and Kalisch's mother both came from Wurtemberg. The two officers became friendly immediately.

General Elster told Kalisch that he had not yet announced it to his troops, numbering 20,000, but he was considering surrender. The American immediately told General Elster that such an historic event should be photographed. General Elster agreed to this too. Kalisch, now promoting his unusual position for all its worth, reminded Elster of Cornwallis' surrender to Washington during the Revolution. He pointed out that a similar ceremony would be more fitting in the circumstances than the usual "table surrenders." Kalisch hastened to add that the German Army would probably be reconstituted after the war and that Elster would probably face a board of inquiry. In facing a board of inquiry, Elster would want some photographs as proof that he surrendered his troops with honor—à la Cornwallis. General Elster was completely persuaded.

Kalisch selected a picturesque crossroads for the surrender scene. He convinced a Frenchman, who owned a house overlooking the area, that he should place his home at the disposal of the press for the historic occasion. All details arranged, General Macon and his staff, representing the American military, and Kalisch awaited Elster's arrival at the appointed hours. General Elster drove up in his staff car—late by a nervous fifteen minutes—stepped out, saluted and extended his apologies. He had had a flat on the way. After Elster's personal surrender, 20,000 goose-stepping troops marched into the area from three different directions before the cameras. The films of this event were used world-wide and many copies were flown into Germany, where they did much to destroy the morale of the enemy. Thanks to Lieutenant Colonel Kalisch, history had been recorded with the co-operation of everyone concerned—including the enemy.

TAPS

The origin of "Taps" is obscure, but there is an amazing story concerning the source of this famous bugle call.

Robert Ellicombe, a captain in the Union Army in the War Between the States encamped near Harrison's Landing, Virginia, was deeply disturbed one night in 1862 by the moans of a wounded soldier who lay in the strip of land that separated the embattled Confederate and Union forces. Unable to bear the cries of suffering, Ellicombe decided to go out and bring the stricken man back for medical attention.

Crawling out on his stomach, Ellicombe reached him and started tugging him back to the Union side. But the trip was too much for the soldier—a young Confederate—and he was dead by the time Ellicombe reached his own lines.

In the course of his duty, Ellicombe started to examine the dead man to identify him. Suddenly, the captain went numb with shock. In the dim light of the lantern, he recognized the dead face as that of his own son. The boy had been studying music in the South and, without telling his father, had enlisted in the Confederate Army.

On the following morning, the heartbroken father asked permission of his superiors to give his son a full military burial despite his enemy status. His request was granted, along with his other request that a bugler arrange and play a series of musical notes that the father had found in a pocket of his dead boy's uniform.

This was done—and that music was the haunting bugle call we all now know as "Taps."

Atomic Power

JOHN MORRELL KEELY

In Philadelphia, in 1874, an amateur scientist named John Morrell Keely made the startling announcement that he had split the atoms of water and had invented a machine to use the energy released.

Scientists flocked to Keely's workshop to see him demonstrate his fantastic invention. Using only a little water as fuel, Keely caused his machine to generate enough power to send a bullet through a 12-foot-thick wall, and break a heavy mooring cable as easily as a piece of thread.

No one could explain Keely's invention. Even men like Edison admitted they were completely baffled.

In November, 1898, Keely was found dead in his carefully guarded workshop. When scientists examined the place, they could make no sense out of the jumble of machinery, tubes, and wires, because Keely had left not a single written record of his experiments.

But most baffling of all was the discovery of a huge 3-ton metal ball which was found beneath the floor of his laboratory. No scientist of that time could explain its use.

To this day, no one knows for sure whether or not, a century ago, Keely actually did stumble on the secret of the atom.

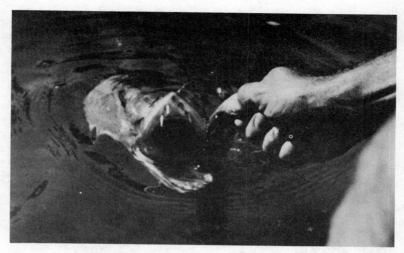

This barracuda has been trained at the Miami Seaquarium to take food, at the surface, from a human hand.

Barracuda

PIRATE KILLER OF THE DEEP

In the tropical waters of the West Indies, the barracuda is more feared than the shark.

With his long snout and huge, sharp teeth, the barracuda's open mouth is one of the most terrifying sights in nature.

The barracuda's hunting habits have been described as those of an old-time pirate's. Lying under any floating cover he can find, the hungry killer waits silently for his prey to pass; then, making a swift dash, he pounces on his unsuspecting victim in seconds.

This piratical trait is instinctive. Born in tidal rivers, the barracuda begins to practice his surprise attack while still a baby less than 2 inches long. At full growth, he will reach a length of 6 to 7 feet, and have moved out into the sea to become the terror of the reefs and coastal waters.

Although they seldom hunt in packs, barracudas have been observed—like a pirate fleet waylaying a golden armada—encircling their victims before rushing in for the kill, a grisly work which their powerful jaws accomplish swiftly.

These jaws are the barracuda's terrible signature. Unlike the shark, whose bite is jagged, the barracuda dismembers a fish, or cuts off a human limb, with almost surgical precision. The bite is so clean and straight because the barracuda's teeth have cutting edges on both sides.

Unpredictable, voracious, no friend to man, the barracuda, in one amazing instance, has been tamed. At the Miami Seaquarium, in a fantastic display of training, this deadly killer of the deep has been taught to come on call, surface, and actually take food from a human hand!

Baseball

A RARE DAY IN JUNE

On a June day in 1909, an obscure ball player named Calvin Dow hit nine home runs in nine times at bat!

The place was an equally obscure little town on the plains of the Midwest—Fullerton, North Dakota.

The All-Stars were scheduled to meet the LaMoores in an afternoon special at Fullerton. At second base for the All-Stars was Calvin Dow, an outstanding player of the area with a reputation as a solid, consistent ball player.

Dow enjoyed the limelight and the cheers of the Fullerton fans. But more than that, he enjoyed the company of one of the town belles, a girl named Stella. Since early in the year, when he had first met her, Calvin had been pursuing the young lady with all his ardor. But Stella, as befitted the fashion of the day, was coy about her courting.

On the morning of this game, Calvin had sought out his lady love to determine if she would be in attendance at the park. She would be, Stella said—and in the company of another of the town eligibles, a young man named Larry.

Calvin was infuriated. "What do you want to go to the game with him for?" he fumed. "I was going to hit a couple of home runs just for you. And after the game, I thought we'd go out and celebrate."

"If you can make good on a promise like that," said Stella, "I'll make good on the promise of a home for you."

With that happy promise in mind, and the constant thought of Stella in the stands seated next to Larry, Calvin Dow took the field for the start of the game.

In the first inning, the LaMoores went down in order and the All-Stars came in to bat.

"Every time I see a pitch this afternoon," Dow said to a teammate as he selected a bat, "I'll see the face of Larry on the ball. Believe me, I'll enjoy knocking the stuffing out of it."

His first time at bat, Dow swung at the pitch and lofted a long fly ball that cleared the fence.

An inning later, another cleared the fence.

And the next time at bat, Dow hit a third home run.

By the time the game ended, Dow had batted nine times and delivered nine home runs—the greatest single display of power in baseball history.

Through the cheering throng, he advanced toward the stands, still carrying his bat. Larry, seeing the bat, decided to leave.

Calvin Dow and Stella were married a week later.

Not many remain who remember that June day in 1909 in Fullerton, North Dakota. But though the mighty Babe Ruth's records continue to fall, it seems safe to assume that the record nine-home-run outburst of Calvin Dow will stand as long as baseball is played.

SLIDE, KELLY! SLIDE!

Every sport has strange twists in its record books, but one of the strangest of all belongs to baseball.

In Allentown, Pennsylvania, in 1893, a 2–2 game was in the last of the 11th inning. Nail-biting suspense gripped the crowd as Cincinnati came to bat, determined to break the deadlock and post a hard-earned victory.

Cincinnati's lead-off batter was retired, and the next batter, "Matches" Kilroy, took a couple of pitches, then swung mightily, and grounded out to the infield.

There still was that all-important third out remaining, and Manager "King" Kelly, one of Cincinnati's best hitters, was due to bat next.

But Kilroy's futile effort apparently had created an insurmountable problem for, in grounding out, he had split the last available bat.

Umpire Tim Durst, one of the most famous and respected of the period, pondered the situation for a few moments and then decided the game would have to be called because, without a bat, there seemed to be no possible way to continue.

He beckoned the two managers to his side and began his explanation. Kelly shook his head and asked Durst to postpone his ruling, arguing he would find a bat somehow.

Noticing a woodpile nearby, Kelly raced over to it, searching for something he could use to swing at the ball. He found an axe and hurried back to the diamond.

"I'll use this to bat," he proclaimed.

Durst shook his head in disbelief.

"Show me in the rule book where it's illegal," Kelly insisted.

Durst began searching through the book. He turned page after page of the small volume, shaking his head as he continued. Finally Durst straightened up, stuffed the book into his back pocket, and shouted, "Play ball." There was nothing in the rules to prohibit the use of an axe as a bat.

The triumphant manager swaggered into the batter's box, hefted his axe, and waited. Twice the pitcher threw, and twice Kelly swung, meeting only air as he struggled with his strange bat.

On the third pitch, however, Kelly connected. The ball soared toward the fence in left field. Suddenly, without warning, the ball, which had been partially separated by the axe blade and further weakened in its flight, split in half as left fielder "Wild Bill" Setley followed its course.

Stunned, Setley watched as half of the ball flew over the fence behind and half dropped at his feet.

Uncertain of what to do, he looked toward the infield and saw Kelly racing around the bases. Quickly Setley recovered, snatched up the half of the ball lying in front of him, and threw it toward the plate. The runner and the ball converged.

From the stands thundered the excited cry of the fans, "Slide, Kelly! Slide!" a phrase which has survived through the succeeding years.

Responding to this encouragement, Kelly slid but the catcher grabbed the ball, whirled, and tagged the Cincinnati captain an instant before he reached home.

Leaping to his feet, Kelly charged the confused umpire, who was about to signal him out.

Durst recognized he was going to get an argument and calmly pointed out that Kelly's slide had not beaten the throw.

"Okay, I agree," Kelly nodded, "but how about the half of the ball that went over the fence? I wasn't tagged with the whole ball."

This was a line of reasoning that Durst was not prepared for and, as he hesitated, a long and heated debate began. No matter how he ruled, Durst realized he stood to lose.

Finally, with the wisdom of Solomon, the umpire stepped back, quieted the adversaries, and announced that he was awarding a half run to Cincinnati. At the same time, he was charging them with a half out.

Thus the strangest score of all time ended a baseball game.

Cincinnati was declared the winner—2½ to 2.

Basketball

BASKETBALL ON HORSEBACK

In Spanish, *pato* is the word for duck. It's also the name of Argentina's wildest, roughest, and most popular sport. Only the very strongest men, the most skilled and daring of riders, can qualify as players in the game that has best been described as "basketball on horseback."

Pato has been played in Argentina for almost four centuries. As early as 1610, a game was played in Buenos Aires during the festival of St. Ignatius of Loyola. A spectator at that long-ago game has left a description of it. He wrote:

"Two groups of horsemen collect and two areas are marked off about a league [three miles] apart. They then take a duck [*pato*] and insert him in a leather boot, which is sewed up, leaving his head outside.

"The boot has two or more handles; one of each of these handles is gripped by the strongest man on each team, and they tug for the *pato,* spurring their horses until one of them finally breaks away with it. His rival usually crashes to the ground.

"The first man then goes into a gallop and the rival team chases him and tries to surround him and grab one of the handles of the *pato.* The other team resists this, and both teams

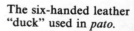

The six-handed leather "duck" used in *pato.*

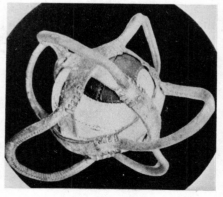

struggle until one of the teams manages to reach one of the assigned points, upon which it is declared the winner."

Because of the ferocity of the game, both the church and the government severely criticized it, and for the next two centuries repeatedly tried to have it banned. Finally, in 1882, *pato* was outlawed.

Then, in 1937, Alberto del Costello Posse started a movement to have the sport of *pato* revived. Posse drew up a whole new set of rules that "civilized" the ancient sport. The chief reform was to replace the unfortunate living duck with a ball bound around with four (later six) leather handles.

Today *pato* teams consist of four mounted players to a side, and the size of the playing field has been greatly reduced. It is now only about 600 feet long and 250 feet wide.

Scoring occurs when a player seizes the *pato* and dashes down the field to his goal. There he hurls the *pato* through an iron hoop about 3 feet in diameter. The hoop is mounted on a pole 7 feet high and is netted at the bottom to catch the *pato* after it drops through the hoop. The *pato* in the net is proof that it has passed through the hoop.

The horses used in *pato* are small native polo ponies, intelligent animals noted for their speed, stamina, and quick response to a player's moves. *Pato* games are played in six periods of eight minutes each, with four-minute intervals for changing horses.

Strict regulations keep players from injuring each other or their horses. A typical play in *pato* (and a real crowd-pleaser) is "lifting." This occurs when a fast-riding player swings far down from his saddle and swoops up a fallen "duck."

THE ONE-MAN TEAM

There have been some great teams, some great players, and some weird results since James Naismith invented the game of basketball at Springfield College, Massachusetts, way back in 1891.

But there never has been a more dramatic scoring in any game, by any player, than one posted by a gentleman named "Lone Star" Lubel, who put on a performance that would make a fiction writer blush if he even considered using it as a part of his story.

"Lone Star" Lubel was a member of a very good San Antonio All-Star team, eight fast men who dominated play in their area of Texas. So it was no surprise, when the city staged its annual tournament, that the All-Stars were right in the thick of the fight and methodically played their way into the finals.

For the better part of that championship game, things went as programmed. The All-Stars led handily most of the way with only one problem marring an otherwise fine performance.

The problem? Foul trouble.

Almost from the opening whistle, the referees began calling an unusual number of fouls on the favorites. By halftime several members of the team were in big trouble. Early in the second half, threat became reality. One by one, the All-Star players were waved to the bench.

Finally, although the All-Stars continued to hold their lead, they were reduced in number to just the regulation five players remaining on the floor. Then, early in the final quarter, one of those five players fouled out.

But that was not the end of the team's dismemberment. Within a few minutes, three other players were sent from the floor. Now, with still three minutes left to play, the All-Stars were down to just one man—ole "Lone Star" Lubel. Worse still, their lead had been sliced to a precarious 5 points just before the last men were chucked out of the game.

It now remained for Lubel to play those final three minutes all by himself if the team was not to forfeit the championship. No one man, of course, could possibly fight off the efforts of five.

But Lubel was determined to give it his best try. He just wouldn't quit, not even when his opponents quickly scored a basket and cut the lead to 3 points. A lonely figure on the court, Lubel took the ball down court, dribbling furiously, trying to kill time.

Precious seconds ticked away with "Lone Star" unable to get off a good shot. Suddenly he lost the ball and found himself chasing five men again, trying desperately to get it back.

More seconds flew by before the opponents could get that sure shot. But score they did, and the lead was cut to one point. And there was still more than a minute to play.

Again Lubel came down the floor, and again he lost the ball to superior numbers. Again the opponents scored.

"Lone Star" Lubel and his seven benched teammates were now a point behind. The opponents, content with their lead, decided not to press Lubel quite as closely. After all, they reasoned, if they fouled him, his free throw could tie the game. They decided just to keep him well away from the basket and let him run out the clock, and prevent any desperate attempt to get off one final shot.

It was exactly the strategy "Lone Star" hoped they would use. Dribbling around near center court, he kept a sharp eye on the clock. As the hand moved down to 10 seconds, Lubel suddenly wheeled and raced toward the basket.

Five men rushed toward him. But just before they reached him, Lubel leaped high in the air and arched the ball toward the basket. Breathlessly, he watched its flight, then nearly collapsed in joy as it hit the backboard and caromed through the rim.

Beards

Mat Phoon is a typical mother in the tribe in Burma. Members of this tribe are completely covered with long angora hair.

Bees

MILKING FOR VENOM

In Greenwood Cemetery, in Manchester, New York, lies one Timothy Ryan who died in 1814. His epitaph, in the tradition of that time, describes vividly the cause of his demise.

> "A thousand ways cut short our days,
> None are exempt from Death;
> A honey-bee by stinging me,
> Did stop my mortal breath."

These funereal words are a reminder of the fatal potency of the venom carried by bee, hornet and wasp—those swift invaders who have ruined more picnics than rain.

For most of us, fortunately, a sting from one of these insects usually causes nothing more than local pain, some sneezing or a headache. But for those who are highly allergic to the venom (as many as 500,000 people in the United States alone), a sting may cause death in a few minutes. It is considered probable that as many as 2,000 people die each year from insect stings, although most such cases are listed as heart attacks or shock.

Researchers have long known that fresh venom will desensitize victims, but until recently getting fresh venom in large enough quantities posed a problem. Bees and wasps are not easy to control, and very often the venom was deposited only in the aching fingers of the handlers.

The gauzy-winged troublemakers met their masters a few years ago in a group of chemists—O'Connor, Peck, Rosenbrook and Erickson—then working at Montana State University, now at Texas A.&M. University.

In a fantastic process called "milking," these scientists put bees, hornets and wasps into a light sleep by chilling them in a refrigerator. Groggy, with folded wings and no fight in them, the insects are then individually propped upright, against a small half-cylinder of brass, and bound into it securely with a tiny girdle of aluminum foil.

Looking like a sleepy papoose on a shiny backboard, the in-

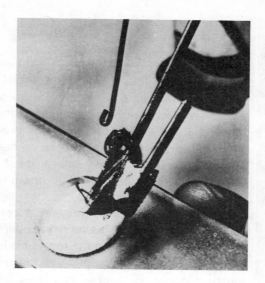

How to milk a bee. An electric charge which does not hurt it causes the bewildered insect to discharge its venom.

sect is then brought suddenly to life by means of a brief electrical charge. That does it!

Shocked wide-awake now, and fighting mad, the insect immediately contracts the muscles of its stinging lancet and lets go with a spurt of venom—right into a sterile dish.

By this unique new method, several hundred bees, wasps or hornets can be processed for venom removal by technicians in a single day. This yields enough venom for initial desensitization for hundreds of treatments.

An electric-shock device developed at Cornell University can be mounted on a beehive to produce honeybee venom in large amounts.

Except for feeling unusually hungry and thirsty, the insect suffers no damage at all through being milked.

Beetles

BRAWLER OF THE INSECT WORLD

Having a drop too much isn't a social error limited only to man. Other animals are known to go on occasional benders. There are beer-guzzling dogs and horses, robins who fall off telephone wires after stuffing themselves with fermented holly berries, and bears who fall asleep on highways after too much apple-eating. These boozy bruins are the victims of their own body heat which acts like a "mountain still" on the apple juice in their stuffed stomachs.

But the strangest of all tipsy creatures is an insect called the stag beetle. He gets his name from a pair of huge, deerlike antlers which protrude from the top of his head. His head, in turn, surmounts a body as completely armored as that of a medieval jousting knight. He looks—and is—a fighter.

What sets the stag beetle apart from the many other belligerent, combat-happy insects, however, is his notorious reputation as a drunken brawler. High on the fermenting sugar-laden sap of trees and bushes, male stag beetles rush to engage each other in a terrible duel to the death, each insect using his branching horns as vicious weapons to slash, impale, and tear apart the other, just as the enraged stags of the forest maim and kill when fighting for supremacy of the herd.

The World's Biggest Bug, the Goliath. Here it is attacking a banana at the American Museum of Natural History in New York.

BUSTER THE BUG

He is called *Goliathus goliathus,* which is like saying "giant giant." But the name fits him well, since this monster beetle from Africa is the biggest bug in the world. Stretched out, he measures 6 inches or more in length and has a wingspan of 8 inches.

The Goliath beetle is rarely seen, even in his native Africa where he lives in the steamy treetops of the jungle. From the high concealing branches, he hangs like a monkey. If disturbed, he will slash at his assailant with razor-sharp claws.

A bite by one of these outsized insects can be very painful. But they don't bite with their mouths. Instead, they use the natural "hinge" located between the wing case and the front part of the body, dropping their head downward to open the hinge and then snapping it back to close on the enemy.

Beetles are clumsy flyers. Except for occasional noisy, bumbling flights to neighboring trees (lured by love, perhaps), they stay close to their leafy pads. They seldom make it to the jungle floor, unless by accident. The way back up to the top is just too difficult.

The only living Goliath beetle ever known to be in the U.S.

was one seen several years ago at New York's Museum of Natural History.

Affectionately called "Buster the Bug" by an admiring staff, the Goliath had been secretly left one Christmas Eve on the museum's doorstep. He was found inside a covered coffee can lined with grass, obviously an effort made to protect him from the wintry blasts.

Buster was installed in a fine, temperature-controlled glass house, was fed a lush diet of ripe melons, mangoes and tomatoes, gained weight (almost half an ounce) and seemed happy to do nothing else but loll around as the museum's star attraction.

Only one sticky little incident marred this coleoptera (the scientific name for beetles) idyll. That was when Buster's fame spread to the Immigration Department. The Department, which takes a very dim view of any insect being imported into the United States, promptly declared Buster an undesirable alien and ordered his demise.

But Dr. John C. Pallister, chief entomologist at the museum, would have none of that and went to bat for his rare bug.

It is very hard for anyone to win an argument with a scientist. So in the end Buster was allowed to stay on at the museum. He was given a special "passport," and Dr. Pallister promised that "adequate safeguard measures would be employed to prevent escape."

Buster remained an attractive resident at the museum for the better part of a year. He had a steady stream of visitors but held a special fascination for children. The reason for this awed interest in the giant bug was probably expressed by a small girl who anxiously asked: "They don't live around here, do they?"

Bible

THE WORLD'S SMALLEST BIBLE

The printed pages of this Bible are approximately one half the size of a postage stamp and require a magnifying glass to read. The book fits into the ring displayed in the man's hand. This Bible was printed in Scotland in 1895.

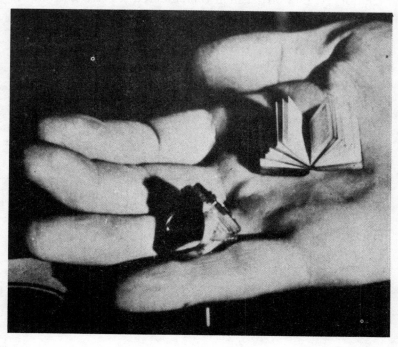

WATER ON THE SINAI DESERT

In the spring of 1921, a group of British soldiers faced death from thirst on the Sinai Desert, in Egypt.

They were a small desert patrol which had become lost in a furious sandstorm and had run out of water. In desperation, they decided to dig in the sand, hoping to find a well.

Suddenly, one of the men remembered a passage from the Bible, the one referring to Moses striking the desert rock and bringing forth water for the children of Israel. He pointed out to his companions that this was the same Sinai Desert, and that there was a rock ledge nearby. Why not, he asked, try to find water just as Moses had done?

The tortured men, willing to believe anything, immediately started to swing at the rocky ledge with a small pick-ax they carried. Then, as they struck out frantically, a miracle occurred . . . a trickle of clear, sweet water came out of the face of the rock.

The rock was actually soft limestone, and part of it covered a hidden spring. This water kept the men alive until they were rescued . . . proving that an Old Testament miracle could be repeated in the 20th century.

This bird may not look spectacular but she is rare. Her tongue is a sensitive thermometer. She uses it to check the temperature of her hatching eggs.

Birds

THE TEMPERATURE BIRD

Old as the dodo and just as strange, but still enjoying life, is Australia's amazing mallee fowl, a bird who can actually tell temperature.

The mallee, anxious for motherhood but scorning the tedious business of nest-sitting, buries her eggs in mounds of earth as high as 3 feet. As a substitute for her own body heat, the mallee mother-to-be keeps the eggs warm by covering them with decaying organic matter before she builds the mounds over them. The heat given off by this organic material turns the earthy nest into a fine incubator, and the clever fowl is free to pursue other interests while her brood hatches. Mindful of her maternal duties, however, the mallee returns frequently to test the temperature of the mound and make sure it is kept always at the same comfortable level.

The mallee tests the temperature by means of its long, sensitive tongue, with which it probes the interior earth of the mound after driving its bill in right up to its eyes. If the bird finds that the mound is growing too hot or too cold, she corrects the temperature variance by one of two methods, either by opening or closing the mound, or by raising or lowering its height.

So well can this strange bird detect temperature that even a change of less than two degrees will cause her to take frantic corrective action.

OPERATION OSPREY

The magnificent Canadian Rockies, near Banff, were the scene some time ago of a unique struggle over homestead rights between a mighty railroad and a militant osprey, a giant species of fish-eating hawk.

The osprey, a mama-in-waiting at the time, elected to build her big, untidy nest high up among the wires on top of a Canadian Pacific telegraph pole.

Although Mrs. Osprey was delighted with her new quarters, the railroad was less than happy. Not only did their unwelcome tenant interfere with the normal flow of messages sent over the lines, but she was also accused of fouling up broadcasts on the Canadian network whose national programs were fed the individual radio stations over these same wires. Obviously, the bird must be persuaded to leave.

A number of nuisances were attempted to get Mrs. Osprey to break her one-sided lease, but all efforts failed. She liked her reedy home among the wires, the view was fine and it was handy to fishing; in short, except for a slight humming noise, it was as near perfection as a hawk could ask.

The railroad finally decided upon drastic action; the bird would be dispossessed by having her nest uprooted. But when word of this proposal got out, it was found that the osprey had an army of friends who would not tolerate her removal. So the osprey stayed, had her young and, when the air grew chill, flew off with her little brood to seek a more clement climate. The railroad heaved a sigh of relief, removed the deserted nest and relaxed.

The following spring the osprey returned to build a new, even larger nest among the very same wires!

But a happy ending was at last arrived at, a solution that pleased the bird, satisfied her friends and brought honor to the railroad. A special cross-bar with a platform attached was erected on top of the pole. Then, with Mother Osprey circling around making loud, rude noises, and occasionally dive-bombing in for a sharp look at the work in progress, the linemen carefully transferred the sprawling nest—now containing three eggs—to its new perch above the wires.

When an osprey's nest interfered with the transmission of messages over communications lines, workmen moved the nest, with eggs in it, as the mother hovered nearby. The osprey, after early misgivings, accepted her new location gracefully.

The triumphant osprey was delighted with her new home (a much higher, better view of the Rockies), and the railroad was happy, too (all messages and programs coming in loud and clear).

THE DODO WITH TWO RIGHT FEET

One of Austria's greatest collectors of art was Emperor Rudolph the Second, the 17th-century ruler who spent so much money on art that his court was frequently put on short rations.

Emperor Rudolph's favorite artist was a man named Saverey who had painted a famous picture called "Landscape with Birds."

This canvas was done in 1628 and shows a dodo bird, a big, awkward creature, unable to fly, who then lived on the island of Mauritius in the Indian Ocean.

Saverey's painting of the dodo bird was the only one ever made from a living dodo, so some years later, when the dodo became extinct, Saverey's painting of the bird was widely copied.

But Saverey had made one mistake. For some reason, he painted the dodo with two right feet. And ever since then all the artists who have copied Saverey's dodo have continued to make the same structural error.

So the poor, clumsy dodo bird, gone from this earth for centuries, must go down through posterity with two right feet!

Robins have been known to get drunk on the bright red berries of the Florida holly. This shy, wild bird routinely greeted this man, ate from his hand and learned to get its water ration from the park's drinking fountain.

Boxing

FOOT BOXING IN THAILAND

By nature the people of Thailand are peaceful, living quietly in a fairyland setting of Buddhist shrines and religious pageantry. But when it comes to boxing their nature changes drastically. The Thailand version of boxing allows almost every form of attack except biting. The boxers wear no shoes. Instead they wear ankle supports to relieve strain on their legs.

This is how a Thai boxer practices.

Feet and arms flying, two young Thai boxers battle in Bangkok's Raja-
dammden Stadium.

THE "MICHIGAN ASSASSIN"

The career of Stanley Ketchel, probably the greatest middle-weight champion of all time, was as tragic as it was brilliant.

The origins of this great champion are partially obscured by the fact that murder seemed to haunt him almost from birth. His mother was only 12 years old when she bore him, and she was murdered while her son was still a youngster. Shortly after, his father also was murdered, and the now-orphaned 14-year-old ran away to take up life among the faceless men who made up the many hobo jungles at the turn of the century.

In order for a youngster to survive as a hobo, he had to learn to take care of himself, and Ketchel soon proved that he was especially adept with his fists.

By the time he was 17, he had convinced himself that he should desert the hobo life and try boxing as a means of making a living. In just four short years he polished his crude skills into the superb boxing form that brought him the world's middleweight championship. At the age of 21, Stanley Ketchel became a king of the ring.

It was a heady jump upward, and one for which the grossly under-privileged youth was totally unprepared. High living became his passion.

As a result, the same year that Ketchel won the championship, he lost it to Billy Papke. But Ketchel had had a taste of the spotlight, and wanted more than anything to be on top. He regained his crown before the year was out.

Now began his greatest period of glory. Popularly called the "Michigan Assassin," he met and defeated all comers within his class.

Then, looking for new fields to conquer, he challenged Jack Johnson, the reigning heavyweight king. When the two men stepped into the ring, Johnson outweighed his smaller opponent by 45 pounds. The fight was scheduled to go 15 rounds. Rumor had it that the two had agreed, in deference to the weight difference, to disdain the knockout and rely strictly on their boxing ability.

For the first 11 rounds Ketchel and Johnson put on a dazzling exhibition. It was a fight that many still call one of the boxing classics of all time.

But Ketchel was well aware that Johnson was in command, and this stung his pride. Early in the twelfth round Ketchel threw caution to the winds and swung a mighty right that caught Johnson just below the ear. The heavyweight champion went down. But that was Ketchel's mistake.

Johnson bounced back to his feet and, as Ketchel charged in for the kill, swung a right uppercut that knocked the smaller man out and kept him unconscious for several minutes.

After the Johnson fight, and between periods of carousing, Ketchel met and defeated a couple of additional challengers from within his own division. Then, less than a year after the Johnson fight, Ketchel traveled to Conway, Missouri, to take a brief vacation from the bright lights and get into shape for his next bout.

In Conway, on a lonely farm, Ketchel met Goldie Smith. She was a young, blonde, vivacious girl who cooked for the farmhands. Their acquaintance quickly ripened into a torrid romance. What the handsome middleweight champion had not reckoned with, however, was that his interest in Goldie had interrupted the romantic ambitions of one of the farmhands. This time, more than fists would be involved in the fight for supremacy.

Despite repeated warnings from the disgruntled suitor, Ketchel continued to press his advantage in the love bout. One night, returning from a date with Goldie, the champion was confronted by his furious rival. When the fighter sought to go on the attack, he was shot down in cold blood. He died almost instantly, murdered when he was only 23.

Ironically, the woman who was the cause of his death died at the hands of yet another man only a few months later, and the man who had murdered Ketchel was also shot to death.

The life story of Stanley Ketchel is the shortest and most violent in all sports history.

THE MAN THEY AVOIDED

They called him the Boston Tar Baby and his feats were legendary. He probably was the greatest fighter ever to step into the ring. But, search as you may the boxing record books, you won't find the same of Sam Langford listed among the champions of the world.

There was a reason. It wasn't because he lacked boxing skill. It was because Sam was black. In the days when he fought, few white boxers were anxious to put their titles on the line against a black man.

Though Langford fought many men who were champions or destined to become champions, the title simply was not at stake whenever he climbed into the ring. So his dream of becoming the heavyweight champion of the world never was realized.

Sam Langford began his professional career in 1902. Before he ended it, 21 years later, he had climbed through the ropes more than 600 times. A little simple arithmetic will show that that was approximately once every 12 days.

Moreover, he had met the best. During just one year, for example, the Boston Tar Baby fought two world champions and one who would hold a title within a few months.

That year was 1903, and Langford started it with a fight against Joe Gans. Gans, the favorite, had won the lightweight championship just the year before.

For 15 bruising rounds the two battlers put on a show that is still remembered as one of the greatest fights of all time. When the final bell had rung, Sam Langford was declared the winner. However, he was over the weight limit, and because of this technicality Gans retained the title.

Weeks later, Langford took on a second champion. This time he fought Joe Walcott—the welterweight king of that day, not the Jersey Joe Walcott of more recent years. Again the fight went 15 rounds, and Sam had to settle for a draw. Even had he won, it would have made little difference. The title was not at stake.

Before the year was out, Langford also squared off against Jack Johnson, a young heavyweight challenger then, who was also a black man. Langford lost this fight in the closest of decisions. Johnson, wearing the world heavyweight crown only months later, remembered the Langford fight so well that he never again stepped into the ring with the Tar Baby.

So it went through the years—Sam fighting in all divisions and generally defeating anyone who would meet him. And along the way, piling up a record of 98 knockouts—a record that placed him second on the world list up to that time.

But even a man of Sam's skills could not avoid being injured when he chose to fight so often. Over the years, the fights began to take their toll, and by 1923 Sam Langford's eyesight was weakening.

Finally Sam challenged the heavyweight champion of South America and his challenge was accepted. The smart money was all on the champion. The Boston Tar Baby, as everyone knew, was over the hill—a spent, half-blind fighter whose superb ring skills had been badly eroded by time.

But Sam had something going for him that nobody counted on. It was the force of his burning desire for a title that so long had been denied him. It fueled his aging body, sharpened his boxer's wits, put spring in his tired legs—it won Sam the fight, and a championship at the age of 45. And he did it with eyes so dimmed he could barely make out the form of the man in the ring with him.

Bridges

THE WORLD'S SMALLEST DRAWBRIDGE

Sailing enthusiasts wishing to explore the Great Sound off Bermuda find they must pass through Somerset Bridge, which joins Somerset Island to the mainland. Passers-by are always willing to lend a helping hand as they steer the mast of your boat through the narrow 18-inch opening, and then replace the center board of the bridge so that waiting traffic can be on its way.

Bullets

THE BULLET COUGH

On Thanksgiving Day, in 1936, two Minnesota boys named Harold and Charlie Peterson decided to go hunting with a man who worked on the family farm.

The two brothers and their companion were good hunters, but accidents can happen to the best of marksmen, and that day a bullet from the hired man's gun accidentally struck young Harold in the face, opening a large hole in his cheek.

When the wounded youngster reached the hospital, it was found that the bullet had lodged at the base of his skull, so near the spinal cord that the doctors did not dare operate to remove it. The 15-year-old boy was told that he would have to take his chances and live with the bullet in his body for the rest of his life. Fortunately, it gave him no real trouble and in time he almost forgot about it.

Then, in 1960, Harold, then 39 years old and running the same family farm, felt that he might be coming down with a sore throat. A few days later he had a violent coughing spasm. He coughed and coughed, and finally he coughed up a bullet—the same soft-nosed rifle bullet that had lodged in his neck 24 years before.

Bulls

BULLS ON THE LOOSE

Spain has brought the art of bull-fighting to its peak, say those who follow this spectacular and bloody sport. And the Spanish festival of The Running of the Bulls at Pamplona each July (before the bull fights commence) is a sporting event which attracts tens of thousands of spectators from all over the world.

At this festival, the bulls are set free from their pens to charge down the main street of the town in pursuit of the men and boys who run before them. In this event, the bull is in charge, and many a desperate runner falls under the crushing feet of the speeding animals. This time it is man, not the bull, who is bloodied.

In Colombia, fighting bulls play their part in another kind of sport, bull-vaulting.

Pole-vaulting over a fighting bull as it charges past is a dangerous sport. But it is not a new one. The great Spanish artist, Goya, depicted such a daring leap in an etching he made in 1815.

Bull-vaulting in South America is mostly done by only the boldest matadors. But it is also a popular sport on breeding farms where young hands practice and dream of the day when they, too, will become bull-fighters.

The racing bulls speed down the track in teams.

THE RACING BULLS OF MADURA

It is post time at Ambunten, in the South Pacific. There is a stillness at track-side. Offshore, the Strait of Surabaya is a shining carpet of green. Soft breezes drift through the coconut palms.

There's a sudden trumpet blast. Someone waves a flag.

And they're off!

But these are no smooth-limbed race horses thundering down the grassy straightaway. They are heavier, stronger, less graceful. Their flying legs are shorter, and they run closer to the ground.

They are the racing bulls of the Indonesian island of Madura—bulls that run at high speed for short distances and train for the races on raw eggs and beer. During the racing season—August through November—they eat as many as 50 eggs a day, and also feed on herbs and honey.

The island of Madura, only 3 miles out from Surabaya, the capital of East Java, is called the Island of Beautiful Happenings.

The bull races of Madura are the only ones in the world, and the bulls on this Indonesian paradise are not trained for track performance alone. Like bulls everywhere else, they also have breeding duties, and from them spring some of the finest bulls in the world. The Madurese also export cattle to the Java mainland, to the surrounding islands, and even abroad.

On Madura, the races are government-operated and are open only to home-bred bulls. The racing bulls are excessively pampered, their food is the best available, and their diet is rigidly controlled. They are bathed, groomed, and massaged daily.

On their way to the race, the bulls are hung with bells and gilded trappings, and brightly colored parasols are held above them, to keep the sun out of their eyes. The bulls approach in pairs, and their gaudily clad drivers carry straps of red, yellow, or blue.

Marching past the stands, each pair of bulls is further accompanied by its supporters and its own marching musicians, playing drums and flutes.

Finally the bulls are stripped for action and all the decorations are laid aside. Following the blast of a trumpet, they amble onto the track and take their places before the stands to await the starter's flag.

There is no winning by a nose or a head on Madura. It's the legs that count, and the winners are the bulls whose forelegs are first to cross the finish line.

The racing rules are less complex than on the world's thoroughbred racing strips. The distances are about 150 yards and there are *three* placing judges. A number of heats are run with winners racing winners until only three teams are left. These three teams run in the final race for first, second, and third prizes.

Despite the island's miles of white sandy beaches, tropical scenery, and the treasures of the ancient Sumenep kings, its greatest attraction is the race track at Ambunten and the magnificent racing bulls.

The racing bulls of Madura are dressed in handsome trappings for the parade that takes place before the races start.

Camels

THE GREAT AMERICAN CAMEL EXPERIMENT

The first mention of a camel ever being seen in America was made in 1709, when one was reported to be in the colony of Virginia. Why the animal was there and what became of it later are not recorded.

But we do know what became of the seventy-nine camels that were brought to the United States in the spring of 1856.

They came to America through the tireless efforts of Jefferson Davis, who was then Secretary of War under President Pierce.

Davis had long championed the use of camels for carrying military freight in the desert regions of the American Southwest. He felt that, for transporting supplies to the widely scattered forts throughout that area, camels would be far superior to the Army horses and mules then in use.

Camels, he argued, were the logical animals for such terrain. They could live off the sparse, dry vegetation of the land, and they could go without food or water for as long as two weeks. Furthermore, camels could carry loads up to 500 pounds for long periods of time, loads so heavy they would break the back of a horse or mule.

Davis' plan was at first widely ridiculed, but eventually he secured the funds he needed for his "experiment," as he called it, and the camels were purchased and brought to the United States. On their arrival in Texas they were permanently quartered at Camp Verde, and from there carried supplies out to other forts in the Southwest.

Unfortunately, the camel is not a charmer. He is bad-tempered and given to biting, is stubborn to the extreme and smells like a leather-tanning factory after a fire. Neither the Army hostlers in charge of the humpbacked animals nor the Army horses and mules who were quartered with them could abide the presence of the odorous camels. As for any nearby cattle, they panicked simply at sight of the alien creatures.

The camels had not come to the New World alone. They

were accompanied by several Arabs who were to instruct the Army hostlers in the care and training of their new charges. But the Arabs spoke no English and the Americans spoke no Arabic, and so all instructions had to be given through signs and gestures.

This communication gap led to many frustrating encounters. One of these occurred shortly after the animals arrived in Texas, when it was noticed that they were showing markedly curious behavior even for camels. They appeared sluggish, and something was definitely wrong with their gait. It was not until a puzzled officer investigated that the cause of the camels' trouble was found. They were drunk.

The Arabs, being teetotalers, did not know what to do with the beer they were handed as part of their daily ration, and so they poured it into the camels' watering pails. The Army handlers, seeing this, thought beer must be part of the camels' menu, and so they supplied the animals with large amounts of it. The camels liked the new beverage, lapped it up in quantity and then staggered around for the rest of the day.

The Arabs did not, however, remain a problem for long. Finding life in an American Army camp tedious, all but two of them took off and disappeared into the untrackable hinterland that was then the American Southwest. They were never heard from again.

The first sustained test of the camels came when twenty of them were taken on a survey trip by Army engineers. That was in June, 1857, and the route was from Fort Defiance, New Mexico, to Fort Tyron, California. On the long trek, the camels carried all the food and water for the men and their horses, lived off the dry land and required little care. In every way they proved that, as pack animals in such terrain, they were superior to mules.

This superiority was just starting to be acknowledged by the military when the whole camel experiment blew up. The Civil War was upon the country, and no one cared what happened to camels in the Far West. Jefferson Davis, the man who sparked the idea, was no longer around to defend it; he had become President of the Confederacy.

For a brief time, the camels were also involved in the conflict. They were, surprisingly, captured early on by the Confederate troops as a prize of war, only to be recaptured shortly afterward by the boys in blue.

But there was no continued interest in the camels. So the camels became an exotic casualty of the Civil War. Several years later they were sold off to circuses and to Nevada silver miners who used them to pack out the ore.

During their years with the Army, many camels had escaped into the desert and reverted to a wild state. They found the desert congenial as a natural habitat, and they survived and reproduced well there. Often, small bands of them were seen roaming across the arid land.

But these small herds gradually vanished, the victims of cattlemen steadily advancing westward and of Indian hunters who found the camels an excellent source of fresh meat.

The last sighting of a band of wild camels was made in 1880. As late as 1903, however, a single camel was found with a seedy traveling circus in San Antonio, Texas. The animal was identified by the Army brand on its flank and was the last survivor of the seventy-nine original camels and their descendants.

Nothing remains now to mark the great American "camel experiment."

This camel-wrestling match is taking place at Aydin, Turkey, near the Aegean Sea.

CAMEL WRESTLING

In Turkey, camel wrestling is a major sporting event, especially in the area around the Aegean Sea. The big humped-back animals actually engage in a long shoving match, with an occasional bite thrown in to get the opponent to move off. The camels are never badly hurt and the winner is the camel who simply doesn't give up.

Cars

FIRST CROSS-COUNTRY TRIP

In 1903, a New England doctor named Nelson Jackson, who was on a vacation in San Francisco, made a bet that he could drive clear across the continent in that new-fangled invention called the "automobile."

A few days later, the daring doctor bought himself a 2-cylinder, 20-horsepower, chain-driven car and—with a companion—headed east on his pioneer journey.

The trip covered 6,000 miles and 11 states. The top speed attained was 20 miles per hour, and the roads were so bad that sometimes Jackson made no more than 6 miles in a single day.

Frequently, he was stopped dead by breakdowns. Even minor repairs took days because tires had to come all the way from Akron and spare parts from Cleveland.

Once a farmer's wife purposely misdirected him so that her sister, who lived 50 miles away, could actually see a "horseless carriage."

But the intrepid Jackson pushed on as fast as he could go and he finally made the East Coast. It took him 63 exhausting days and cost him $8,000 to win a $50 bet . . . but he was the first man in history to cross the American continent by car.

Catfish

WALKING CATFISH ATTACKS DOGS!

Not long ago a woman in the Miami area was awakened early one morning by the frantic barking of her dog. Looking out the bedroom window, she saw the cause of the commotion. The family dog was being attacked by a fish—and right on the front lawn!

The air-breathing walking catfish, which inhabit fresh water and are native to Africa and south Asia, were first brought into the United States as exotic aquarium novelties. It is suspected that they entered American waters accidentally by escaping from a Florida holding pond a few years ago. Now they are entrenched by the millions in the fresh waters of southeastern Florida, where conservationists consider them a disaster and report them officially as out of control.

It is easy for walking catfish to live out of water. In addition to gills, they are equipped with rudimentary lungs and can survive on land for extended periods of time.

They can also walk considerable distances over moist ground by stumping along on their strong pectoral fins. Generally, they do their traveling on damp or rainy nights. In this way, they are able to move from one freshwater source to another and establish new colonies.

Florida is particularly suited for the migration of the walking catfish. The state has the warm climate the fish needs and also provides it with many lakes, ponds, streams and man-made waterways for habitat.

Although the walking catfish are thought to be tasty by African and Asian standards, Americans do not find them palatable, and so they have no economic value. Worse still, they drive out edible fish.

The alien invaders are omnivorous feeders on fish eggs and insect and fish larvae, and devour everything in sight. Once they are established in any body of water, it is just a matter of time before all the other fish—including game fish—disappear. Other fish cannot compete with the aggressive newcomers for food, and so they either leave or starve to death.

This albino catfish is air-breathing, but it doesn't walk overland—it's confined to the Miami Seaquarium in Florida.

The migratory fish are also prolific breeders and have no natural enemies. From one small Florida pond in which they had become entrenched, game wardens seined them up to get a head count. The dismayed wardens found that the unwelcomed residents of the pond were living in a population density of 3,000 pounds to the acre.

Cats

COOL CATS

Most of the old beliefs concerning cats have disappeared, but some persisted until very recent times, and a few still do. One of the strangest untruths about cats was that tigers could not climb trees, a belief long held by men who should have known better. As late as the 1920's, Frank Buck, who had treed a tiger and taken pictures of it, couldn't wait to hasten home and show his evidence to several still-doubting naturalists of his acquaintance. Actually, all cats, with the single exception of the cheetah, are good climbers. The long-legged cheetah, who can hunt like a dog and is the speediest animal on earth (for short distances, it can make up to 70 miles an hour), is the only member of the cat family that does not have retractable claws and is, therefore, without grasping ability.

Contrary to popular opinion, cats, wild or domestic, are not afraid of water. Sensible creatures, they don't like being wet or uncomfortable, but they are excellent swimmers when the need for this skill arises. The director of the Frankfurt Zoo makes mention of a cheetah who once fell overboard in the Red Sea and then swam calmly about for half an hour until it was rescued.

Some cats have taken to the water voluntarily. Tigers, on a number of occasions, have been known to swim from the Malay Peninsula to the island of Singapore by way of the Johore Straits, navigating this mile or more of rough water without any difficulty.

Among the little domestic cats, a yellow tom bearing the unlikely name of Thumbles (he had an extra "thumb" on each forepaw) became a living legend on Chesapeake Bay because of his uncatlike devotion to water sports. Not only was he an accomplished gunwale-walker and mast-climber on the fast little sloop he "commanded," but he was a born swimmer and liked nothing better than dropping over the side and swimming across for a brief visit with any neighboring craft.

Cats are widely recognized as animals with an instinct for

elegance, but none has ever been able to indulge this aristocratic bent so fully as a magnificent white Persian called Nicodemus.

As one of the most highly paid cat models in the business, Nicodemus, groomed right up to his ear tufts, spent most of his time before a camera, his snowy person usually glittering with priceless jewels or draped in boneless languor around the neck of a beautiful woman.

A hard-working "career" cat, Nicodemus once faced a severe financial setback when a witless joker singed off his long, white whiskers. In a business based on beauty, a cat without whiskers is a cat without a job. But a fashionable New York wigmaker came to the rescue and glued to Nicodemus' soft muzzle a glistening horsehair moustache which, undetected, served until his own grew back.

CHEETAH VS. GREYHOUND

Here's a race which should drive the rail birds up into the grandstand. At a dog track in Aldershot, England, a cheetah was matched against a greyhound. Kid Spots, in the lead, ran away with the race. The cheetah, despite its leopardlike appearance, is easily tamed.

Chess

A GAME OF CHESS IN MOROCCO

Late in the 15th century, when the Moors were fleeing Spain, the sultan of Morocco imprisoned a politician named Yuseph on the charge of treason.

Yuseph, finding time heavy on his hands while awaiting the sultan's decision on his fate, prevailed upon a friendly guard to play chess with him. Both men were excellent players, and the guard grew so interested in the game that he played it every day.

Finally, a message arrived from the sultan with an order for the immediate execution of the prisoner. The guard was very disappointed. The two men were in the middle of a close game and he hated to lose his partner. The prisoner, eager for even a few more hours of life, talked the guard into delaying the execution and continuing the match.

Late that day, while the men were still playing the same game of chess, another messenger arrived, this time with news that the sultan was dead.

After he had given this news to the guard, the messenger then turned to the prisoner, fell on his knees before him, and addressed him as the new sultan of Morocco. Unknown to the guard, that political prisoner, whose life was saved by a chess game, was none other than the brother of the dead sultan, the man who had imprisoned him.

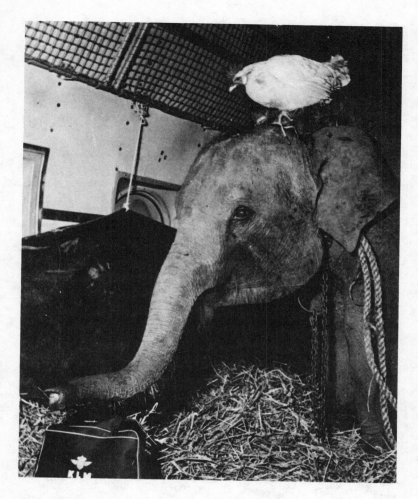

Chicken

<u>THE ELEPHANT GIRL</u>

KLM, the Royal Dutch airlines, flies a great many elephants from the Far East to zoos all over the world. For some unknown reason the elephants' jangled nerves during flight can be soothed only by perching Elephant Girl, an ordinary white chicken owned by KLM, on their heads.

Toy Town—This model of Madurodam, in Holland, is built to scale. It is 1/25th the size of the actual buildings and people.

Child's World

MADURODAM, SMALL TOWN

In The Hague, capital of Holland, is the smallest town in the world.

Scaled accurately to 1/25 their actual sizes are perfect models of everything that goes to make up a typical large Dutch town—houses, churches, airfields, canals, barges, radio towers, shopping centers, factories, cars, schools, windmills. You name it, it's there.

This amazing miniature town—the most complete in the world—is really a memorial, erected by the parents of George Maduro to honor their brave son's death in World War II. The manual labor required to build the town was volunteered by students from all over the world. Today, students still contribute time to help operate the attraction. It is the only "town" where the blind can see, for only those who are sightless are permitted to touch any of the models.

But most amazing is that the "smallest town in the world" is maintained for the benefit of the "smallest university in the world." This unique university is the Netherlands' Students Sanitorium which provides students found suffering from tuberculosis with medical treatment and a college education at the same time.

Children can play around the structures of the miniature world of Madurodam.

Looking down on the roadway with its moving cars and trucks, one hardly notices the tracks.

Christmas

CHRISTMAS NIGHT IN NO-MAN'S LAND

On Christmas night, in 1916, a company of New Zealanders were holding down a sector of the Western Front. There had been heavy fighting all day long, but now the sound of the guns had almost ceased and there was a lull in the battle which was welcomed by the men of both sides.

Suddenly, from the enemy lines the commander of the New Zealanders, Captain Greshley, heard a voice call out in German. Looking over the top of the trench, he made out the figure of a German soldier coming toward him carrying a white flag of truce. Safely at the trench, the German at once made the reason for his visit clear: It was Christmas, he said, so why not call a short truce, and in the spirit of the holiday, have the men on both sides talk to each other and enjoy a few moments of peace.

Captain Greshley agreed, and soon the New Zealanders were scrambling out of their trenches to greet the Germans who had already thrown down their guns, and before they knew it, they were all singing "Silent Night, Holy Night." Greshley was asked how come a New Zealander could speak German so well. The captain explained that he had been born in Germany, but that his parents had died while he was a child and he had been sent to live with an uncle in New Zealand. There had been a younger brother, the captain went on, but he didn't know where he was. The German soldier stared at the captain. "Was your name originally Greisler?" he asked. The captain nodded. "Then," said the soldier, "I'm your brother, Max Greisler."

THE WORLD'S SMALLEST CHURCH

The Reverend Lewis West of Hudson, Massachusetts, holds services in his 5′ by 11′ church. The edifice seats four people, and there are usually a hundred people congregated outside on Sundays.

LIGHT OF GENIUS

One of the most clever tasks of design and engineering was accomplished by Filippo Brunelleschi, an Italian architect who lived in the 15th century.

When he constructed the dome on the Cathedral of Florence, this Renaissance architect left a small opening in the top through which a shaft of light streams every June 21. The opening, in its relation to the sun, was so precisely arranged that the sunbeam shines squarely on a brass plate set in the floor of the sanctuary. For over five centuries this ray of light has never failed to cover the plate completely.

Brunelleschi knew that once there was the slightest divergence of light from the plate it would mean that the cathedral had shifted its center of gravity and the structure would have to be bolstered to prevent its collapse. The cathedral, however, was so perfectly designed that it has stood firmly on marshy ground for over 500 years.

CHURCH OF BONES

All Saints Church in Sedlac, Czechoslovakia, is decorated with the bones of an estimated 10,000 persons. A fierce plague and a war with the Turks resulted in the death of 30,000 people who were buried in the church graveyard in one year. In 1600 the bones were taken from the graveyard to redecorate the church after soldiers had looted it of its ornaments.

Mountain of skulls.

Chandelier of bones.

Circus

THE CLOWN GRIMALDI

One day, in the year 1835, an Italian doctor who treated only diseases of the mind was visited in his Florence clinic by a man whose face was a tragic mask of despair.

The man said that he suffered constantly from anxiety, was exhausted from lack of sleep, could not eat, avoided all his friends. So deep and prolonged was his melancholy, said the unhappy man, that he now felt that only by taking his life could he escape the horror of living.

However, he had learned that the doctor was famous for treating cases of depression, and the man had now come seeking the physician's help.

The doctor examined his patient and found that, despite his mental condition, he was in excellent physical shape. What the man needed was simply to learn how to laugh again.

There was a circus in town at that time, and a marvelous clown named Grimaldi was its star performer. Night after night, the clown had people rolling in the aisles with his comic antics and zany humor. He had the critics raving, he was the darling of the city. The clown could make anybody laugh, so the doctor prescribed an immediate visit to the circus for his melancholy patient.

"You must go tonight," the doctor advised. "Grimaldi is the world's greatest clown. He will make you laugh. He will cure you of your sadness."

"No," replied the sad-faced man. "He cannot cure me. You see, I am Grimaldi."

An 1835 illustration of the clown Grimaldi in action in the circus. All clowns today are called "Joey" in honor of Joseph Grimaldi.

PINK LEMONADE

During the summer of 1857, the Mabie Circus was making a tour through the South when one of the clowns suddenly decided to leave the troupe. The manager called on the ballyhoo man, Pete Conklin, to fill in.

Conklin did pretty well, but when he asked for a raise, the manager said Conklin wasn't that good. So Conklin quit in a huff. But because he was broke, he tagged along with the circus as a lemonade-seller. Lemons were expensive in those days, so Conklin made his lemonade with tartaric acid and sugar.

One hot day, Conklin did such a brisk business that he ran out of lemonade. Rushing into a nearby tent, he picked up a bucket of water, stirred in some tartaric acid, and was in business again. It wasn't until he poured the first glass that he noticed that his new lemonade was pink. He couldn't imagine how the color had changed. But he decided to make the most of it.

"Strawberry lemonade," he shouted. "Try the new strawberry lemonade." People did try it, and today pink lemonade is sold at every circus.

And how did Conklin's lemonade get that color? Well, a performer's red tights had just been soaking in that bucket of water!

Clothing

THE MAGIC CAPE

In 1597, a young Spanish sailor by the name of Juan Combe returned to Madrid from the New World, full of stories about his adventures among the Indians. Juan also brought back an unusual garment . . . a wonderful cape which the superstitious people said must have magic qualities. Juan explained that there was nothing magic about it, that such a cape was widely used by the Indians.

But the people grew more suspicious of the power of Juan's cape, and finally the unlucky man was brought before the local court.

The judge examined the curious garment, questioned Juan at length and then gave his verdict.

Juan, said the judge, was guilty of wearing a cape through which water could not pass. Therefore, Juan was interfering with the will of God, who sent the rain to drench us. Such evil interference was witchcraft and was punishable by death.

So Juan was executed, and all because he wore a raincape made of crude rubber . . . a substance which was then unknown in Europe but which had been used for centuries by the Indians of South America to keep themselves dry.

Courts

A LATE DECISION

In 1843, in the city of Pskov, Russia, two noblemen became the fathers of sons at the same time. One father secured a fine French nursemaid for his child. But she did not remain long; the second nobleman stole her away by offering higher wages. This infuriated the original employer, and he sued in court for the woman's return. But the case dragged on endlessly, year after year.

One day, in Moscow, while Czar Nicholas the Second was reviewing his troops, a horseman arrived with a message. General Kuropotkin, the Czar's minister of war, took it and read the message. At first he looked puzzled, then he started laughing, and, turning to the Czar, read the words out loud:

> "We, the Semstov Court, have decided that the nursemaid, Amelie Petitjean, be held to return to her original employer where she shall immediately resume her duties as wet nurse to the infant Alexi Nicholayvich."

When General Kuropotkin finished reading, the Czar asked him who the infant mentioned in the court order might be. Grinning broadly, the general replied: "Your Majesty, I am that infant."

The legal action brought more than 50 years before was finally won in 1899, the same year that the "infant" became Russia's minister of war.

DEPUTY GOVERNOR

In 1879, when Arizona was still a territory, a man named Beecher was tried for murder, found guilty, and sentenced to be hanged.

However, the sheriff felt that Beecher was innocent and continued a search for proof. Finally, he found evidence that he knew would clear Beecher, but time was running out, as the condemned man was to be hanged the following morning. So the sheriff wired the governor asking for an immediate stay of execution until a new trial could be arranged.

This message was received at Phoenix late at night. The telegrapher on duty, a man named Randall, realized the urgency of the message and went at once to the governor's house. But the governor was desperately sick and could not be seen. And no one else was available to give a stay.

The telegraph operator was sure that the governor would have given a stay automatically in such a case. After all, a possibly innocent man might be executed if the hanging were not delayed.

Randall made a decision. Just before dawn he sent a message clicking out to the waiting sheriff. "Stay granted," the message read. And it was signed: "H. Smathers, Governor . . . by E. Randall, Temporary Governor."

Beecher was later proved innocent, and because of this no charges were pressed against Randall for impersonating the governor.

The Rhone Valley cow-fight.

Cows

THE COW-FIGHT

It's the camel-fight in Turkey (see page 77), the cock-fight in
Mexico, the ram-fight in Austria, the bull-fight in Spain, but to
the Swiss these are no match for the cow-fight held each year
in April in the Rhone Valley. The entries come from all over
Switzerland; even the monks of the St. Bernard Hospice, so famous for their dogs, enter a cow from their large herd.

The long-horned, black-haired bovine beauties who participate in these unique tournaments have been bred exclusively
in the Val d'Herena, one of the side valleys of the Rhone River.
The animals are small but very strong, with a reputation for
being prolific milk-givers, and for having a rare fighting spirit.

The owner of a herd generally has two or three combative
cows eligible to fight the previous year's "Queen of Queens."
These contenders are all "queens" of their own individual
herds, having won their position by sheer aggressiveness.

The object of their fight (which takes place naturally) is to decide which cow will be Queen of the Queens for the coming year.

Shortly before the big fight, the queens, wearing garlands of flowers and with heavy brass bells dangling from their massive necks, are brought down to the town of Martigny, and put on a special diet of bran and white wine to make them stronger.

On the day of the contest, the cows are taken to a special open arena on a nearby hillside. Like race horses, the animals begin to show excitement as soon as they enter the enclosure, where they paw the earth and pull down the little fir trees standing at the edge of the big ring.

When the "queens" have reached the proper pitch of excitement, they are let loose and enter at once into combat with whichever cow is nearest. Locking horns, bucking, kicking, charging each other, bellowing in anger, the fighting cows—sometimes as many as twelve at once—make a thundering and unforgettable sight as they battle for supremacy.

This curious fight rages around the arena for an hour or more, while one by one the beaten, exhausted cows withdraw voluntarily until only a single cow is left in the field. This animal, later, will be paired off against the titleholder in a battle which will not end until one of the two cows is decisively vanquished. The winner will then be crowned Queen of the Queens among all the herds of the high Alps for that year.

Crime

ROBBERY ON MADISON AVENUE

One day, in 1946, a holdup man boldly entered a jewelry store on New York's Madison Avenue. There were no customers in the store and the holdup went off smoothly. When he'd taken all the jewelry he could gather up, the bandit left, got into a car parked outside, and drove off. Only then did the frightened jeweler dare to call the police.

There were no clues for the police to go on, so they proceeded to question all those who had been passing by when the bandit drove off from the store. But the getaway car had been noticed only by an old man out walking his dog. And he couldn't describe the car. He could only say that the license number added up to a total of 35.

The police stared in astonishment. Then the old man explained that it was a hobby of his to add up license plate numbers. Perhaps, he said, if they gave him a little time, he could remember the numbers which had added up to a total of 35.

Finally, he did remember all the numbers on the license plate of that get-away car. The car was traced and found, and so was the thief. And all because an old man liked to amuse himself by adding up license plate numbers while walking his dog.

SEEING IS BELIEVING

One day in 1910, a traveler boarded the London-to-Liverpool Express, and settled back for the trip with a newspaper and a big cigar. He was alone in a first-class compartment until, just before the train started, a young woman jumped aboard and sat down opposite him.

After the train started, the woman suddenly spoke to him, demanding 50 pounds sterling ($250).

When he refused, she took off her hat, rumpled her hair, and tore her blouse. "Give me the money," she threatened, "or I'll call the train guard and have you arrested for attempted rape."

Thinking hard, the man continued to puff on his cigar. Suddenly, he had an idea. Reaching up carefully, he pulled the emergency cord. This surprised the woman, but when the guard appeared, she accused the man of attacking her.

"Is this true?" asked the guard.

"No," said the man, "and here is my proof." He held up his cigar; the long ash on its end proved he hadn't moved from his seat.

THE PRISONER OF MONACO

In 1912, a prisoner was sentenced to death in Monaco. According to custom, an executioner had to be brought from France, but when the man appeared he demanded 10,000 francs to do his unpleasant job.

The prince of Monaco said this was too much—his little country couldn't afford it. But the executioner refused to come down in price, and returned to France. A cheaper executioner could not be found, so the execution was held up indefinitely.

Meanwhile, the doomed man, who was poor and had no place to go anyway, was quite comfortable in jail. But he began to be a financial burden on the country. He was the only man in jail and, as the weeks and months drifted by, the cost of guarding and maintaining this one prisoner mounted higher and higher.

Finally, a solution was reached. If the man did not attempt to escape, he could live in jail under minimum security and would be paid a small monthly allowance for the rest of his life. This would pay for his small comforts and care. The prisoner agreed, and that allowance was paid to the day of his death, 30 years later.

THE PIRATE AND THE WINE JUGS

A few centuries ago, when the New World was very new, the Caribbean was infested with pirates who preyed on the great Spanish galleons that sailed from South America to Spain laden with rich treasure.

One of these pirates was a man named Bartolomo. Although the Spaniards had captured Bartolomo a number of times, they had never been able to hang him. He was a clever man, and no prison could hold him. He always escaped before his trial.

But the pirate had one weakness. He could not swim. The Spaniards learned of this and the next time they caught him, they clapped him into a ship's brig and then anchored the vessel far out in the water.

But soon again Bartolomo was free on shore, and laughing at his infuriated captors. What they didn't know was that one night the pirate had worked his way out of the brig and made his way on deck. Finding two big, empty wine jugs, he quietly lowered them into the water, dropped quietly overboard himself, and then, using the jugs like water wings, silently floated to shore and freedom.

The deadly Nile crocodile and his "flying toothpick," the Egyptian plover.

Crocodiles

THE FLYING TOOTHPICK

The crocodile, which is found all around the world within the broad belt of the tropics, is the most feared of all the giant reptiles. Compared to this evil-tempered monster, his alligator cousin is a pussycat.

The armor-plated body of the crocodile is lithe and long. (Some have been known to reach a length of 30 feet.) He moves with lightning speed and can kill a man with a lash from his powerful tail.

But it is his mouth that is really frightening. The jaws of a crocodile can snap shut on its prey with a thousand pounds of pressure. In his long, tapered head his teeth are set like a row of deadly weapons. Nor does he have to worry about this natural arsenal failing him, because his 70 teeth are endlessly replaced as he loses them.

The huge teeth also intermesh, giving the reptilian mouth the look of a murderous zipper. The croc's charmless appearance is further emphasized by his front choppers which thrust upward through a marginal groove on his upper lip to jut, tusklike, above his pointed snout.

Though his teeth serve him well, the crocodile *does* have a dental problem. Unlike the alligator, this big saurian does not have a tongue. That means he has trouble freeing his teeth of debris after devouring his frequent meals. The Nile crocodile solved this grooming problem eons ago, when he formed a strange partnership with the Egyptian plover. This bird keeps the big reptile's teeth clean by feeding on the particles of food left lodged between them.

Apparently the bird's host is content with his "flying toothpick" as the plover is the only living thing that the crocodile has never been known to attack.

CROCODILES AND ALLIGATORS

Given the common name "lizard" by both the ancient Greeks and the exploring Spaniards, the crocodile and the alligator show a fearsome similarity. But despite their obvious kinship, the natural ranges of these heavy-scaled reptiles meet at only one place in the world, in the southern part of Florida; nowhere else are they found together in the wild.

Aside from this area, alligators exist only in one small section of China along the Yangtze River. Crocodiles, on the other hand, may be found almost anywhere around the world within the broad belt of the tropical zones. Crocodiles can live only in a very warm climate; alligators can survive in a slightly colder environment.

Although both these ferocious reptiles, with their bony armor-plated bodies and deadly snapping jaws, are descended from the same ancient family of prehistoric monsters, they have never been known to mate with each other.

There are a number of differences between the two. The alligator is very dark in color with a heavy, even chunky, body; the crocodile is lithe and light-hued. The crocodile seeks salt or brackish water; the alligator prefers fresh streams. The female alligator builds an elaborate nest of mud and wet grass for her eggs, while the mother crocodile simply deposits hers in a hole along the water's edge. Both reptiles are vicious, but the crocodile is far more evil-tempered, swift and aggressive than its somewhat lethargic cousin.

The greatest differences between the two reptiles are in their heads and mouths. The crocodile has a long, narrow head tapering to a point, while the alligator's head is broad, almost rectangular in shape, with a blunt snout. It also has a tongue, which the crocodile does not.

Both these saurians boast huge teeth which are endlessly replaced by new ones as needed, but where the 'gator enjoys the regular use of eighty of these enameled weapons, the croc has to make do with only seventy. The teeth of both intermesh when the jaws are closed, giving each reptilian mouth the look of a murderous zipper. To this charmless appearance, the croc adds the exposure of two or more of his big, lower front teeth,

A look into an alligator's mouth.

generally the fourth tooth on either side. Thrust through marginal grooves in his upper "lip," these jut, tusklike, above his deadly snout when it is closed. The alligator does not share this dreadful-dragon look; its lower teeth disappear into upper-jaw pits.

These dangerous creatures of swamp and river are not only voracious eaters but are inveterate cannibals as well; if there is one thing a saurian likes for dinner, it is another saurian. They are the worst predators of their own young.

Because their intermeshing teeth make the sidewise motions of chewing impossible, both reptiles must swallow their food whole, in large chunks snapped off by their powerful jaws. The labor needed for one of these monsters to digest the horny hide of another is formidable. Digestion is made possible with the help of large stones swallowed regularly to act as "grinders" in the stomach, and a bountiful supply of a digestive juice so strong that a single drop of it on a man's hand feels like a burn.

Both crocs and 'gators frequently drown their victims before swallowing them. If their prey is too large to get down in one piece, as it often is, the reptiles clutch their victims tightly in their mouths and revolve furiously in the water, hoping, by this violent thrashing, to break up their too-large meals.

When this fails, the victim is often carried to the reptile's fetid den along the water and is left there to putrefy, thus making the captor's grisly job of breaking up and consuming his meal considerably easier.

The American crocodile is somewhat smaller than the alligator—which averages about 9 to 12 feet in length—and rarely exceeds 16 feet; but the estuarine crocodile of South Asia is a fearsome giant, as well as a notorious man-eater. In one of these huge monsters, caught in the Philippines, was found the complete body of a man with only his head missing.

The largest estuarine crocodile ever heard of was found near Bengal at the end of the 19th century. This nightmare reptile measured a fantastic 33 feet from tip to tail, and was 14 feet around. His skull may be seen at the British Museum in London.

Vienna.

Dancing

THE WILD DANCE

Who would ever have thought that the Old World city of Vienna could dance itself into a frenzy.

Well, it did. Back in the 1700's a new dance hit the Austrian capital. It paired the dancers off in wildly revolving couples, and was the opposite of the slow minuet.

Overnight, the lively dance became a citywide craze. Huge ballrooms sprang up by the dozens; their doors were never closed and mobs of eager dancers surged in at all hours. Rotating orchestras played around the clock. Intoxicated by the dance, people neglected their work, abandoned their children, left their sick untended.

Foreign observers were stunned by what they saw. A touring British actor wrote: "The people of Vienna have a dance mania ... they dance from 10 o'clock at night to 7 the next morning in a continuous frenzy." Another writer described droves of people actually pawning their possessions for money to dance.

Artists depicted the city as the scene of an endless carnival, the people whirling themselves into exhaustion, their faces demented. Press and pulpit thundered against the evil. Doctors warned that the dance was deadly. Couples had taken to competing with others to see how many times they could whirl around the dance floor at top speed without stopping. Sudden death often followed these contests.

And what was the dance that had turned Vienna into a city of madness? It wasn't the Disco. It wasn't St. Vitus Dance. Would you believe it was the waltz?

Reindeer roundup in Lapland.

Deer

REINDEER ABOVE THE ARCTIC CIRCLE

Dag Hammarskjold once said that the life of Lapland is "tied to the ancient rhythm of reindeer breeding."

The reindeer, to the Arctic Lapp, is his most vital possession, providing him with transportation, food, clothing, bone utensils, even medicine, in the form of powdered antlers.

The herding of reindeer has made nomads of the Lapps, forcing them to follow their animals endlessly as they roam the vast silent tundra in search of fresh vegetation to feed on, or to take to the coastal mountains to escape from the pestilential mosquitoes.

Once a year the Lapps round up their herds. I have been in Swedish Lapland during one of these reindeer roundups, when all the foraging animals in a particular area are gathered together and driven into a huge, public corral made of logs and

Lassoing the reindeer in Lapland.

wire. Once all the reindeer are inside the corral, which may
hold several thousand milling animals, the big gates are pulled
shut and the Lapps enter to separate their own reindeer from
those of other herders.

The Lapps have no difficulty sorting out their own animals,
easily identifying them by means of a "branding" notch cut
into their ears at birth. As soon as a herder spots one of his

own deer, he sends his lasso singing through the air, captures the bucking animal neatly around its branching antlers, and leads it off to one of the small corrals reserved for the individual herds. The annual roundup is the only means by which a Lapp can make an accurate check of his roving stock.

The reindeer may be the first animal in history to have felt the tightening restraint of the lasso, as the Lapps were using the rope for herding centuries before the American West was discovered. One of the earliest mentions of reindeer herding was made in a 9th-century letter written by Norway's King Ottar to Alfred the Great of England, in which Ottar spoke of his fine herd of 600 animals.

It is estimated that about 300,000 reindeer, most of them in domestic herds, roam over the European Arctic of Finland, Sweden and Norway; how many are in Siberia is anybody's guess.

Alaska has a lot more reindeer than European Lapland. A

A Lapp woman milking a reindeer. Reindeer milk is four times as fatty as cow's milk, but very scant in quantity. For this reason, when twin calves are born, one of them usually dies for lack of food.

count made some years ago placed the number at about 700,-000. Reindeer are not native to North America, and the flourishing community of Santa's helpers in Alaska dates back only to 1891, when an American missionary, Dr. Sheldon Jackson, imported a herd of 16 animals from Siberia to help the Eskimos augment their dwindling supply of seal meat. The minister's experiment was a success, and reindeer-raising supports many native Alaskans today.

A reindeer can never make a sneak attack. Due to the curious structure of its ankles, it clicks when it walks like a Spanish dancer with castanets.

Its rough hide is covered with coarse hair which it never sheds. Each hair is like a tiny, air-filled tube, and this makes the animal so buoyant in the water that it is able to swim with most of its body above the surface.

Unlike other antlered animals, there is no double standard among reindeer; the female as well as the male sports a multi-pronged headpiece. In the male, however, the antlers are larger and have more points, sometimes as many as 60.

In snowy Finland, reindeer-drawn sleds are a common means of getting around. To meet the hazards of increasing traffic, an official reindeer driver's school is operating at Pohtimolampi, in Finnish Lapland. To get his license, a prospective driver must demonstrate that he can manage with only one rein, not fall out of the wobbly "pulkka" (sled), and convince the reindeer to stop.

Finland was also the first country ever to penalize a man for drunken reindeer-driving. In 1956, a man in the little town of Kittela was fined $30 for this strange traffic offense. The Finnish driver's license notes this possibility and warns that drunken drivers of reindeer face the same punishment as do drivers of cars.

Sled-driver Alarvikka, Finland's Counsellor of Economics, officially opens his country's first reindeer-drivers' school and successfully demonstrates the tricky technique of one-rein control.

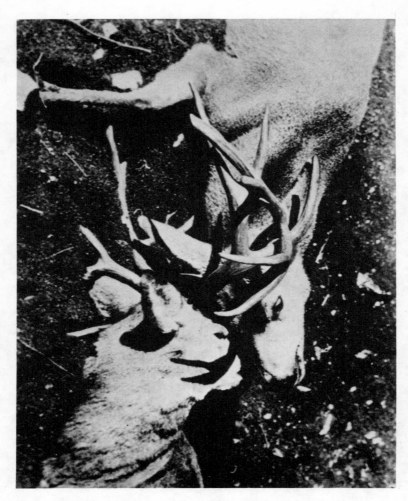

These buck deer, firmly locked together when their antlers became entangled during a battle, were unusually lucky. They were dicovered while
still alive, and their rescuer sawed them apart.

DOOMED ENEMIES

One of the most fascinating sounds is the bugling call of buck deer sending out their signals for combat at the start of the mating season.

As autumn approaches, small herds of deer find their way, as if by prearrangement, to certain wide meadows hidden high up in the wooded mountaintops. Here, with their does and young standing by, the big bucks who lead the herds announce their presence by trumpeting out a challenge to all comers.

The battle sought by these bucks is as much for possession of another's females as it is for the safe enjoyment of their own, for these polygamous animals are always in need of more wives at the mating season.

With the tines of their heavy bone antlers honed to stiletto sharpness from constant rubbing against stone and tree trunk, the encounter that takes place between two raging bucks is always a mortal one. When it is over, one buck must always be left dead in the field, while the mutilated victor trots off, followed docilely by his own family and that of the vanquished buck as well.

Sometimes, however, there is no victor. Slashing and stabbing at each other in their primitive fury, the bucks' many-branched antlers often become inextricably locked; then, bound together in a grotesque union, the doomed animals stagger blindly about for days, the air torn by their bellows of pain, anger and fear. Finally, with their does looking on quietly, the two enemies, overcome by hunger and exhaustion, drop to the trampled, bloody grass and die together.

Disease

BEFORE PASTEUR

During the reign of Queen Anne, in the early 1700's, the city of London was in continuous mourning. The royal children were dying, one by one, from some mysterious disease.

Every known remedy was tried, but still the children died. Finally, a tight guard of soldiers was stationed around the palace, standing shoulder to shoulder. They were instructed to blast constantly on their trumpets in the superstitious hope that the noise would somehow keep death away.

No one, of course, was allowed into the palace. No one, that is, but the royal milkman. He was permitted to pass through the line of soldiers because he carried the cool, fresh milk that the fevered children drank so eagerly.

Unwittingly, this innocent man also carried death. This was long before the days of pasteurization and that innocent-looking milk was filled with the fatal germs of typhoid, a disease which was then incurable.

Although her children did not all die of typhoid, Queen Anne, the last of the Stuarts of England, died without heirs. She had borne 17 children but not one survived her.

Dogs

<u>CROSSING GUARD-DOG</u>

One of the oldest religious shrines in Europe is at Montserrat, Spain. On the way there is a place where a cog railroad crosses the road. Since 1892 the crossing has been guarded by dogs taught to run out and bark when the train was coming. The railroad was discontinued in 1957, but the dogs are still there entertaining tourists who throw money at them to be collected by their one-armed master.

The Australian dingo's bite is much worse than his bark. The dingo is one of the world's most voracious predators, and his jaws are strong enough to tear the flesh right off a victim's bones. However, the dingo does not bark at all when he is hunting, and when he does make a sound it's a howl and not a bark.

THE DINGO

This rough-coated animal with its wary, cold eyes and alert stance is the dingo, the wild dog found only in Australia.

Looking like both fox and wolf, but with all the structural characteristics of a true dog, the dingo is believed to be descended primarily from the ancient wolves of Asia. How the dingo got to the vast island that is Australia is a mystery but it is thought that it probably arrived many thousands of years ago with the first aboriginals who found their way down from India.

A swift and voracious predator, the dingo has jaws that are remarkable for their savage strength, enabling the animal to tear away completely the flesh gripped in its bite and so kill its prey by shock alone.

But what sets the Australian wild dog apart from most of the canine world is that it must hunt in silence, for the dingo does not know how to bark. Barking is a comparatively recent development among dogs, perhaps learned in an effort to imitate man to whom they have voluntarily given their love and loyalty. But the dingo still remains a savage. It looks upon man as its enemy and, having no desire to communicate with him, has never learned to bark.

Ichimonji is the only donkey in the world who owns a set of gold-filled dentures valued at $2,000. They were given to him by the doctors and students of the Tokyo Medical School when he lost his last natural tooth at the remarkable age of twenty-nine.

Donkeys

THE DONKEY'S TEETH

Ever since man and beast entered into domestic partnership, they have been supporting and befriending each other to great mutual advantage.

Man, to be sure, has been by far the greater beneficiary in this joint trust, but he makes up for this edge by frequently giving his dumb companions very unorthodox—but useful—assistance.

Some time ago, Ichimonji, a popular pet donkey at the big Tokyo Zoo, fell prey to the ravages of his 29 years and lost all his teeth. Visiting tots, arriving at the zoo with bundles of juicy carrots, wept at sight of their ancient little friend who could no longer chew their vegetable offerings.

Touched by this, the zoo authorities called upon the Tokyo Medical School to do something about the situation. Their plea was answered.

Doctors and students alike fell to with a will and, providing Ichimonji with a $2,000 set of gold-filled false teeth, they fully restored to the shaggy little pet his former capacity for carrot-munching.

Ichimonji's dentures.

Ducks

THE PENTHOUSE DUCKS

Man has long had a fondness for ducks and not just for those that come to the table.

The waddlers make amusing, even affectionate pets. They are amiable, clean and never have to be brought in from the rain.

The ancient Greeks, noting the drake's intricate courtship dance, gave the birds a semi-sacred status by keeping them in honor of the gods of fertility and love.

The Romans also were partial to ducks and kept them in special roomy enclosures called "nessotrophias" which were complete with ponds and feeding stations.

And in 1525, the city fathers of Zurich issued a stern warning to small "wicked" Swiss boys who stood on bridges and cast stones at unsuspecting ducks below. Furthermore, stated the ordinance, parents would be held accountable for their small frys' anti-duck behavior.

However, no ducks have enjoyed such a downy time of it as the five who once lived at the Peabody Hotel in Memphis, Tennessee.

Called Daphne, Daisy, Denise, Daffy and Donald the Drake, the sleek mallards were housed in the posh penthouse of the Peabody. A special detail of room service provided them with all necessary quacker comforts, including their steady gourmet mixture of grain, grated carrots, cabbage tops and lettuce.

It's not all fun and fine pin feathers, though. The ducks also did their bit for the hotel.

Every morning at 7 o'clock, the ducks were ushered onto an elevator and whisked down to the lobby. There, the small platoon marched to a fine marble fountain, hopped into its clean artesian-well water and swam about happily for most of the day.

Promptly at 3 o'clock each afternoon the ducks were returned to their penthouse pad. This time, though, the passage

The famous Peabody ducks get the red-carpet treatment from the hotel staff.

of their little webbed feet across the lobby was made with pizzazz.

A red carpet was rolled out for them and in single file they waddled over this to the waiting elevator to take them to their quarters. Along the way they were flanked by an honor guard of bellmen. Needless to say, a large, admiring audience was also on hand for their daily departure.

The ducks did not stay at the hotel continuously. Every couple of months the resident group was sent to a farm outside Memphis for rest and recreation, and a relay team was sent in.

Dugongs

CREATURES OF MYTH

It is hard to believe that these all too solid animals are the stuff of which myths are made, but the tantalizing mermaids of legend were actually these solemn, unlovely creatures which go by the name of dugong, a corruption of the Malayan word "duyun."

Dugongs are often found in the Indian Ocean, the Red Sea and off the coast of Australia. A harmless aquatic mammal, the female dugong has a curious habit of standing upright in the water, half her body above the surface, to feed her young which she suckles by holding tightly against her breast with her short fore-flippers. When the first bold mariners of the ancient Mediterranean world ventured into the mysterious waters of the South Pacific, they mistook the nursing dugong, unknown in their native seas, for a woman with her child and brought back to Europe the first startling tales of mermaids. By the accretion of folklore, the beautiful mermaid later acquired a siren song with which she lured enraptured sailors to their death beneath the billowing waves.

The frightening mermaid myth persisted for centuries until some brave sailors finally closed in on a dugong and exposed her for what she really was, a glum, blubbery-visaged sea cow whose natural charm was such that she must have difficulty attracting even another dugong. And as for emitting a siren song, her discoverers found that she could not even talk.

The dugong is lumpish in contour, brownish-gray, has a flat, double-lobed tail and grows to a length of more than 10 feet. It is caught by some aboriginals who eat its flesh, which is not very palatable, and who sell its skin for leather. Most prized of all dugong products is its oil, which is sometimes used in the treatment of tuberculosis.

In 1944, a 12-foot-long Australian dugong weighing more than a ton found itself off the coast of Punta Arenas, Chile, far away from its native seas. For reasons unknown, it dragged its huge bulk out of the water and began to waddle through the streets of the city, giving the natives the fright of their lives. After covering about three city blocks, the dugong was ready to abandon its impromptu sightseeing tour. It had already turned around and headed back toward the sea when the Chilean police arrived on the scene and dispatched it with two shots from their guns.

A harmless dugong created a panic in the streets of Punta Arenas, Chile, when it hauled itself up out of the sea and began to waddle clumsily through the town. Alarmed policemen killed it with two shots, believing that they were dealing with a dangerous monster.

The eagle swoops down on the lizard.

Eagles

EAGLE VS. LIZARD

A golden eagle raised by Dan and Jule Mannix is trained to hunt and retrieve quarry. These photographs show the eagle swooping down on a giant 8-foot iguana lizard, preparing for the attack, and then, with its powerful claw, pinning it to the ground. The lizard thrashed about until it was exhausted and the eagle flew back to its owners with the subdued reptile in tow.

The end of the lizard.

KIDNAPPED BY AN EAGLE

In the village of Leka, some miles north of Trondheim, lived a little 4-year-old girl by the name of Svanhild Hansen. On the bright Sunday morning of June 5, 1932, little Svanhild was playing happily in the yard of her parents' farmhouse when she was suddenly startled by the menacing sound of massive, flapping wings. Looking up, she saw an enormous eagle swooping down upon her. Before the terrified little girl could even cry out for help, the huge bird had clutched her dress tightly in its sharp talons and was carrying her off, rising higher and higher above the familiar earth.

The eagle carried the child for more than a mile to the end of the valley, where it flew to a mountain and dropped her down on a narrow ledge of rock. The ledge jutted out about 800 feet up the mountainside, and was about 50 feet below the eagle's nest. Apparently, the bird had intended to take the child to its nest, but the burden proved too great for that distance, so he dropped the child short of the nest.

Little Svanhild's parents had not witnessed the capture of the child by the big bird of prey; and although they knew she had been carried away, they were not able to see just where the eagle's flight had ended.

It was the eagle himself who finally showed the frantic parents where he had dropped his little captive. Time after time, the great bird swooped and soared over the high ledge. He made no attempt to pick the child up again, but his repeated flights attracted the attention of the Hansens and told them plainly that their child must be hidden from sight on the rocky outcropping.

With a search party from the village, the parents started out to rescue their little girl. It took seven hours to climb the steep and dangerous mountainside and reach the narrow ledge on which the child lay. There they found her unharmed and sound asleep. Except for some scratches and bruises, a tear-stained face, and a dress that had been shredded by the bird's sharp talons, little Svanhild showed no other evidence of her frightening ordeal.

Here Svanhild Hansen and her husband display the tattered dress she wore on the morning of June 5, 1932, when she was suddenly picked up by a swooping eagle and carried through the air for more than a mile to a mountain ledge 800 feet above the floor of the valley in which she lived.

Svanhild is now a young woman, married and living in the town of Rorvik. Recently, in a newspaper interview, she retold the story of her terrifying flight with an eagle, and showed again her treasured memento of that amazing experience—the rumpled, talon-ripped little dress she wore on that unforgettable day.

Earthquakes

LEWIS GALDY'S LUCK

In 1692, the city of Port Royal, on the island of Jamaica, literally slid into the sea when it was struck by a giant quake. Many had predicted that Port Royal, a corrupt city of pirates and cutthroats, would one day suffer God's judgment and be destroyed. The disaster, therefore, surprised no one, least of all the handful of pious men who were swept to their doom along with the sinners.

One such man was Lewis Galdy. When the first shock came, Galdy was buried deep beneath the earth. He remained conscious, understood what had happened, prayed for his soul and resigned himself to death.

A few minutes later, the ground shook a second time, the earth opened up, and Galdy found himself sailing high into the air and out over the churning water. He landed in the harbor unhurt and clung to a piece of wreckage until he was rescued.

Galdy lived for 47 years after his amazing experience. He died in 1739 and on his tombstone is the story of his miraculous escape.

Elephants

THE KING OF BEASTS

Without question, the elephant is the true King of Beasts. Like all royalty, his person is inviolate and, with the exception of men and mosquitoes, no other animal dares to attack him. When, in a fit of anger, he rampages wildly over the land, all creatures scatter before him; when he is at peace, the most timid browse near him without fear.

The strength of the elephant is awesome; he can uproot a forest giant or toss a car on its side with ease. An African bull elephant (the Indian elephants are smaller) often weighs in at 5 tons, his heavy hide accounting for about 15 per cent of this weight, and his big 8-to-9-foot tusks adding another 200 pounds each.

These stately beasts grow to be more than 10 feet tall. The most famous elephant was Jumbo.

P. T. Barnum acquired Jumbo in England in 1882 and, giving the animal's height as 12 feet from floor to shoulder, billed him as the "tallest elephant in the world." As the canny showman never allowed Jumbo to be officially measured, this claim could not be disputed. However, when Jumbo lost an argument with a locomotive at St. Thomas, in Canada, Barnum gave his hide to Tufts College and the secret was out. The taxidermists who mounted his huge skin measured the dead animal and pegged his height at 11′ 4″—not quite Barnum's figure, but still close to the world record for any pachyderm.

The elephant enjoys some natural gifts denied lesser animals. He grows new teeth as the old wear out and often renews his choppers to the extent of six full sets in a lifetime, which is about 50 years.

To insure against the discomforts of dehydration, an elephant is equipped with a body recess, separate from his stomach, in which he can store as many as 10 gallons of water at a time.

The first elephant ever seen in the United States was brought

Elephants on the road are an unusual traffic hazard in South Africa's famous Kruger Big Game Reserve. If the majestic Jumbo (above) lost his temper, he could topple the car behind him with ease, but he doesn't even know there are humans inside because their scent is masked by the fumes of the motor.

to Boston in 1796 by a Yankee shipowner. Little is known of this bulky immigrant, except that she was a female named Buffon and was exhibited briefly.

Along about 1805 came Old Bet, the elephant credited with being the mother of America's carnival business. Old Bet was brought to Somers, New York, by Hackaliah Bailey (no relation to Barnum's partner) and was later exhibited as the star attraction in the first permanent circus ever to hit the sawdust trail in the United States. Her worthy memory is honored in the town of Somers by a hotel, a statue and, in 1959, the founding of America's first circus museum.

Since Old Bet's day, thousands of elephants have been brought to the United States, but only a few babies have been born here, as elephants do not breed readily in captivity.

The first baby elephant born in America made her historic appearance in Philadelphia on March 10, 1880. She was named Columbia and was a gifted circus performer until the age of 25, when she had to be put away because of her increasingly bad temper.

The gestation period for an elephant is about 21 months, and the weaning of the youngster often continues well into its fourth year. Because of this prolonged dependency, many very young calves sold to circuses for training are still in need of mothering, and they would die of loneliness were it not for the curious herd custom among elephants of endowing each baby with an "aunt."

In the wild, as soon as an elephant becomes pregnant, an older cow becomes her constant, helpful companion. When the pregnant female starts her accouchement, the "aunt," like a massive midwife, takes over. She shoos away unwanted visitors, bellows in sympathy when she hears a cry of pain, and, finally, kneels down beside the laboring animal and massages its sides gently with her knees.

After the delivery, the "aunt" goes everywhere with the mother and the little one, and stays with them until the baby is weaned and on its own. Should anything happen to the mother meanwhile, the attendant elephant adopts the little orphan.

Responding to these herd customs in captivity, the kindly "aunts" comfort the homesick little waifs bought by zoos and circuses, and, by taking over all the duties of the absent mother (except that of feeding), they keep the babies from pining away. Without these "aunts," few young elephants would survive in captivity.

Rival elephants scramble for an oversized soccer ball during an exhibition match in Thonburi, Thailand.

This is Sunja, the only water-skiing elephant in the world.

ELEPHANTS AT PLAY

When did you last root for your favorite elephant soccer team?

Well, the people of Bangkok do. The Thais have a couple of elephant teams making the sports circuit there, and the pachyderms are packin' them in. These bulky contenders are no threat to Pelé, of course. They lack the great Brazilian soccer player's skill and speed at making a pass, or taking off with a break-away dribble. But the elephants are great crowd-pleasers, and they certainly have given soccer a brand-new look.

You may never see an elephant on snowy ski slopes, but you can see one skimming over the water on out-sized skis. Her name is Sunja. She makes her home at Cleveland's Sea World of Ohio, and she's the only skiing elephant in the world.

It took Sunja's trainer, Dave Blasko, 3 years to make a water skier of his 3,000-pound charge. Now the young elephant skims the water with remarkable skill and grace, considering her size, and thoroughly enjoys a breezy run on nearby Lake Geauga. Blasko does have one problem, though. It's hard to fit Sunja for skis. Sporting goods stores seldom carry her jumbo size—21 feet long and 7 feet wide.

THE TUG-OF-WAR

Recently, in Bangkok, 70 strong young men pitted themselves in a tug-of-war against an elephant. The elephant, after standing still for a while, decided to move off. The whole straining man-team was carried along with him. It was no contest at all.

A tug-of-war rarely lasts very long. Even when teams are evenly matched, there is always that moment of shifting or slackening on the part of one team which works to the advantage of the other. A strong, quick tug at such a time brings instant victory to the alert opposition.

However, this was not the case with a tug-of-war which took place during some competitive games held in Jubbulpore, India, in 1889.

It was early afternoon when the match started, and it was scheduled to be a best two-out-of-three event. But it didn't work out that way; there was no second tug. The two teams were so evenly matched that they huffed and puffed, and pulled and tugged, and slipped and strained for the incredible time of 2 hours and 41 minutes before one team managed to drag the other over the line for the first time.

It's quite understandable, therefore, that as the exhausted tuggers lay on the ground struggling to regain their strength and their breath, the two captains met and willingly agreed that once was enough. There would be no two-out-of-three in this match.

Two hours and 41 minutes had been consumed dragging the losing team a total of only 12 feet. This represents an average speed of 0.00084 miles per hour.

That must certainly be the slowest winning-game time on record.

Some 70 men battle one elephant in a tug-of-war in Bangkok, Thailand.

Holy Beggar of India lifts a child with his eyelid muscles alone.

Because of his deep faith this Indian fakir feels no pain even when hundreds of pins are stuck into his flesh.

This Indian fakir will earn religious merit by twisting his foot behind his neck and over his shoulder.

An Indian yogi lets a truck roll over his chest. He says special breathing and muscle control allow him to survive with no ill effect.

Shinto in Japan is a religious cult similar to that of the fakirs in India. Here 12-year-old Eike Nagumo walks over burning coals, praying for the return of her father, who disappeared during the Red Army's invasion of Manchuria.

Falls

WIDEST FALLS IN THE WORLD

Iguassu Falls, Brazil, has a 10,000-foot crestline, twice as wide as Niagara Falls.

It's petrified—that's why it doesn't flow.

146   Falls

THE FROZEN WATERFALL

Until recent years, this natural wonder of the world was almost unknown outside of Asia Minor. It is the "Frozen Waterfall" of Pamukkale and is located at Hierapolis, in a remote region of Turkey.

Although it is found in a year-round mild climate, this icy-looking cataract is in no danger of melting. It is a petrified waterfall, formed entirely of limestone, and its Turkish name means "Cotton Castle."

This marvel of nature is the eons-old result of natural hot springs which gush from the earth less than a mile above the falls. The water from these springs is filled with calcium carbonate which cools and hardens into chalky white limestone. It flows through numerous channels down to the cliffs of Pamukkale where it trickles over the rim to form stalactites which hang like huge icicles on a frozen cascade.

Limestone terraces are also built up at Pamakkale and on these the action of the water dripping endlessly down from above has scooped out shallow pools. As these pools fill and overflow, their water drips down to form new stalactites, thus creating a series of waterfall upon waterfall.

The Romans once came to Pamukkale to take the curative baths afforded by the hot springs. They built an elaborate spa and the ancient ruins of this are seen today by travellers who also come to bathe in the springs.

The petrified waterfall of Pamukkale is almost twice as high as Niagara. And when the sun shines on this crystalline cataract it creates a spectacle of dazzling beauty unmatched anywhere else in the world.

UPSIDE DOWN FALLS

On Oahu Island in Hawaii is the startling sight of Upside Down Falls in the Koolau range of mountains. The waterfalls start a downward plunge over the cliffs and then are suddenly lifted and tossed back up in the air. A powerful updraft of wind causes the phenomenon.

REVERSING FALLS

One of nature's curiosities is the Reversing Falls at New Brunswick, Canada, where the St. John River meets St. John Harbor. At low tide the river rushes downstream through a 350-foot gorge and reaches the harbor by a 26-foot descent; at mid-tide the fall is submerged and the water is as calm as a mill pond; and at high tide the inrushing flood forces itself upstream through the gorge in a chaos of boiling eddies and whirlpools.

Fathers

FATHER'S DAY

Presented with an unusually large bill for his son's expenses, Charles Dickens once lamented in mock despair: "Why was I ever a father?"

The most indulgent father was without question Don Simon Patino, the Bolivian tin tycoon who, on the occasion of his daughter's wedding in 1929, handed her a staggering dowry of $22,000,000, the largest ever given.

What father had the most children? Well, in the Western World the palm must go to Niccola the Third who ruled the independent Italian city of Ferrara from 1393 to 1441. During his long reign, through a succession of wives and mistresses which shocked even his free-and-easy age, he fathered almost 300 children.

Though fathers are said to prefer that their first-born be a boy, they have a special feeling for their little girls. In 1947 an affectionate father wrote a letter to his recently married daughter, speaking warmly of her happiness, of how proud he had been as he walked with her to the altar, of the lonely gap her departure had left in the family's life. He ended with the words ". . . your old home is still yours, and do come back to it as much and as often as possible . . . Your loving and devoted, Papa." Although universal in its thought, the letter is unique in that the home referred to is Buckingham Palace, the father was King George VI and the glowing bride he wrote to is now Elizabeth, Queen of England.

Fathers don't always prefer their first-born to be a boy. Theodore Deitsch of Los Angeles, a few years ago, was so stunned with joy to have a daughter that he could hardly break the cigar-passing news. The reason for his elation? His new baby was the first girl to be born in his family for three generations, a period spanning more than half a century.

Festivals

<u>JAPANESE KANTO FESTIVAL</u>

In Akita City, Japan, the Kanto Festival is held each year to invoke divine help for a good harvest. A kanto is a long bamboo pole with several horizontal ribs from which hang as many as 50 lanterns. The young men of the city try their skill at balancing "kanto" on their hands, foreheads, shoulders and hips.

Finance

THE TALLY AND THE STOCKS

Everyone is talking about stocks today, but the subject isn't new.

In 11th-century England, people were plagued by the dishonesty of moneylenders who frequently overstated the amounts they had loaned.

To overcome this abuse, King William the Conqueror started a system known as the "tally," a word which comes from the Latin and means "stick."

This "tally" system was simple and completely foolproof. Every time money changed hands, lines were drawn across the face of a wooden stick indicating the amount of the loan. Then the stick was split down the middle, with the creditor retaining one half and the debtor getting the other. In this way, the debtor had what amounted to an exact "carbon copy."

The "tally" system continued in use until 1543, at which

The original stocks were like these. The tally stick was marked to indicate the amount of the loan.

time all the sticks in England were called in and stored in the cellar of the House of Commons.

More than a century later, the government decided to destroy these sticks by burning them. Unfortunately, the sticks—now dry as tinder—exploded in the furnace and burned down the House of Commons as well.

But the "stick" still lives on in our financial life, because it is from this word "stick" that we get our present-day word of "stock," meaning a security.

Firewalking

KUDA BUX

Many years ago, I produced a very unusual radio program over the NBC network. At that time, there was an unpaved parking lot in New York's Rockefeller Center, and I hired it for 24 hours.

In the center of the lot, I had a pit dug that was 20 feet long, 3 feet wide, and 3 feet deep. I had the pit filled with oak logs, which were then set on fire and allowed to burn all day. That evening, I had charcoal spread over the hot logs. By 10 o'clock that night, the pit was filled with a 2-foot-deep bed of white-hot ashes that registered 1,400 degrees F.

Then the broadcast began. As an announcer walked beside the pit, describing what he saw, a young holy man from India named Kuda Bux walked calmly, his legs and feet bare, through the entire length of that burning pit, sometimes sinking almost to his knees in the searing ashes.

Immediately after this amazing performance, three medical experts—my own doctor father among them—examined Kuda Bux' feet. They found not a mark on them. In fact, they were not even warm.

Kuda Bux walking on hot ashes.

Fish

FRESH-WATER LAKE
WITH SALT-WATER FISH

Lake Nicaragua, Central America, is the only fresh-water lake in the world which abounds in salt-water fish: tarpon, sharks, sawfish, etc.

The lake was once a huge bay until, eons ago, a series of volcanic eruptions closed off the mouth of the bay with piled-up lava. The big salt-water fish were trapped in the new "lake" and, as the water lost its salt through evaporation and became fresh, the sharks, sawfish and others adapted to this change in their watery world.

The author is holding the "saws" of three sawfish caught in the lake.

Flamingoes

<u>BIRDS ON THE MARCH</u>

Under the direction of Hedley Edwards, a troop of Bahamian flamingoes performs military commands at Ardastra Gardens in Nassau.

Food

EATING LIKE A PARAKEET

A study of parakeet eating habits has exploded the popular idea that birds have tiny appetites. Instead, it showed that the average parakeet eats nearly 100 times its own weight annually in seed, cuttlebone, gravel and water. Because the parakeet weighs only about 1¼ ounces, this actually means that it consumes about 8 pounds of food a year. To eat at the same rate, a man would have to devour some 16,000 pounds of food annually instead of his normal consumption of 1,300 pounds.

The famous athlete, Milo of Crotona, who lived in ancient Greece, was a top wrestler. He was a big, powerful man, and he was always hungry. He devoured everything in sight.

One day, when he was unusually hungry, he outdid himself and captured the world's record for big eating. During that day, Milo managed to polish off a whole calf weighing 150 pounds.

A modern man, Ted F. Ey of Rochester, New York, once demonstrated how to eat "like a bird."

With his pet parakeet, "Frenchy," watching from his shoulder, Ey breakfasted on wheat cakes, with the rest of his day's "bird rations" before him—45 pounds of meat, poultry, potatoes, vegetables, fruits, eggs, milk and other foods!

THE HOT DOG IS BORN

Everybody loves a fair, and the great World's Fair held in Chicago in 1893 was a terrific hit. People flocked to see it from all over the world, as it had, among other new attractions, the first Ferris wheel.

But it was a food concessionaire by the name of Anton Feuchtwanger who was to make a lasting impression on American life.

Anton had come to America from Bavaria with many old recipes, and now, at the fair, he was selling a specialty of his homeland.

However, because this specialty had to be served piping hot it was difficult to handle, so fair-goers passed it up for more conventional nourishment.

Anton tried everything to get people to eat his food. He even provided white cotton gloves to protect the hands of his customers, but most of them walked off with the gloves.

Finally, Anton hit on a solution. He would prevent burned fingers by simply putting his specialty between the halves of a long roll.

From then on, Anton was a success. The food he served was the spicy sausage known throughout the world today as the "American hot dog."

COFFEE

During the 16th century, Europe was introduced to a new drink made from a small, exotic fruit. The drink had come from Turkey, but before that the fruit had been used for centuries in Africa. African nomads had crushed the fruit into balls of fat, and had used these as their sole ration on long desert journeys.

The drink was said to have almost magical powers. It could allay fatigue and bring renewed strength; it could restore victims from the paralyzing effects of shock, or of poisoning.

So great were the powers ascribed to this drink that many Europeans believed it was touched by witchcraft. It became known as the "infidel" drink, and European churchmen banned it.

However, in 1592, Pope Clement VIII came to the Vatican. He was a wise and sensible man, and it was he who cleared the reputation of this new beverage by issuing an order which approved the new drink as fit for Christian consumption.

This controversial drink was our everyday coffee . . . the only beverage ever to be officially Christianized.

SAUERKRAUT AND CAPTAIN COOK

In 1772, Captain James Cook, the great English explorer, was preparing his ship—the *Resolution*—for a voyage to the South Pacific.

In those days, the greatest danger on a long sea voyage was from scurvy, which Cook believed had something to do with a sailor's diet. When he found out that the Germans seldom had scurvy and always carried barrels of sauerkraut with them on their voyages, Cook decided to feed his crew the same thing.

The captain knew his English sailors would never voluntarily eat this sour "foreign" food, no matter how good it was for them. So he had barrels of sauerkraut put out on deck and then had signs put up over the barrels which read: "For Officers' Use Only."

Captain Cook's strategy worked. No sailor was ever seen to take any of the sauerkraut, but day by day the contents of the barrel grew less and less.

But most important of all, during all that long voyage not one sailor aboard the *Resolution* ever came down with scurvy. The sauerkraut provided the dietary elements needed to prevent the disease.

Franklin

SAVED BY RESPECT

In 1763, George III of England appointed a popular young lawyer to be governor of New Jersey.

The young governor was well liked by the people until the American Revolution erupted in 1776. Then it was discovered that, although born in the colony of Pennsylvania, the governor sympathized with the British.

As the war grew more intense, the governor used all his power to help the enemy. He secured intelligence information for the British, and violently denounced his own people, saying that he would kill three Americans for every British sympathizer who was killed.

The American patriots, in their turn, called the governor a spy and a traitor, and swore to capture him and avenge themselves.

The Revolutionary Congress of New Jersey finally ordered the governor's arrest, and he was captured shortly afterward. But he was not shot. Instead he was imprisoned in Connecticut until 1778 when he was sent to England in exchange for some American prisoners.

And why was the governor's life spared? It was spared because of the love and respect that Americans held for his father. For that governor, who was hated as a traitor, was William Franklin, the son of the great American patriot, Benjamin Franklin.

Memorial in
Berlin to the
lottery ticket.

Gambling

THE LOTTERY TICKET

On an ancient house in the oldest section of Berlin there was erected a strange memorial—a large bas-relief showing an old man staggering under the weight of a heavy door. The plaque commemorates the story of a long-dead cobbler who once lived on that site.

A patient, long-time but very unsuccessful buyer of state lottery tickets, the cobbler used to paste each ticket he bought to the door of his house, thus insuring himself against loss of the precious little piece of paper.

One day, when he had all but given up hope of ever being a winner, he received the startling news that his ticket had drawn first prize in the lottery. It was a sum large enough to keep him in comfort for the rest of his life.

The happy old man rushed to the door and tried frantically to peel off the winning ticket which he had pasted up with all the previous useless stubs. But he had done a fine job of pasting it on, and now he could not detach it.

However, the ticket was needed to collect. So he took the heavy door off its hinges, hoisted it on his back, and then tramped laboriously off to the lottery office where he claimed and received his prize.

Giants

JOHN HUNTER AND THE GIANT

During the 18th century, there lived in London a famous surgeon by the name of John Hunter.

The doctor owned a fantastic collection of skeletons which he used for teaching anatomy to young medical students.

However, there was one skeleton the doctor wanted but could not have. It belonged to the famous Irish giant, a man named Byrne who stood close to 9 feet tall.

Although the "giant" was still very much alive, Hunter let it be known that he would someday have the Irishman's bones.

But Byrne did not go along with Hunter's plans. So he gave instructions that when he died his body was to be weighted down and cast into the sea.

Shortly afterward, Byrne did die. But he never made it to his watery grave. Instead, on its way to the sea his hearse was held up by masked men who overpowered the driver, then made off with the giant's body.

The gruesome highwaymen were never identified. But a few weeks later, students entering Dr. Hunter's surgery found an imposing new specimen in his bony collection—the skeleton of a man that stood almost 9 feet tall.

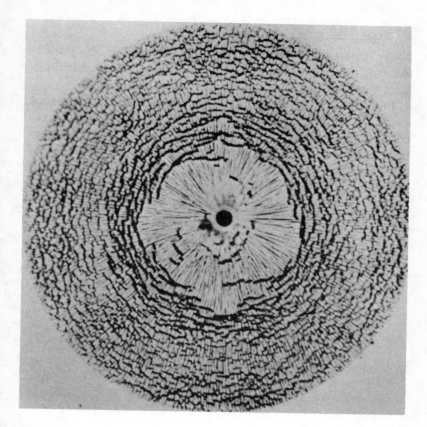

Glass

<u>GLASS BREAKING</u>

When glass breaks, the cracks move at nearly a mile a second—more than 3,000 miles an hour. This photograph was made at an exposure of one millionth of a second. The black spot in the center is the end of the metal plunger that struck the glass, shattering it and causing the cracks that radiate from the center to form a perfect circle, proof that they all moved with equal velocity.

MARGARET OF AUSTRIA

Early in the 16th century, Holland was ruled by Margaret of Austria, the clever daughter of the German emperor Maximillian, who was then the most powerful ruler in Europe.

In those uneasy days of intrigue and murder, rulers took every precaution against sudden death. Margaret was no exception. She feared death by poisoning, and because it was believed that pure rock crystal would disclose the presence of poison, she would drink from nothing but a goblet made of this rare mineral.

One day a servant, handing Margaret a drink, dropped the goblet to the stone floor. The shattered crystal was carefully swept up, but one tiny fragment flew unnoticed into Margaret's slipper.

The splinter of glass worked its way into her foot which soon became painful, then grew red and swollen with infection. By the time doctors were called, gangrene was far advanced. Immediate amputation was necessary but the great Margaret of Austria did not survive the ordeal.

Ironically, she died of poisoning caused by the very crystal she believed would protect her from death.

The tree-climbing goats of Morocco. Vegetation is scarce on the ground so the goats regularly feed on the leaves of trees.

Goats

THE "MINER'S COW"

The goat was once called the "miner's cow" because he gave milk but cost nothing to maintain. Goats will eat just about anything lying around, and when there is nothing left on the ground, they will climb trees and eat the leaves.

Goats have provided man with more than milk and meat.

In Europe, the coarse hair of the agile animal was once used for wigs, and in India fights between battering rams are still a popular spectator sport though the government officially frowns upon it.

In 1955 the people of Jaboatao, a small city in Brazil, wanted to get a message to their lazy and corrupt local government, and so they ran a goat named Fragrant for the city council. The horned candidate won the council seat with 468 votes.

In Roseburg, Oregon, the local goats have won fame as weather prophets. Residents of the town now look to see what a herd of wild goats on nearby Mount Nebo are doing when they want to know what the upcoming weather will bring.

If the herd is grazing high up on the mountain side, then the day will be sunny. If the goats are nibbling halfway down the slope, then cloudy weather will be around for a while. And if the goats are near the base of the mountain, then haul out your boots and raincoats.

A local man checked the weather movements of the goats and found that they were 90 per cent accurate as compared with the 65 per cent accuracy of the weather bureau.

Golf

ARMLESS GOLFER

Tom McAulife of Buffalo, New York, an armless golfer, played an average round of 98. Tom's drive went about 135 yards.

THE WORLD'S STRANGEST GOLF COURSE

The moat of the historic fort of El Morro in San Juan, Puerto Rico, has been made into a 9-hole golf course. Sand greens, fairways running under bridges, and 90-degree dog-legs make this course a tough par 27.

The hole leaves little room for a slice.

The author on the par-3 third hole.

GRAND-SLAM GOLFER

Even before he scored his famous "grand slam" in 1930, Bobby Jones was a golfer to be reckoned with. He won a neighborhood championship when he was only 6. At 14, he was invited to play in the National Amateur. Between 1923 and 1929, the young man from Atlanta collected a total of nine national championships.

But then came the "grand slam"—victories in the four major tournaments of the age: the U.S. and British Amateurs, and the U.S. and British Opens. Jones's claim to immortality was assured.

The year 1930 will be remembered as the year of the greatest golfing accomplishment in the history of the game. It all started in England, where Jones had gone to play as a member of the Walker Cup team. The Walker Cup competition pits the finest golf amateurs of the United States against those of Great Britain.

After his contribution to the American victory, Jones stayed on to play in the British Amateur. After squeaking through some of his early matches, he put it all together; in the finals, he routed Roger Wethered 7 and 6 to win that title for the first time in his career.

A few weeks later, he entered the British Open championship, which is for both amateurs and professionals. Once again his mastery paid off, and he shot a 4-round total of 291 for a 2-stroke victory.

Then, with half of the coveted grand slam locked securely in his golf bag, he returned to the United States and a roaring welcome.

The question of whether he could accomplish the impossible was now on every sports fan's mind.

He entered the U.S. Open, and after three rounds he appeared to be a shoo-in to win the third leg of his quest. He had piled up what appeared to be an insurmountable 5-stroke lead and seemed to be coasting. But there was trouble ahead.

Jones struggled through the early holes of the fourth round, watching nervously as his lead began to slip. Finally he came

Bobby Jones' famous swing.

up to the ninth hole, desperately needing to get his game back together in order to preserve his chances.

That hole, at Minneapolis' Interlachen golf course, was a challenging 485 yards long, with a small lake placed directly in front of the green. It was a par-5 hole, and most of the golfers were cautiously playing short of the lake on their second shot. Then, hitting an easy short iron onto the green, they were happy to settle for a safe par on the tough hole.

But Jones knew he needed something better than that if he was to restore his own confidence and get back into winning form.

Teeing off on the dangerous hole, the young Georgian hit a perfect drive. As he approached the ball for his second shot, he made a fateful decision: he would shoot the works and go for the green. Pulling a fairway wood from his bag, he stepped up to the ball, hung over it for a long moment, and then swung with all the power he could summon.

Unfortunately, Jones had topped the shot slightly, and he realized it immediately. His heart sank as he watched the ball slow up and descend toward the middle of the yawning lake. But instead of disappearing into the water, the ball skipped once, continued on its flight, and finished up just a few feet short of the putting green.

For a moment there was a stunned silence. Then the thousands of gathered spectators shrieked in disbelief. The ball had struck a lily pad in the middle of the lake and ricocheted to a perfect lie on dry ground. Miraculously, Jones had the opportunity for the birdie he wanted.

It was exactly what he needed, and Jones went on from there to win his third straight major championship.

Now only the U.S. Amateur crown stood between him and history, and that event was anticlimax all the way. He literally waltzed to the championship—defeated his final opponent by the unbelievable margin of 8 and 7.

A few weeks later, with no other worlds to conquer, the 28-year-old hero announced his retirement from competitive golf. Then he sat back to watch as two generations of golfers struggled to equal the mark he had established. No one has ever accomplished it. The great grand slam of 1930 remains in the books as one of the finest hours of any golfer in the game's history.

Long-horned grasshoppers, sparring.

Grasshoppers

CANNIBAL GRASSHOPPERS

The vast insect world, with its uncountable creatures who buzz, hum, flit and crawl, is nature's true battlefield, frequently marked by forms of aggression and violence unknown in higher orders.

The giant long-horned grasshoppers, which I first saw on a desolate plain in Turkey, near the Syrian border, are ferocious fighters and greedy cannibals. With their powerful jaws tearing each other to pieces, they engage in battle which can only end in dismemberment and death, generally for both insects. With the terrible cunning of instinct, these savage creatures try first to rip off each other's legs, as the grasshopper's "ear" is located in the knee, and without its hearing it is deprived of one of its protective senses and is more vulnerable. If one of these meadow monsters is able to survive, it will eat the victim; often, it is its last living act.

Most fearsome of all insect killers is, undoubtedly, the praying mantis, that deadly pious fraud whose powerful forelegs, seemingly clasped in worship, are really poised for speedy death. These "arms" of the mantis are like a pair of sharp cutting tools, able to hold and pierce at the same time. In this terrible embrace dies not only the prey or enemy of the female mantis, but her male partner, as well: after he has served his purpose in their joint act of reproduction, the male is killed and devoured at once by his savage mate.

So strong are the pincer-like arms of the praying mantis that one naturalist has reported witnessing the amazing spectacle of this long, delicate insect actually holding in her viselike grip a still-living, very terrified frog which she was slowly eating.

When giant grasshoppers fight to the death, the ground is littered with the fragments of the losers. Frequently the winner of a battle is so badly wounded that it also dies. The survivors, if any, gorge themselves on the dismembered bodies of their victims. Here, the winner has half-devoured his opponent already.

Graves

HEADSTONE IN PARIS

This unusual headstone in the cemetery in Montmartre, Paris marks the graves of a man and his wife. An inscription reads "Life has separated them; death has reunited them."

HAYDN GOT AROUND

Joseph Haydn, the great Austrian composer, died in 1809 and was buried in an old Vienna cemetery.

One night, shortly after his burial, two men opened the grave and severed Haydn's head from his body. They did this in the belief that an examination of the master's skull would disclose the secret of his genius. It did not, but one of the men kept the head until his own death in 1839. Then the grave-robber's widow, anxious to get rid of her ghastly treasure, turned the head over to the family friend who was a doctor.

The doctor kept the head for 13 years, then gave it to a professor who was the director of Vienna's famous Pathological Institute.

Eventually the professor died and by his will Haydn's head was given to the Vienna "Society of the Friends of Music."

About this time, the public became aware of the pitiful progress of Haydn's head. There was then a great public outcry and, at the insistent demand of the people, the head was transferred for the last time. On June 5, 1954, there was a new burial ceremony and the head of the great musical genius, Joseph Haydn, was finally reunited with his body, thus ending a posthumous journey of almost 145 years.

Haydn's head on exhibit in the Vienna Pathological Institute.

"THE TOMB"

When the founders of the great Washington Cathedral laid down their rules concerning the use of the church, they strictly limited the number and kind of burials to be allowed there.

Half a century ago, the beloved wife of a stone-carver who had worked for years on the cathedral died, and her husband asked the bishop for permission to have his wife buried within the church. Gently, the bishop explained to the workman that this would be impossible, the rules of the founders did not allow such a burial. The man thanked the bishop, and nothing more was ever heard of his request.

Not long ago, however, another old stone-carver confessed to church officials that the man who had lost his wife so long before actually had succeeded in burying her in the cathedral, just as he had wanted to do.

The sorrowing man had his wife cremated and later, while he worked on a scaffold near the roof of the cathedral, he had placed her ashes behind a stone high up on the church wall. Then he had set the stone in place forever. No one now will ever know where these ashes lie hidden, as the old stone-carver himself died years ago.

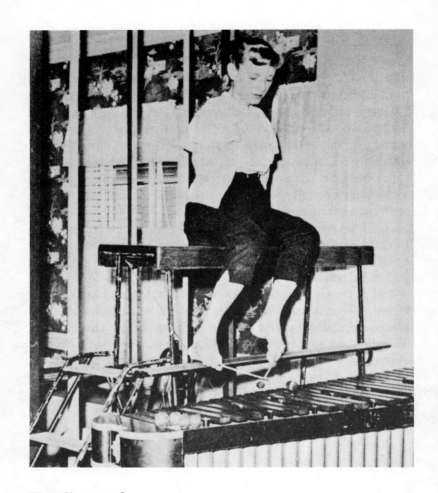

Handicapped

<u>THE WORLD AT HER FEET</u>

Born with a handicap that would have overwhelmed most people, pretty Mrs. Mary Kurtz, a Venice, California, housewife and the mother of two children, can perform endless household chores. Besides washing dishes, changing her infant son's diaper, applying lipstick, knitting, writing, ironing, and shopping, she can play the marimba, as you see here.

Heroes

NO-GOODS

A letter found in the old files of the Post Office shows that William Faulkner, Nobel Prize-winning author, was once fired as postmaster of a little Mississippi town. Seems he just wasn't up to the job.

This makes Faulkner a member of the Order of Famous No-Goods. Mark Twain, George Bernard Shaw, Albert Einstein, Napoleon, Charles Dickens, Thomas Edison, Michelangelo were all, at one time, looked upon as only a cut above the village dolt.

One of these towering "failures," Winston Churchill, was born in 1874.

Churchill was never a good student. Brilliant and restless, he was bored by formal learning. While attending Harrow, an exclusive preparatory school, he managed to work his way to the very bottom of the class and come close to being tossed out permanently.

Once given a paper to do in Latin—a dead language he never did master, or see the use in doing—he returned it bearing nothing more than a large ink blot surrounded by brackets, and his name signed in big, bold letters.

Churchill took the entrance examinations for Sandhurst, the military college, three times and just managed to squeak through on the last try, with the help of intensive tutoring. This led one examiner to exclaim that young Churchill "couldn't have gone through Harrow, he must have gone under it."

The great statesman did not find enjoyment in looking back to this time. Sir Winston wrote later that "I was, on the whole, considerably discouraged by my school days.... It is not pleasant to feel oneself so completely outclassed and left behind at the very beginning of the race."

JOHN PAUL JONES

The body of John Paul Jones lies in a magnificent crypt at the United States Naval Academy. But his remains almost failed to reach their stately resting place.

After the Revolution, which he had served so brilliantly at sea, Jones was completely forgotten by his countrymen. He lived in lonely poverty and was found dead in cheap lodgings in Paris in 1792.

Only a few people knew him. One of these was a Frenchman who believed that America would someday recognize Jones for the hero he was, and would want his body back. So, at his own expense, this not rich but generous man had Jones's body placed in a heavy lead coffin which was then completely flooded with alcohol and tightly sealed.

The burial took place in a small graveyard on the outskirts of Paris. The mourners consisted of only three men.

For years Jones was forgotten. Then, Horace Porter became our ambassador to France. As a boy, the ambassador had read about Jones and had grown to venerate him as a hero. Now, Porter vowed, he would find Jones's grave and have the remains brought home.

Porter's search ended in success. On July 6, 1905—the anniversary of Jones's birth—America's greatest naval hero started his journey back to the United States and the honored burial he deserved.

And thanks to the vision of an obscure Frenchman, the body of John Paul Jones could be identified because it was still "wonderfully preserved" 113 years after his death.

John Paul Jones, one of America's great heroes.

The body of John Paul Jones, with honor guard, being returned to the United States for burial at the Naval Academy.

CHANGED HISTORY

One dreary night in Paris, in 1794, a young man walked alone on the bank of the Seine. He was bitterly despondent, and had made up his mind to die.

His short span of 25 years had been filled with hardship. As a child, he had been poor. Then, while in his teens, his widowed mother and her children had fled from their homeland for political reasons. For years they had lived on French charity, as refugees.

Then the young man had entered the army, and by his own brilliance and personality he had risen to a high rank. But it was a time of political unrest in France, and his political opinions were on the wrong side. So he was arrested, relieved of his command, and expelled from the army. He was completely disgraced, without funds, and without a future. His only wish now was to die. He would find peace in the dark waters at his feet.

Suddenly, a figure loomed out of the night, and called to him. It was an old army friend, and when he heard the young man's story, he was deeply touched and insisted upon helping him. This act of kindness on his friend's part proved a turning point in the young man's life . . . and also in the history of the world. For the despondent young man, intent on suicide, was none other than Napoleon Bonaparte.

THE CHURCH PISTOLS

In 1799, John Church, a wealthy New Yorker, fought a duel in which he used a handsome set of pistols handmade for him in London.

His opponent in the duel was Aaron Burr. Burr's shot went wild and Church's bullet only nicked a button off Burr's coat, but both men were satisfied.

Two years later, Church lent his pistols to Philip Hamilton, son of Alexander Hamilton. Philip had challenged George Eacker, a lawyer, to a duel for making insulting remarks about the senior Hamilton.

The duel was fought on New Jersey's Weehawken Heights, a famous dueling ground overlooking the Hudson River. At the last moment, Philip decided to hold his fire. But Eacker did not hold his and young Hamilton died.

Then, on July 11, 1804, a duel was fought between two political giants of that time—Alexander Hamilton and Aaron Burr. And again the Church pistols were the chosen weapons. Both men were familiar with them; Burr had used the pistols before, and Hamilton knew that one of them had killed his son.

The men met on Weehawken Heights at daybreak. Arrangements were quickly made and the command to fire given. As two shots blasted the morning air, Hamilton fell, mortally wounded by Burr's bullet.

Just as his beloved son had done before him—and using the same fateful pistols—Alexander Hamilton had held his fire and paid with his life. His gun had discharged accidentally as he fell.

The Church pistols were never again used for dueling.

Hockey

POINT-A-MINUTE PLAYER

Everyone knows that ice hockey is one swift, bruising, bone-cracking sport. But just how rough life is for the puck-and-stick supermen surfaced only recently in a study made by the University of Michigan's Medical School. The doctors there found that a hockey player, during his professional life, can expect to receive 14 severe lacerations around the head, and that one of these will also be a facial fracture. He will also lose two or more of his teeth. No other game can make that grim claim.

But despite the violence of the game, it is becoming more popular each year. And there's no scarcity of men who want to get out on the ice to batter and be battered, and score big.

However, no matter how hard a top hockey player may try to add up goals today, it is doubtful that he'll ever be able to equal the record set by Frank McGee who once starred with the old Ottawa Silver Seven.

But to better understand McGee's story, it is necessary to look back even beyond the years of his stardom. Ice hockey was born in Canada more than a hundred years ago, and it bore only faint resemblance to the game which has vaulted near the top of spectator sports in recent years.

Originally, teams sported seven players and the goals were mere upright posts, anchored in the ice. There were no nets, no blue lines, no red lines, and no face-off circles.

Yet even in those early days, it was an exciting sport, and in 1893 it so stirred the interest of sportsman Frederick Arthur that he added something to it that has become the *pièce de résistance* of the hockey world.

Arthur, who was Lord Stanley of Preston, the son of the Earl of Derby, became so fascinated by the breathtaking action of ice hockey that he bought a trophy—for less than $50, incidentally—and decreed that it should be presented annually to the amateur team champion of Canada. That trophy, to this day known as the Stanley Cup, continues to signify that its holder is the champion of the hockey world, although now it is presented to the professional champions.

The Stanley Cup competition has been marked with some of the greatest pressure performances in hockey history, and Frank McGee provided one that probably never will be surpassed.

Hockey is generally a low-scoring game. As a matter of fact, the feat of one player scoring three or more goals in a single game is rare enough to have a designation all of its own—the "hat-trick," a name reputedly derived from the offer of a felt hat by a Canadian hat manufacturer to any player who managed the achievement.

Despite the rarity of this "hat-trick," some players have managed to achieve or approach the difficult feat in rather remarkable time.

For example, Peter Elko, of the Eagle River (Wisconsin) Bobcats, didn't actually post the hat-trick, but he did manage once to score two goals within 13 seconds. Bill Mosienko of the Chicago Black Hawks holds the record for the fastest "hat-trick" on the books. The Chicago star took just 21 seconds to score three times.

However, even these amazing feats pale in comparison to the act of Ottawa's Frank McGee. Moreover, McGee's amazing performance came in a Stanley Cup series game. That series was only 11 years old at the time and pressure for the trophy was at its height.

The Ottawa Silver Seven's opponents for that series was a team of stars from the far reaches of the Yukon. So impressive had they been in their native area that a millionaire Dawson City prospector decided to pay all the expenses for his favorite team to travel to Ottawa—clear across the country—and challenge the defending champions.

Traveling was neither fast nor easy in those times. It took the Yukon team 23 days (via dog sled, boat, and train) to reach Ottawa.

Maybe it was the tiring experience of that long and difficult journey that took the starch out of the Dawson City seven. Or, maybe the Ottawa entry was simply too good. Whatever the reason, the defending champions simply skated the invaders off the ice in their first meeting and won the opening game of the Cup's usual best-of-three series by an overwhelming 9–2 score.

It was a humiliating experience for the visitors, and when the time came for the second game they were determined to reverse the outcome.

But determination was not enough. Flying Frank McGee took charge from the very beginning of the game. By the time the ice chips had settled back to the rink's surface, McGee had scored the incredible total of 14 goals. His teammates added a few more and the Ottawa Silver Seven amassed an overwhelming 23–2 victory.

Now 14 goals certainly is a triumph in itself. But McGee posted an even more amazing display midway in that stretch. In one short span of 8 minutes 20 seconds, he slammed in an unbelievable eight goals—nearly one per minute.

Somewhere in this fabled world of hockey, someone may have put on a demonstration that approaches that of McGee, but never in Stanley Cup competition.

The story should end there, but it doesn't. Most of the fans in the stands on the night of that remarkable performance were totally dazzled by McGee's explosion of goals. What they didn't realize was that he always played under a severe handicap.

Frank McGee was blind in one eye.

Horses

TRIPLE DEAD HEAT

On October 10, 1903, in New South Wales, Australia, a horse race was held that ended in a *triple* dead heat. The three horses finishing together were High Flyer, Loch Lochie, and Bardini. The race was rerun and *again* the three horses hit the finish line in a triple dead heat! This is the only record of its kind in all of racing history.

King's Own, who made a record high jump of 8′3½″, takes the barrier easily here at his home farm in Elberon, New Jersey. Fred Wettach, his owner, looks back at the height of the jump to see if the big gelding has cleared the top pole.

A herd of wild horses has been flushed from a canyon onto the open desert.

WILD HORSES HUNTED IN NEVADA

In Nevada, and across the country, raged a controversy over the practice of mechanized wild horse hunting in Nevada. The issue was first brought to light by Velma Johnston, known as "Wild Horse Annie" because her father's life had been saved as a child when he was fed milk from a wild mare. One day "Wild Horse Annie" witnessed a horse hunt accidentally. She learned that airplanes were used to flush out the horses from canyons onto the desert plains, where they were greeted by

Run down by a truck, a mustang is about to be lassoed by a hunter.

Held fast by tires attached to the lasso, the horse comes to a frightened halt.

The exhausted horse waits for his captors to catch up.

fast-moving trucks. In the trucks were men who lassoed the mustangs just before they reached the point of exhaustion. The lassoes were tied to tires, which were kicked off the truck as soon as the noose was around the horse's neck, thereby stopping the animal in its tracks. The hunters then tied them up and loaded them into trucks which took them to slaughter houses. The horse meat was used in dog and cat food.

There were advocates of the mechanized hunts. They claimed that the horses were a degenerate group of feral—animals who were once domesticated and reverted—mustangs that do nothing but eat up the grasslands reserved for sheep and cattle. In ten years these hunters had reduced the number of wild horses in Nevada from almost 100,000 to about 10,000.

In September, 1959, President Eisenhower signed a bill preventing the use of planes and trucks in wild-horse hunting. And the woman responsible for this humane law was "Wild Horse Annie."

Three hunters tie up
the horse and await the
truck for loading.

The finishing step is loading the mustang onto the truck which will take it
to the cannery.

THE AMERICAN HORSE

In 1788, Justin Morgan, a poor schoolmaster living in Vermont and badly in need of funds to support his family, went down to Massachusetts to collect an old debt. But his debtor couldn't pay up and Morgan had no choice but to take in barter the only goods his impecunious friend had, a horse and a colt.

Morgan sold the horse, but could not get rid of the colt. Although the colt's sire and dam had been of mixed Arabian stock, the young horse did not resemble them and, being small with short legs and a very delicate head, had nothing to recommend him to the Vermont farmers who wanted big horses. The colt was considered a freak, and just wouldn't do.

But the schoolmaster, to his own surprise, was eventually to have those cagey farmers eating their own words. Noticing the massive shoulders, superb endurance and quick intelligence of the little animal, Morgan entered him in stock contests throughout the state, and soon the rejected horse was a sensation, gaining a reputation for being able to "outdraw, outwalk, outrun and outtrot every horse that was matched against him."

But the debt-ridden Morgan could not keep his now valuable horse and was forced to sell him in the late 1790's. Subsequently, the animal passed through the hands of a succession of owners throughout Vermont, siring hundreds of fine colts as he went. When the great horse died at the advanced age of 32 from a neglected leg injury, he was already recognized as the foundation sire of a fine new breed. Called Justin Morgan, after his scholarly master, the colt once held in such contempt lived to give his name to the first truly "American" horse.

Today, there is another "American" horse on the scene. It is the Quarterhorse, a term used to describe a fleet, lightweight animal that can go like the wind for a quarter-mile and then suddenly peters out.

The ancestors of the Quarterhorse were brought to this then horseless continent by the early Spaniards exploring Florida. When the Amercian West opened up, these horses trekked out with the pioneers. Later, they came to be used almost exclusively by cattlemen and, as time went on, they were carefully bred for those "cow-pony" qualities most needed on the long, hazardous trail drives in which vast herds, often numbering more than 2,000 longhorns, were driven overland for months at a time through harsh, dry wasteland and hostile Indian country.

Eventually, on the big Western spreads the perfect ranch animal was developed, the American Quarterhorse, embodying to perfection those special traits needed for working cattle. The Quarterhorse is small and strong for endurance, fleet and quick-stepping as a dancer for the flashy art of rounding up, cutting out and roping. Above all, he is cooperative and alert to quick commands.

Houdini

THE MASTER ESCAPE ARTIST

Among Harry Houdini's many feats was escaping from a straitjacket while suspended by his heels 40 feet above New York City's Broadway.

Hunting

A SHOT IN TIME

Hunter's luck! Those words have summed up a thousand great stories. But here are two episodes in which Lady Luck really outdid herself for the man with the gun.

Newton Smith of Cuero, Texas, was out deer hunting several years ago and spotted a handsome buck just a few yards ahead of him. The deer was standing motionless, within easy range, and outlined against a background of underbrush.

Smith was an old hand at hunting, so he quietly and carefully hoisted his rifle to his shoulder, took deliberate aim, and fired a single shot at that deer. His target staggered briefly and then slumped to the ground. But before Smith had moved from his hiding place to claim his trophy, he was stunned to see a second deer—standing shoulder to shoulder with the first one—also go to its knees and then roll over dead.

This was too good to be true.

Smith now started toward the two deer lying in the clearing before him. Suddenly he paused at the sound of some unseen creature thrashing around in the brush against which his original deer had been outlined.

Moving cautiously, he crept forward, sidled around the pair of deer, and began poking gingerly in the brush. There he discovered a third deer, also in the final stages of death.

Smith's single shot had passed through the first deer and then had struck the second one standing immediately behind the first. The bullet had passed through that second deer also and had continued on to hit a third hidden in the brush some 15 feet behind the original two.

Thus, with one shot, Smith had scored an amazing three kills.

But the Texan's story can only be categorized as mild compared to the amazing experience of a man named Lawrence Myatt on a hunting trip in Maine's lonely backwoods.

One evening, Myatt and his guide, Will Boucher, were stalking down a path leading to a water hole when a big buck bounded into view. The animal was directly ahead of them but slightly out of range.

The men froze in their tracks, and the guide then quickly drew Myatt into the nearby brush. As they watched in silence, the deer slowed in his flight, edged up toward a pond, and prepared to drink.

Boucher slipped his arm about Myatt's shoulder and whispered, "You stay right here. I'll circle around and get on the other side. As he begins to move out of the clearing, we'll get him. Don't fire until I signal."

Myatt nodded and waited silently as Boucher slipped into the brush and began to make his way toward the other side of the clearing.

Seconds passed—although they seemed like hours—and then the tense Myatt heard his guide shout, "Okay!"

Simultaneously, gunshots echoed through the woods. The startled deer threw up its head, paused briefly, and then bounded off into the sheltering trees.

Myatt, bitterly disappointed by his miss at a range of less than 60 feet, rose to look around. There on the path beside him lay a small mass of lead.

The hunter reached down, picked up the blob of warm metal, and found himself looking at two bullets that were fused together. Both Myatt and Boucher had fired at the same time, each—unwittingly—directly at the other. And their bullets had met in mid-air.

And so Myatt says of himself: "I'm now known as the man who would have been shot if I hadn't shot the shot that would have shot me."

India

THE EAST INDIA COMPANY

In the middle of the 17th century, the ruler of India was the Shah Jehan, builder of the fabulous Taj Mahal.

The Shah was a happy man until the day that a flash fire horribly burned his favorite daughter, Padshah.

Nothing could be done for the girl by the palace physicians and she was doomed to die. Then the prime minister made a suggestion. There was an English doctor at the town of Surat ... perhaps he could help the child.

The Shah immediately sent off his fastest couriers who brought back the young doctor, Gabriel Broughn by name. Not only did Dr. Broughn save the girl, but he kept her from being scarred as well.

The overjoyed Shah then offered the doctor anything he wanted as a reward.

But the doctor asked only one favor ... that the British people be allowed to trade freely, and in peace, with India.

This request was granted, and eventually the English set up trading posts throughout the country. These posts were the beginning of the most powerful trading company in the world—the famous East India Company which paved the way for British rule in India.

The author with an Indian friend at the Taj.

MARBLE "PALACE"

In 1629, the emperor of India, Shah Jehan, went on a campaign to crush a rebellion in his kingdom. As always, his wife went with him on the long, arduous march. But she was ill and pregnant, and on the way she collapsed, gave birth to a daughter and died. The empress was only 39 years old at that time, but the little girl was her 14th child.

The emperor was beside himself with grief. He carried his wife's body home, constantly wore the white robes of mourning, and went into seclusion.

Then one day, he appeared and gave orders that a beautiful "palace" was to be built for his wife. The body would lie there, he said, but it was never to be called a tomb. It was to be called by the Indian word "mahal," meaning "palace"—and his wife was never to be spoken of as dead but as merely resting within her palace.

That "palace," which the emperor built for his beloved dead wife, is the most breathtaking structure ever created by man ... a dazzling wonder of marble and jewels which is known throughout the world today as the Taj Mahal of India.

198   India

INDIAN TIGER HUNT

Around the start of the 20th century, two Englishmen living in India went on a hunting trip to try and kill a tiger that had been terrorizing a local village. A number of the inhabitants had already become his victims.

The hunters picked up the tiger's tracks very quickly, and started into the jungle after him. But the tracking was long and hard and, while sitting down to rest, both men dozed off for a few minutes.

Suddenly, a loud ticking sound brought them wide awake. Before them, coming through the trees, they saw the savage tiger. Fortunately, the men had kept their guns in their hands. Now fully awake, they sprang to their feet, took aim, and fired. The bullets found their mark and the tiger died instantly.

Back at the village, the men told the village chief of their experience. Both of them were mystified as to why they had heard the loud ticking sound which had awakened them to their danger.

The chief listened to them in amazement. Then he spoke.

The official hunter of the village had died not long before. He had been a great marksman and had brought down many man-eating tigers. For this, the ruling Nizam had given the man a watch, a watch with a most powerful tick. When the village hunter died, he had been buried almost on the spot where the two Englishmen had killed the tiger. And the hunter's watch, with its loud tick, had been buried with him.

HOT MILK AND A COBRA

In 1872, while on a hunting trip, the viceroy of India woke one night with a feeling of pressure on his body. Opening his eyes, he saw that a cobra had coiled up on his chest.

The viceroy, although terrified, kept his head and remained still. He knew that his slightest move would cause the cobra to strike and kill him.

The viceroy lay unmoving for an hour. Suddenly, in a shaft of moonlight, he saw a man coming through his tent door. The man came silently toward the bed and then, seeing the cobra, he put his finger to his lips, turned, and left the viceroy's tent.

In a short time the man returned carrying in one hand a large jug of steaming hot milk and, in the other, the cover of the jug. He placed the jug as near as he could to the head of the cobra.

It was not long before the cobra sensed the nearness of great warmth. Uncoiling slowly, the snake glided from the viceroy's chest and disappeared into the jug. The man clapped the cover on the jug, and the cobra was securely trapped.

And the man who saved the viceroy's life? He was a thief who had been looking for rich pickings in the royal camp.

Italy

STREET CLEANING IN VENICE

Venice's roads are waterways, and the "street sweepers" keep the canals as clean as possible with their nets.

Ivory

THE CANTON BALL

The first step is to shape the ivory into a perfect, polished sphere. In the second step, holes equidistant from each other are hand-bored into the sphere to the center. The size of the holes diminishes as the holes approach the center. An L-shaped cutting tool then cuts the inner balls apart. The finished ball with its free-moving concentric "ball within balls" has all been carved with primitive tools from a solid piece of ivory. This Canton Ball contains 26 fragile concentric balls. All ivory balls are made for export, to impress foreigners with Chinese art and carving ability.

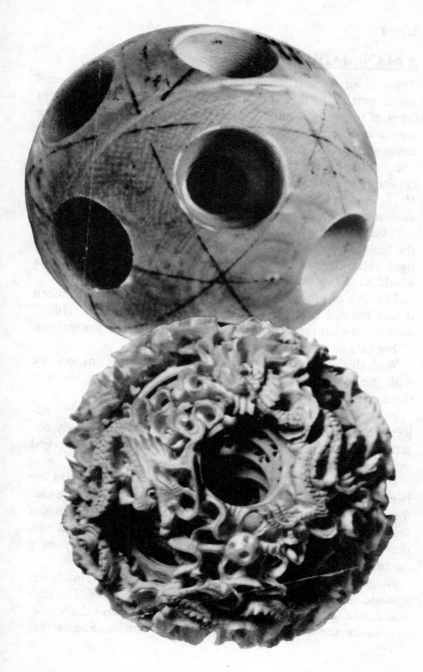

Liger

A MAN-MADE ANIMAL

There is an ancient legend in the American West, a legend which persists to this very day, that among the snowy, silent crags of towering Mount Shasta, there lives a band of strange creatures different from all others in nature. Of course, they are never seen.

By coincidence, "Shasta" was also the name of a unique creature, unknown in the wild, who lived quite openly at the Hogle Zoo in Salt Lake City. She was that great rarity in the animal world, a liger.

A beast of lithe beauty and ferocious strength, "Shasta" was the female hybrid of a male African lion and a female Bengal tiger. (Had the sex of her sire and dam been reversed, Shasta would have been called a "tiglon.")

The idea of producing a liger started at the Hogle Zoo when it was noticed that the tigress "Daisy" and the lion "Huey" were somewhat tamer and more tractable than the general run of big cats.

With this in their favor, the keepers at the zoo went to work with the idea of bringing about an eventual mating between these two different animals.

For some time the tigress and the lion simply occupied adjoining cages. Their reactions to each other were carefully observed, and their awareness of each other patiently encouraged in a friendly direction.

Finally, it was decided that the "get acquainted" period between the two cats had lasted long enough, and a day was set for the big lion to enter Daisy's cage. That first encounter was a touchy business for the men at the zoo, but, as it turned out, they needn't have worried. Daisy and Huey found they were meant for each other and set up housekeeping at once.

Shasta, the mixed-up little liger born of this union, made her historic appearance at the Hogle Zoo on May 6, 1948. The staff was elated, and the baby's birth was noted around the world.

Because she weighed in at a scant 12 ounces, Shasta was

Shasta is the first liger ever born, and possibly the only one who ever lived to reach maturity.

taken from her mother and raised carefully on a bottle, like a household kitten. When she outgrew both bottle and household, the handsome hybrid was returned to the zoo and placed in a private enclosure.

At full growth, Shasta weighed a strapping 375 pounds and enjoyed superb health. This in itself is an amazing feat, for few ligers ever live to reach maturity.

Shasta had the head of her tiger mother and the leonine body of her father, but with stripes. Her temperament was not quite as high-strung and suspicious as a tiger's, but she was unusually violent in her likes and dislikes. To a giant tortoise who once shared her cage, however, she was completely indifferent.

On occasion, Shasta displayed a lion's "playful" mood, but, said Gerald de Bary, then Director of the Hogle Zoo, "She is not tame and gentle, as some of our keepers can testify through past experience with her lightning-quick paws."

Shasta had no offspring because ligers are sterile. Nor could she ever have been born outside a zoo. In the wild, the inherent hostility of one species toward another would have doomed the kind of union from which Shasta sprang. But beyond that, her lion father and tiger mother could never even have met, as the natural ranges of tigers and lions do not anywhere coincide. Shasta, the beautiful liger, was a completely "man-made" animal!

Lincoln

LINCOLN—BOOTH

One stormy night in March, 1865, the famous American actor, Edwin Booth, stood on the platform of the Jersey City railroad station. He had just finished a successful run of *Hamlet* at the New York Winter Garden, and he was now on his way to visit his sister in Philadelphia.

Railroad tickets were then sold on the open platform, which was dangerously crowded that night as people milled around the conductor trying to buy sleeping-car space.

Suddenly, a young man standing beside Booth was violently jostled and, losing his footing, plunged to the tracks, falling into the empty space between two cars. At that very moment, the cars started to move; the train was getting underway.

Horror-stricken, Booth threw himself down on the platform, leaned far over the stone edge and, with the strength born of desperate urgency, grasped the terrified young man under the arms and pulled him to safety.

Saved from certain death beneath the crushing wheels of the train, the shaken young man now overwhelmed his rescuer with thanks. Then, looking at him closely, he asked Booth if he was not the famous actor.

Booth acknowledged that he was, and the man smiled with pleasure.

"It's a great honor to meet you, sir. And may I introduce myself. My name is Lincoln—Robert Lincoln. I am the son of the President."

A few minutes later the two men parted, young Robert profuse in his thanks, and Booth understandably elated that he had rescued the President's son.

LINCOLN—KENNEDY

It has often been noted that the past events of history are often repeated many years later. But this old saying has never been more dramatically borne out than in the striking similarities found in the assassinations of Abraham Lincoln and John F. Kennedy.

Abraham Lincoln was elected President in 1860; John Kennedy was elected just a century later, in 1960.

Lincoln was warned not to attend Ford's Theater on the night he was shot; Kennedy was warned not to visit Dallas.

Both men were shot on a Friday, in public view, while sitting happily and at ease beside their wives. Both were shot from behind, the fatal bullet in each case entering the back of the head.

The men who succeeded Lincoln and Kennedy to the presidency were both named Johnson. Andrew Johnson was born in 1808, Lyndon Baines Johnson was born in 1908. Lyndon Johnson was a Democrat, a Southerner, and a former Senator, and so was Andrew Johnson.

John Wilkes Booth shot Lincoln in a theater and was later found in a tobacco storage barn (warehouse); Lee Harvey Oswald shot Kennedy from a book storage warehouse and was found in a movie theater.

Both assassins were shot down before they could be brought to trial.

LINCOLN AND MATTHEW BRADY

When Abraham Lincoln first appeared on the political scene, few people knew what he looked like. In the cartoons of that time, he was always depicted as a crude woodsman.

In February, 1860, when Lincoln made his first speech in New York, he met Matthew Brady who was then making a name for himself with the newly invented process of "wet-plate" photography.

Brady made a portrait of Lincoln and the picture was widely circulated. It showed Lincoln as he really was and completely reversed the distorted public image created by the cartoons.

Lincoln believed that this photograph helped him to become President. Of it, he said, "It dispelled the opposition based on the rumors of my ungainly figure, making me into a man of human aspect and dignified bearing."

At the time his photograph was taken, Lincoln was clean-shaven. But in the following year a little girl named Grace Bedell, who liked beards, asked Lincoln if he wouldn't please grow one for her sake.

Lincoln did grow a beard soon afterward, and he said later that he had done so "in fulfillment of a little girl's wish."

In this fight with a chicken, the dragonlike lizard is the unquestioned victor.

"Macho"

THE "MACHO" COMPANION

High on the cold stony peaks of the Spanish Pyrenees, lives one of the most handsome of all game animals. It is the native wild mountain goat, called the "macho de monte," or "he-animal of the mountain." Weighing upward of 130 pounds, with magnificent 2-foot horns, the strong, fleet and intelligent "macho" is very difficult to bag, and is considered by Spanish hunters to be the most prized of all sporting trophies.

Because the "macho de monte" is rare and inhabits only the craggy mountaintops, it is difficult for anyone even to come within range of the big-horned animal.

When, however, after an exhausting and dangerous climb, the hunter does manage to spot the big mountain goat, he seldom has time enough even to draw a bead on him, as the wily animal rarely exposes itself as a target for very long.

The reason for this elusiveness is due entirely to a "companion beast," a young goat who follows the big "macho" wherever it goes and acts as a lookout for it.

Hiding behind an outcropping of rock, or on some hidden ledge, the young "companion" keeps watch for any strange sound or movement. Noting anything out of the ordinary, it anticipates the approach of danger and signals the adult animal by giving a high, whistling call. At this shrill warning, the big "macho" takes cover immediately—and another disappointed hunter goes back down the mountain, empty-handed.

Marriage

THE GIRL HE LOVED

In 1761, a young Londoner named Nathaniel Bentley became heir to a fortune. He was a handsome fellow and lived an extravagant life until he met a beautiful girl and fell in love. When she accepted him, he was overjoyed and planned a big banquet to announce their engagement.

But on the very day of the banquet, the girl he loved died suddenly. From that day on, Bentley became a recluse. He never went out, refused to see his family and friends, and lived alone in his vast, boarded-up house, allowing no one to enter. Food was delivered and left at the back door.

Finally, in 1809, Bentley died, and the silent, decaying house was at last opened up.

Inside the house, dirt and confusion were everywhere ... except for the dining room. Here, the chairs stood neatly around a huge table that was all set up for a formal banquet, complete with silver, linen, fine china, and bottles of choice wines. And resting on the table before one special chair, where it had been placed by a happy lover years before, was a small bouquet of dried-to-dust flowers tied with a faded blue ribbon.

Nathaniel Bentley had kept faith with his lost love for half a century, waiting patiently for the arrival of a dead guest of honor to a ghostly banquet that never took place.

THE BANKER'S RUNAWAY WIFE

One evening in March, 1835, a French banker named Henri Bernard returned to his Paris home to find three things missing . . . his wife, his cashier, and the contents of his safe.

The servants told him that his wife had eloped with his young employee, and that they had gone to the seaport of Le Havre where they were to take a boat for America the following morning.

Calling for his horses and a fast carriage, the banker set off for Le Havre, which he reached late that night. Making the rounds of the hotels, he finally caught up with the guilty couple at a small inn.

The runaways were terrified when they saw Bernard. They were certain that he had come to avenge himself and pleaded with him to spare their lives. They would return the money, the wife would go back to Paris, just don't kill them.

But Bernard had no intention of killing them. Instead, he asked the cashier to bring him the stolen money. From it, he counted out ten thousand francs and gave them to the startled young man.

The money was his, the banker said, on one condition. That the cashier would leave for America as he had planned and would take the woman with him. His wife, Bernard continued, was a worthless, troublesome creature and he had been hoping to get rid of her for a long time.

The story surfaced later when the cashier tried to rid himself of the banker's wife.

THE TABLES TURNED

On Christmas Eve in 1832, a wealthy man by the name of Malcolm living in Edinburgh, Scotland, gave a party at which he announced that he was going to marry his housekeeper.

His family and guests were stunned. They knew that he had known the woman for almost 40 years, but they also knew that, because of her greed and shrewish temper, he had come to hate her. Everyone was mystified.

Late that night Malcolm shot himself to death, and the reason for his strange announcement became clear. Old and very ill, he had decided to take his life, but not before he played a grim joke on the woman he detested by falsely raising her hopes of marrying him.

His family, of course, were overjoyed. Now his fortune would be theirs, and not the hated housekeeper's.

But like so many other cruel jokes, this one backfired. By right of an ancient and little-known Scottish law, any man who publicly acknowledged that a woman was to be his wife conferred upon her the status of a wife.

The woman he intended to humiliate actually became his legal heir.

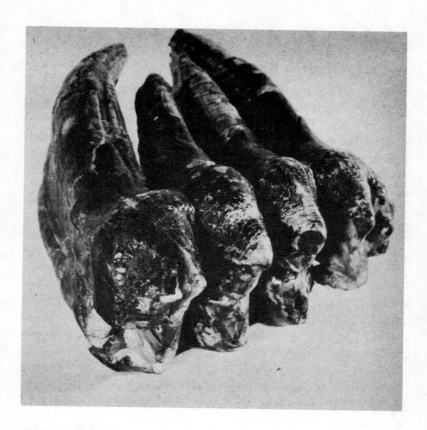

Mastodons

MASTODON'S TEETH

A photograph of the mastodon's "grinder" which David McClure sent to the Dartmouth College Museum. The fossil was found at Big Bone Lick, a great deposit of animal fossils in Kentucky. Mastodons once browsed in great herds and their remains are common in the peat bogs of the Eastern states. This specimen is still used by Dartmouth students for study.

Mining

BLOCK OF SILVER

In 1880, a German doctor named Karl Weiner, who practiced in Peru, made a mercy trip into the mountains to save the sick wife of a poor Indian.

After the doctor treated the woman and saved her life, her husband escorted the doctor down the mountainside. As they made their way along a dangerous trail, the old Indian suddenly made a detour and led the doctor to a small, rocky opening in the face of a steep cliff. Inside, the doctor saw the glittering walls of a fabulous, hidden silver mine.

The Indian told the doctor that the mine was his, and instructed the astonished doctor to dislodge as much silver as he could carry in payment for saving the Indian woman's life.

The doctor did so. But why, he asked, did the Indian keep the mine a secret? The Indian replied that wealth brought only misery, and he wanted his people to be happy. As for the doctor, the Indian said, he would never find the mine again, so its secret would be safe.

And that mine never was found!

But in the Museum of Natural History, in Vienna, there is a big block of raw silver marked "from the collection of Dr. Weiner."

Money

THE FABULOUS BALLAST

From the very beginning of World War II, the little island of Corregidor, in Manila Bay, defended by weary American soldiers, took a terrible pasting from the Japanese on the Bataan peninsula.

Just before Corregidor fell, an American submarine, the *U.S.S. Trout*, received orders to proceed to Corregidor with a cargo of badly needed medical supplies. To accomplish its mission it was necessary to unload all of her torpedoes and all other heavy equipment that could be spared. The *Trout* made Corregidor and spent three days unloading her cargo under fire from the Japanese batteries on Bataan. In order to slip out past the enemy, the sub had to have a heavy ballast for a quick descent. The diving officer wanted bags of gravel, but they were needed for breastworks on Corregidor, shortly to be under siege. Where could heavy ballast be found on Corregidor?

Suddenly, an American Army officer remembered that the banks of Manila had stored $10,000,000 worth of gold and silver on Corregidor—2 tons of gold bars and 18 tons of silver pesos.

This gold and silver was transferred to the *Trout*, and that valiant sub escaped safely ... carrying the most fabulous ballast ever known in all maritime history. It soon transferred the ballast to a cruiser at sea.

THE RABBIT AND THE MONEY

One morning in 1873, a young German forester named Karl Asmis was deputized by the local postmaster to deliver a letter containing a large sum of money to a man living far out of town.

On his way through a forest, Karl shot a rabbit and, thinking it would be easier to carry both the heavy envelope and the rabbit together, he tied the envelope around the rabbit's neck and then slung the little animal over his shoulder.

Suddenly the rabbit, which had only been stunned, came to and, breaking loose, darted away into the woods, carrying the money with him.

Karl returned immediately to the postmaster and reported the loss, but no one believed his story. His father paid back the lost money, but Karl was shunned by everyone in the town.

Years later, a boy playing in the forest pulled down a tree branch, and with it came an old bird's nest. In the nest were remnants of the money and the envelope, as well as the skeleton of a rabbit. The rabbit had been caught and eaten by a wild hawk, which had then lined its nest with the money.

RICHLY DECORATED

In May, 1901, the Dutch steamship *Tambora* hit a submerged reef and sank off a small island in the East Indies.

After the ship had settled, the island natives rowed out to salvage what they could of the ship's stores. One of the natives, arriving after the others had carried off the best items, had to be content with a bundle of soggy small pieces of paper. But it was brightly colored, so he dried it out and used it like wallpaper to decorate his hut.

A few months after this, there arrived on the island a Chinese merchant who made regular trading visits. The man who had found the paper told the merchant that he would like some needles and thread. He had no money, but he would trade him a fine, large fishbone.

The Chinese trader refused, at first, to give anything for the fishbone. But the native was so persistent that the merchant finally agreed to visit the man's hut and see the bone for himself. The trader, however, never did look at the fishbone. When he entered the man's little hut, his eyes popped at the sight of the small pieces of colored paper on the wall. For that native, who was trying to trade a fishbone for some needles and thread, actually had $40,000 worth of Dutch banknotes plastered on his walls.

JOSHUA TATUM, COUNTERFEITER

During the 1880's, a man by the name of Joshua Tatum thought up a daring scheme for making money.

At that time, the lowly nickel and the $5 gold piece, which was called a half-eagle, were very popular. They were just about the same size and looked very much alike, as each coin had a "Liberty Head" on one side.

Tatum decided that if the nickels were gold-colored there would be no difficulty in passing them for half-eagles. With the help of a larcenous jeweler, Tatum put his scheme in operation and then went from store to store passing the counterfeit coins.

His method was simple. He would make a five-cent purchase and then put the gold-plated nickel down on the counter with the "Liberty Head" up. The unsuspecting storekeeper would think the coin was a $5 gold piece and give Tatum $4.95 in change.

The system worked for quite a while, but finally the law caught up with the counterfeiter and he was brought to trial.

But Joshua Tatum was acquitted. It was proven that he had never purchased anything worth more than five cents. The storekeepers, argued Tatum's lawyer, had voluntarily given him the change; Tatum had never asked for any. And how could this be proven? Easily, because Tatum couldn't speak. This clever swindler was a mute and had never uttered a single word in his entire life.

Monkeys

WORKING MONKEYS

If you happened to be "down under" in Australia and thought you saw a bright-faced little monkey at the wheel of a tractor, don't doubt your vision. It was a monkey and he was driving that tractor!

The monkey's name was Johnnie, and he was the only permanent farmhand on the ranch of his owner, Lindsay Schmidt, at Balmoral, a town about 200 miles west of Melbourne.

Schmidt bought Johnnie from a traveling showman, when the little simian was only a few weeks old. Johnnie fitted right into the rancher's family from the start, and Schmidt decided to set the bright little animal to doing a few simple chores around the farm. Johnnie performed so well and liked doing things so much that Schmidt finally tried him out on driving the tractor. Or rather, steering the tractor, because Schmidt would start it and put it in gear. Then Johnnie took over, sitting at the big wheel and steering straight or curved paths according to commands Schmidt has taught him to heed. He even learned to cut-out around trees, boulders and haystacks. While Johnnie drove, Schmidt stood in the back of the truck and threw out fodder for his stock.

When the rancher and his "farmhand" knocked off for lunch, they sat together in the shade of the tractor and enjoyed separate but equal lunch bags, containing soft drinks, sandwiches and fruit.

Johnnie was not the first monkey to be set to work by man. In South Africa, a baboon herded sheep on the farm of a German woman, and did it with all the skill of a trained sheep dog, quickly rounding up strays and bringing stragglers back to the fold. The baboon also had one advantage over a dog in this case. If things got sticky and he found himself caught in a clot of woolly obstinacy, the resourceful baboon would leap on the back of one of his charges and start giving directions. From his elevated position, and his general appearance, the sheep apparently thought he was a man and bowed to his superior authority.

Monkeys have been put to more exotic tasks than sheep-herding, however. Today, in Borneo and elsewhere, it is possible to find monkeys pulling down coconuts for their masters. Such a monkey, attached to a long lead, is sent scrambling up a palm tree, where he picks and tosses down to his waiting owner a ripe coconut. The man can see from the ground whether or not the nut is ripe and signals the monkey when to leave one nut and try another by giving a sharp tug on the lead.

The strangest task ever done by monkeys was undertaken during the 19th century, in Africa. European visitors, returning from Ethiopia at that time, brought back the exotic news that monkeys were used as torchbearers during royal feasts. The animals were trained to sit absolutely motionless, lighting the scene, until after the guests had finished eating. Then the monkeys were rewarded by being allowed to finish off what was left of the sumptuous meal.

Mountain Climbing

"BECAUSE IT WAS THERE"

Why do people climb mountains?

"Well," say the rugged men who climb them, "because they are there."

Few climbers, however, make a career of scaling a single mountain. But that's just what Johann Schraudolph did.

Johann's story actually begins when he was a lad of 10. Born and raised in the tiny Bavarian alpine village of Einodsbach, Johann was exposed to the sport of mountain climbing from infancy. Climbers from all over the world came to his village to work their way up the many huge peaks that surrounded his native valley.

Johann grew up to love mountains and to admire those who risked life and limb to scale the towering heights. At an early age he decided that some day he also would be a climber. But then he began to notice something very strange. None of the climbers ever attacked the sheer cliffs that made up the sides of Mount Madelegabel.

Perhaps it was because Madelegabel was only 8,680 feet high, and not the highest mountain in the area. However, the mountain was locally considered a very tough climb because of the steepness of its walls, and its sharp outcroppings.

Young Schraudolph began to feel that Madelegabel was being unjustly ignored. The thought stayed with him, and finally he decided to do something about it. He would become the first to make the attempt to Madelegabel's stony summit.

On a crisp morning, shortly after celebrating his tenth birthday, Johann made his first try. Struggling every inch of the way, the dedicated youngster stubbornly battled Madelegabel's treacherous formations for many dangerous hours. At last, thoroughly exhausted, he succeeded in reaching the windswept peak of the mountain that nobody wanted to climb.

For most 10-year-old boys, that would have been accomplishment enough. But not for Johann. A couple of months later he set out to repeat his triumph. And once more he succeeded.

Suddenly, the mountain seemed to become an obsession with the boy. Periodically, throughout that year, he repeated his feat. Before the year was over he had scaled Madelegabel's slippery sides seven times.

His fellow townspeople began to whisper behind his back. "There goes that crazy kid who keeps climbing the same mountain."

But their growing ridicule didn't stop him. And year after year, Johann returned to Madelegabel and struggled to its summit. But he did this not once a year but seven times each year, just as he'd done after he first scaled the mountain in the year he was 10.

For 61 years, until he reached the age of 71, Johann followed his strange compulsion to climb the Madelegabel seven times every year.

He became a living legend and, when it was known that he would make one of his climbs, the villagers gathered to watch him start his ascent.

Johann Schraudolph devoted his life to climbing just that single mountain. In the course of the years, he traversed a distance of more than 1,400 miles up and down the stony face of Madelegabel.

It is a strange record in the annals of mountain climbing, and it has never been equalled.

Murder

MARRIAGE AND MURDER

Devil's Island, a small dot of land off the coast of South America, was a French maximum security penal colony that was notorious for the harsh treatment of its prisoners.

One of these prisoners was a young Frenchman named Jean Massot who had been sent to Devil's Island to serve a term of 18 years for the murder of his wife. She had disappeared after a quarrel with her husband.

Massot was arrested, tried, and found guilty of his wife's death, although he steadfastly protested his innocence and the evidence against him was circumstantial.

After serving his full prison term, Massot was released and promptly went back to France. There he met a woman, fell in love, and proposed marriage. But when the couple applied for a marriage license, they were informed they could not get one. It would be illegal.

Why? Well, although Massot had served 18 years for killing his wife, her body had never been found. Because of this, he could not prove that she was legally dead and that he was free to remarry. The authorities reasoned, therefore, that Massot was still technically married to the woman for whose murder he had been sent to Devil's Island.

Music

ONE-MAN CONCERT

One stormy night in 1910, a group of traveling musicians arrived at the city of Riga, on the Baltic Sea, to fulfill a concert engagement.

The weather was so bad, however, and the concert hall so far out of town, that the conductor of the orchestra tried to persuade the manager of the hall to cancel the concert. He felt no one would venture out on such a wild night.

The manager refused to cancel, but he agreed that if no one turned up, the orchestra could leave early in order to catch the night boat for Helsinki, Finland.

When the musicians arrived at the concert hall, they found only one person sitting in the audience . . . a stout old gentleman who seemed to smile at everyone.

Because of this old music-lover, the musicians were forced to play the entire concert. They were, therefore, unable to leave early and catch the boat.

After the concert was over, the old man continued to keep his seat. Thinking he was asleep, an usher nudged his shoulder. Only then was it discovered that the old man was not alive. The musicians had played an entire concert for a dead man!

But in doing this, they also saved their lives. For the boat they would have taken to Helsinki went down that stormy night with all hands lost.

Navy

THE DUEL

One bleak March morning in 1820, two men met in a muddy field in Bladensburg, Maryland, and faced each other in a deadly pistol duel.

One man was James Barron. He had been an officer in the United States Navy but had been found guilty by a court-martial of cowardice under fire and had been dropped from the service in disgrace.

The other man was a commodore in the Navy, and Barron hated him. Not only had the commodore been a member of the court-martial, but he had continued to oppose all Barron's efforts to be reinstated in the service.

Now Barron wanted revenge, and the commodore, although he thought dueling was barbaric and should be abolished, accepted the challenge.

Barron was a crack shot; the commodore was not. So it was no surprise when Barron's bullet found its mark and the commodore pitched forward dead.

But the man who hated dueling did not die in vain. His death shocked the nation and brought about the abolition of dueling in the United States.

That commodore was the great naval hero Stephen Decatur, the man who had become famous for those stirring words: "May she always be right; but our country, right or wrong."

THE SHOT THAT BACKFIRED

During World War II, the American submarine, *Gato,* patrolling off Saipan, sighted a Japanese carrier and opened fire. Her torpedoes scored direct hits and the carrier sank. The *Gato* then submerged, the sea around her peppered with depth charges.

The *Gato* dodged the bombs successfully, but after five hours the captain decided to take a chance and surface.

When the *Gato* reached the top of the water, a new danger was discovered. A depth charge was lying on the *Gato's* deck! The submarine had caught it as she rose through the water.

The *Gato* seemed trapped. The Japanese had spotted her, were bearing down for the kill, and the submarine could not submerge without setting off the depth charge on her deck.

Then a quick-witted sailor had an idea. A life raft was inflated and the bomb placed in it. Before the raft was floated off the *Gato's* deck, a small cut was made in its side so that it would sink. And that raft sank just slowly enough to explode beneath the oncoming Japanese destroyer. The destroyer was blown to bits, and the *Gato* made it safely back to her base.

Octopus

TEACHING IT TO READ

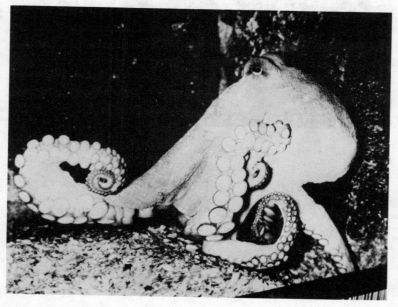

The eyes of the octopus most nearly resemble human eyes. The U.S. Air Force at one time, in doing research, taught this 8-armed creature of the deep to "read" by distinguishing letterlike shapes.

Oil

SPLASH!

An electronic flash at 1/12,000th of a second caught this droplet of oil in mid-splatter hitting a hard surface.

Ostriches

BIG EYE, SMALL BRAIN

The big angry eye of the ostrich occupies more space in his small head than his brain does. But this tiny mind directs the largest bird body in the world.

The flightless ostrich weighs in at 300 pounds and averages about 8 feet in height.

Although he cannot fly, the ostrich is able to cover the ground at 50 miles an hour in giant, 28-foot strides. In South Africa, he is sometimes saddled and used as a racing bird. Only the toughest jockey can ride such a steed since the big bird is erratic and given to sudden, jolting stops, leaps and right-angle turns, which he accomplishes by means of his rudimentary, otherwise useless, wings.

Ostrich-riding can also be a very dangerous sport because the plumed bird is malevolent by nature and uses his legs

Ostrich racing is a sport around the famous ostrich farms of South Africa. Jockeys must guard against raking blows from their ill-tempered mounts' sharp claws.

A herd of ostriches on a "feather farm" in Oudtshoorn, South Africa, the world's "ostrich center."

freely as weapons. One raking blow from his sharp-clawed, two-toed foot could lay a man wide open.

Alfalfa is the principal food of the ostrich, and to keep this nourishment moving comfortably through his 46-foot-long intestine, the big bird adds pebbles to his diet for roughage. When these aren't available, the bird-brained muncher will pick up anything lying around—tin cans, old bottle tops, bits of wire or tennis balls. When this happens, the owner of an ostrich has to dig down and retrieve the harmful digestive aids from the bird's long, flexible throat.

Only the male ostrich has plumes. His body feathers are black and glossy, the feathery white plumes appearing only at the tips of his tail and wings. His wives (the ostrich is polygymous) are a neutral gray and are kept busy laying their 3-pound eggs. Just one of these eggs makes a hardy omelet for a dozen hungry diners.

Now what did you swallow? A tin can, a tennis ball?

The male also aids in the incubation of the chicks by sitting on the eggs at night. This is a protective measure, since his black feathers make him almost invisible in the darkness.

The South African town of Oudtshoorn is known as the "ostrich center of the world" and is the only place where ostrich farming is still carried on. It is also where ostrich farming started in the mid-19th century, when the demand for the birds' handsome plumes made for a profitable worldwide business. But after World War I, ostrich plumes went out of fashion and feather farming collapsed.

Today, the ostriches at Oudtshoorn are raised mostly for their skins, which are used for fine leather goods, and for their small body feathers, which are used to make feather dusters. The ostriches are sheared of these—like sheep—every nine months. Most of these feathers go to France, where tidy housewives still prefer to keep the mahogany bright by means of feather-flicking.

As for the old belief that ostriches bury their heads in the sand, that is definitely not so. The ostrich bends only to eat or drink. And it couldn't even survive among the sand dunes. It is a vegetarian and must live where the green things grow.

Outlaws

THE DOCTOR AND THE OUTLAW

One day in 1874, in Sherman, Texas, a man dying of typhoid fever was brought to the local hospital. The young doctor in attendance, John Burke, managed to save the man's life and, when the patient left, he promised that someday he would repay the doctor.

Years later, Burke moved to Missouri and built up a new practice. One day, while walking to his office, the doctor spied a group of strange horsemen heading for the Moniteau Bank. He realized they were bank robbers, and he recognized their leader as his former Texas patient.

Without hesitating, Burke went up to the outlaw leader, who remembered the doctor immediately. The doctor pleaded with the bandit not to rob the bank. If he did so, Burke said, he would suffer. He told the bandit that the townspeople, who were nervously watching them, would accuse Burke of being an accomplice of the outlaw band and drive him out of town. The doctor would never be able to practice there—or anywhere else—again.

When Burke finished speaking, the outlaw gave a command to his men, said good-bye to the doctor and then, wheeling his horse around, he led his band out of town.

The bandit who that day repaid his debt to the doctor who had saved his life was none other than Frank James, brother of the notorious outlaw, Jesse James.

Oysters

<u>OYSTERS GROW ON TREES</u>

Oysters grow on the submerged roots of mangrove trees along Caribbean shores. The College of Agriculture of the University of Puerto Rico has conducted studies to establish a year-round oyster industry for the island. As many as 50 oysters cling to a single root and you can pick a whole bucketful in 15 minutes. The oysters are small and sweet and they can be eaten at any time of the year. During periods of low tide one can pick the oysters right from the roots without entering the water.

Parachutes

AN AIRBORNE MIRACLE

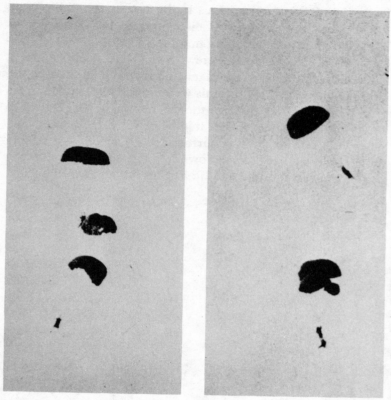

In the picture above left you see Sgt. Marvin O. Smith dangling from the bottom parachute, while above him is the semi-collapsed parachute of Pfc. Charles J. Dye, who is plummeting earthward. On the right you see Sgt. Smith's quick-thinking heroism as he grabs the shroud lines of Dye's parachute, and the two fall safely to the ground. Their swinging comrade above has had a ringside seat at the drama.

SOFT LANDING

Corporal Joseph Aiello of New York was serving with a bomber squadron in the South Pacific in World War II when he flew a mission from his East Indies base to the Philippines. A few hours out, a leak was discovered in the bomber's gas line. Unable to repair it, the pilot descended to 3000 feet, leveled off and instructed the crew to bail out. Aiello jumped, made his count to clear the plane and then pulled the ripcord. Nothing happened; his shrouds were hopelessly tangled in his Mae West. Plunging through the air, he fought desperately to loosen his chute. But he couldn't. Mercifully, he blacked out. When he came to, he was surrounded by medics all talking about a miracle. He'd come down in a big, soft tropical tree, a giant green cushion that had broken his fall and saved his life.

TWO ON A PARACHUTE

Paratroopers in maneuvers over Bedford, Massachusetts, became entangled on their way down. Both men landed safely.

Pearl Harbor

WERE THE JAPANESE TIPPED OFF?

It started in 1932—nine years before the devastating assault took place. In that year Adm. Harry Yarnall staged a mock "sneak attack" on Pearl Harbor to test the readiness of the base and its personnel in the face of a sudden offensive by an unnamed enemy. Everyone concerned, of course, knew who that enemy might be.

The carefully staged (and top secret) attack was planned for early on a Sunday morning. The admiral chose that day because he knew that most of the men on the base would still be asleep at that time. He also knew that those who were astir would be a bit less than alert, the normal state following the usual Saturday night on the town.

At the admiral's direction, the planes took off from U.S. carriers positioned off the coast, swooping in from the Pacific under cover of a dense pre-dawn fog. They took the base completely by surprise.

Flying low over the anchored ships, the "enemy" met almost no resistance and was able, theoretically, to completely "destroy" our fleet at Pearl.

During the mock attack, the Navy had encountered only one difficulty—some bumbling Japanese fishing boats kept getting in the way of the carriers while they prepared to make the "assault" on the base.

At the time, except for being a nuisance, the fishing boats were given little thought. Things would have been different, however, had it been known that aboard those innocent-looking little vessels were Japanese observers who were taking detailed notes of everything they witnessed that day. This information added up to a blueprint for invasion.

And that is what was used as a pattern when the carrier-based planes of the Japanese made their stunning attack on Pearl Harbor on Dec. 7, 1941. They winged in precisely according to the plan used by U.S. planes in the dry run made nine years before. They chose early Sunday morning for their

On December 7, 1941, which President Roosevelt called the "day of infamy," Japanese aircraft sank the U.S.S. *Arizona* and left little above the surface of Pearl Harbor. Today a memorial stands on top of the sunken ship.

attack, and they bombed the same areas which the U.S. planes had "bombed." They imitated the "attack" exactly.

That was the only lucky thing that came out of the tragedy of that "day of infamy." Why? Because in the 1932 exercise, the Navy flyers had been instructed to "hit" only the ships lined up in Battleship Row, nothing else. The Japanese, following that pattern, did exactly the same thing. Only the ships were made the targets of their bombs; the shore installations at the base were barely touched.

In 1941, the enemy completely ignored the giant repair docks. Amazingly, they also passed up the opportunity of setting ablaze an exposed storage "farm" containing 4.5-million barrels of fuel oil. These were highly vulnerable to attack, yet the raiders spared them.

Of what the loss of these would have meant to the United States, Adm. Chester Nimitz later said: "The destruction of the repair docks at Pearl Harbor would have forced our Navy all the way back to the West Coast . . . (and) the loss of that great fuel supply would have been well-nigh irreparable."

But with all the fuel needed still on hand, and with all the vast shipyard facilities left intact at Pearl, the U.S. Navy was able to start immediately on the repairs necessary to rebuild the crippled Pacific fleet. In less than a year, the U.S. ships were again afloat and on the offensive.

And thanks to one more error in a plan too carefully carried out, the U.S. still had the submarine base at Pearl. They didn't knock that out, either. Soon after the attack, U.S. subs were prowling the Pacific, taking deadly toll of enemy vessels.

If the docks and fuel had been destroyed in 1941, the war might have lasted three years longer and Japan might have won!

DRESS OF PEARLS

This pearl Kavacha (dress) is among the items in a fabulous jewelry collection in the Great Temple in Madura, India. On festive occasions the dress adorns the Goddess Minakshi. The entire dress is wired into a simple form containing the soft hues of pearls and corals. Its true value is impossible to estimate.

A STRING OF PEARLS

Several years ago, two ladies, Lucy and Lavinia, from New Haven, Connecticut, decided to spend a vacation cycling about England. Their purpose was to explore the countryside and become more familiar with the people. The pair promised to return with souvenirs for a long list of friends. Limited funds, however, dictated that their purchases be little more than mementos. Therefore, throughout their vacation, the two women made it a habit to stop at small, out-of-the-way shops, buying trinkets that were easily carried in pockets or bags.

Such was their object one afternoon when they arrived in Newhaven, England, namesake city of their home. After checking in at a small inn near the heart of the city, they questioned the clerk about possible souvenir shops where they might pick up yet another bargain.

The young man thought for a moment and then suggested: "You might try Martin's. It's a dusty little shop, two squares down the street. I pass it each day on the way to work, and he seems to have a number of items in his window that might fit your plans."

With great anticipation, the two adventurers hurried to the tiny shop, chatted excitedly as they searched the store's window and finally entered, certain they would find something to suit their fancy. Lavinia took the lead as the smiling proprietor greeted his two visitors.

"We're from New Haven, Connecticut, in the United States," she explained, "and we want to take home something to remind us of our visit to your city. We don't have much money nor do we have a lot of room to pack souvenirs. Could you show us something that might fit those requirements?"

Martin Lazenby thought about the conditions a moment, his eyes roving over the many items in his shop. Suddenly, they lit up. "I think I may have just the thing for you," he answered.

Moving toward a nearby shelf, he picked up a small Bible and turned to face the ladies. "Possibly this will do," he offered.

He watched their expressions and, detecting no excitement,

began looking elsewhere around the cluttered room. His eyes finally spied a string of beads, suspended from a nail that was driven into the wall.

Followed by the shoppers, he moved toward the beads, lifted them from the nail and offered them to the ladies. "These aren't much," he acknowledged, "but they do fit your needs. They're small and I can let you have them for a shilling."

Lucy accepted the string of beads and began inspecting them. "Do they have any historic background?" she asked.

"None that I am aware of," Lazenby answered. "But, they're the only other thing I have in the shop that you might be interested in."

Nodding, Lucy turned to Lavinia with a questioned glance. When her friend nodded, she turned back to the owner. "We'll take them," she smiled. "However, I notice the string is quite worn. Could you restring them for us?"

"I'm sorry, madam," Lazenby answered. "I don't do such work. Possibly someone else in town may be able to help you."

"That's no problem," Lucy smiled. "We'll have a couple of days in London before our boat sails. We'll have it done when we get there."

On their arrival in London, Lucy looked in the telephone directory to select a shop in which to have the beads restrung. She happened onto the name of Lucy Coghill Company, a distinguished jewelry firm, close by the ladies' hotel. Struck by the coincidence of names, she took her dusty find to the shop and explained what she wanted done.

"Can you leave them overnight?" the clerk asked.

"Oh, certainly. I'll pick them up in the morning," Lucy agreed.

When the two returned, they were greeted by the excited manager of the firm.

"Could you step into the office for a moment?" he inquired.

As they entered his plushly furnished office, Lucy noticed her beads had been laid out on a piece of white material in the corner of a massive desk. Their appearance had changed remarkably. From a chair along the wall, a second man rose and started toward them.

"There," the manager said, gesturing toward his desk, "is your shilling-strand of beads, as you described them to my clerk yesterday."

"But, they look so different," Lucy squealed in delight.

"And, well they might," the other man cut in. "May I ask where you got them?" he continued.

"At a small shop in Newhaven," Lucy answered. "But, why? Is something wrong?"

"Nothing's wrong, young lady. As a matter of fact, you've done something British researchers have been unable to do for more than three hundred years. Let me explain," he continued. "I'm from the British Museum. We've been searching for these 'beads,' as you describe them, for years."

The official then backtracked into English history to tell his story.

In 1542, the explanation started, King James V of Scotland and his wife, Mary of Guise, became the parents of their only child, also named Mary. When the baby was only a week old, the king died. Immediately, the child was named Queen of Scotland.

Six years later, her mother insisted that she be sent to France to be educated as a Catholic. At age 16, the young Mary married the French crown prince, or dauphin. A year later, he became Francis II, king of France; but he ruled only a year before his death.

Four years after Mary's return to the throne of Scotland, she married her cousin, Henry Stuart, Lord Darnley, who persuaded his wife to begin persecution of the rising Protestants. The action set off a revolt.

In the next few years, the Queen began to hate her husband, and took on lovers. The first of these, David Rizzio, an Italian musician acting as the Queen's private secretary, was stabbed to death by a pair of irate Scottish noblemen. It was rumored that Lord Darnley had been at the bottom of the plot.

Soon, she had taken another lover, James Hepburn, Earl of Bothwell. Several weeks later, the house in which Lord Darnley was living was blown up, and the Queen's husband died in the explosion. Almost immediately, she married the Earl of Bothwell who, many were certain, had murdered Darnley.

The act was too much for her Scottish subjects, and the Queen was forced to give up her throne. She was succeeded by her son, who later became King James I of England.

The deposed Queen tried to raise an army with which to regain her throne. There was no support for her in Scotland, however, and she was forced to flee to England, where she sought the protection of her cousin, Elizabeth, who was Queen of that country.

Because Mary had a secondary claim to the British throne, she soon came under suspicion when several plots to murder the English Queen were discovered, and Elizabeth ordered Mary to be beheaded.

"That," the official of the British Museum continued, "should have ended the story of Mary, Queen of Scots. Unfortunately, it didn't. We know from old records that one of Mary's lovers or husbands had given her a string of black pearls. Although we do not know which one, we do know that Mary was extremely proud of those pearls and that she wore them quite often.

"She was a very vain woman," the official continued, "and she proved it at her execution. The records show she was dressed in black satin on that day, and her undergarments were made of red velvet. For that reason and the fact she loved the pearls so dearly, we believe it may have been possible she wore that necklace when she went to the block. Whether she did or did not, has never been proven. However, we do know that the necklace was never seen again by anyone who recognized it until you brought it in here yesterday."

The two ladies looked at each other and could only shake their heads in disbelief.

Then, the official spoke again.

"The loss was discovered shortly after Mary's death. First, Queen Elizabeth asked her private agents to investigate and see if they could find the missing necklace. They turned up nothing. As the years passed and word of the loss became generally known, more and more agencies joined the search. Officials of the British Museum, Scotland Yard and hundreds of private investigators have remained baffled for more than 350 years. Now the search is over.

"As you can see, this is a very valuable find. It helps fill a gap in our history. The Board of Governors of the British Museum has authorized me to offer you five thousand pounds—that's about $25,000 in your money—for the necklace of black pearls. For the sake of our history, will you sell it to us?"

Not a sound intruded in the silent room. Once more, the Americans looked at each other. Finally, turning toward the official, Lucy, unable to speak, nodded her agreement.

Thus, the necklace was restored to its rightful place in British history and found a proud spot in the British Museum. Here, nearly 400 years after it had disappeared, the necklace is on display for visitors to marvel at.

And, in Newhaven, England, Martin Lazenby, who didn't profit by his transaction with the American ladies, did benefit indirectly. For souvenir-hunting tourists, Martin's tiny shop became a popular stop.

SPANISH TREASURE UNCOVERED

While exploring the ruins of a 400-year-old Spanish village, Dr. Joseph M. Cruxent discovered this fabulous cache of over 3,000 pearls buried only 2 inches under the earth. Valued at well over $300,000, these pearls have lost little of their luster in 400 years.

Pigeons

PIGEON APARTMENT HOUSE

The pigeons of San Juan, Puerto Rico, have this apartment house all to themselves. The luckiest birds have the tower apartments.

"G.I. JOE" PIGEON

One of the most outstanding flights recorded for any homing pigeon during World War II was made by a dark, check-splashed bird named "G.I. Joe," early on the morning of October 18, 1943.

On the day before the flight, the British 56th Infantry Division had requested air support from headquarters to assist them in breaking the stubborn German defensive lines at the heavily fortified village of Colvi Vecchia, in Italy. However, soon after this message was sent, the British suddenly succeeded in making a surprise breakthrough; without warning, the German resistance collapsed completely and the British troops overran the little town.

But this unexpected victory, the British quickly realized, would be a disastrous one for them unless they could get word through at once to call off the air support they had so recently requested. If not, they would certainly be massacred by their own planes, as they now occupied the very position they had asked to have bombed!

It was at this point that they made a dismaying discovery; they could not get word of their danger to the airfield. All communications had broken down in the hectic advance. There was no choice now but to entrust their urgent message to one of several pigeons always kept on hand for just such a desperate emergency.

"G.I. Joe" was the pigeon chosen to carry this life-or-death message, and it was a fortunate choice. Flying swiftly and unerringly over the battle-torn land, the courageous bird covered 20 hazardous miles in minutes, arriving at the military airfield just in time to intercept the takeoff of the Allied Air Support planes which were warming up on the runways.

The successful completion of this historic flight saved the lives of more than one thousand British soldiers.

In 1946 the Lord Mayor of London personally presented "G.I. Joe" with the Dickin Medal for gallantry under fire, and this honor was followed by special Congressional recognition in the United States.

"G.I. Joe" had been hatched on March 24, 1943, at the U.S. Army Pigeon Section in Algiers, North Africa. He was later taken to the Tunisian front, then to Bizerte and from there to the Italian front.

After World War II, "G.I. Joe" was brought to the States and housed in the Army's Churchill Loft, a special loft built just for pigeon "heroes" at Fort Monmouth, New Jersey. All such heroes had flown 20 or more combat missions.

On March 23, 1957, the Army Signal Corps deactivated their Pigeon Breeding and Training Center at Fort Monmouth and sold off all their highly trained birds—1,018 of them—at a public auction, which was attended mostly by racing-pigeon fanciers seeking fine birds to improve their flocks. The birds were sold in pairs, male and female. The Army, however, did not sell the 15 pigeons still remaining in the Churchill Loft but, instead, gave their heroes away to selected zoos throughout the country. "G.I. Joe" was given to the Detroit Zoo, where he remained a happy attraction until his death on June 3, 1961.

The United States Army first started training and using homing pigeons in 1878 during the Sioux uprisings in the Dakotas, and continued using these birds by the thousands in every war until Vietnam. The use of homing pigeons by the military reached its peak in World War II, when 56,000 birds were in service. The birds had a fantastic rate of success in completing their dangerous missions; those that failed were almost always battle casualties.

The use of birds as messengers dates back to antiquity. When Roman chariot drivers set off to enter out-of-town competitions, they often took with them swallows dyed the same colors as their prized two-wheeled vehicles. After the race, the winning driver would immediately release his birds who, winging homeward, would by their colors inform the eager townspeople which of their favorite sons was bringing home the trophy.

Today, in some areas of the South Pacific, the big frigate bird, an aggressive, virtually mute creature, able to soar almost endlessly on his long, narrow wings, is still trained to carry messages between neighboring islands.

G. I. Joe, the carrier pigeon who saved a thousand lives during World War II, was awarded a medal by the Lord Mayor of London.

Dagwood prefers volleying without a paddle.

Dagwood has a left-hand forehand and no backhand.

Ping-Pong

CAT PLAYS NET GAME

Morning exercise for Ted Matson of Portland, Oregon, is a Ping-Pong match with Dagwood, his cat. Dagwood, using his paw for a paddle, has a game each morning before breakfast with his master. Matson wins just a little better than half the games. In one exchange Dagwood returned the ball fifteen times.

Platypus

THE WORLD'S STRANGEST MAMMAL

"It's a hoax," said the European scientists when they first set eyes on the Australian platypus. "Such an animal can't exist."

With a tail like a beaver, covered with brown and orange fur, a bill like a duck and some inner organs like a reptile's, the warm-blooded platypus, native only to Australia, is the world's oldest and most primitive of mammals.

Although it is a mammal, the platypus lays eggs like a bird. Unlike bird eggs, however, those of this curious mammal have springy shells, tough as leather.

The 2-foot-long platypus is a fine swimmer and always lives close to the water. It hides in burrows on land by day and swims all night hunting down its food. During the night, the platypus eats food equal to half its own weight on a diet that ranges from worms to crayfish.

It also carries a weapon for protection, a sharp spur, equipped with a poison sac, on each hind leg.

At breeding time, the female platypus tunnels far into the earth and makes a warm, tight nest of leaves and tree bark at the end of the passage. Then she seals off the tunnel with more leaves and lays just two eggs.

The platypus babies, at hatching, are only half an inch long and totally blind. They cling to the mother's skin and she feeds them with milk through pores that open up in her chest by means of rubbing.

The Australian platypus is a mammal, but it lays eggs. It has a bill like a duck, a tail like a beaver and it swims like a fish. Scientists thought it was a hoax when they first saw it.

Porpoises

High-jumping porpoise is enticed by the food which the author is holding out. Dolphins are a variety of porpoise in the *Delphinus* genus.

THE GREATEST OF ALL DOLPHINS

The graceful, warm-blooded, affectionate dolphin, whose intelligence was noted 2,000 years ago by the great Roman naturalist, Pliny, is now considered to be man's most likely partner in his next scientific breakthrough—verbal communication with a lower animal. This fascinating, seagoing mammal will be the prime candidate for such a dialogue; not only is the dolphin brainy and cooperative, but a dolphin has already been taught to say a few words.

When, and if, the day of the discoursing dolphin arrives, we may learn the answer to one baffling question: why did his ancestors, who once lived and walked on land, decide to go back into the sea again? We may also learn at last the whole story of Pelorus Jack, the greatest of all dolphins.

At the northern end of New Zealand's vast South Island lies French Pass, a narrow strait of dangerous water long used by daring coastal skippers as a shortcut between Tasman Bay and Pelorus Sound.

Sometime late in the 1800's, a big, handsome dolphin took up his abode in these troublesome waters and soon gained fame for his habit of meeting approaching ships and guiding them safely through the hazardous pass. Eventually, he came to be known as Pelorus Jack, after the sound in which he lived.

Pelorus Jack followed faithfully a self-imposed schedule. Every day he waited at the mouth of the sound and, as each ship appeared, the dolphin would swim out to meet it, rubbing against its sides like a cat, snorting and blowing in pleasure. Then, crisscrossing its bows, the animal would accompany the ship through the rushing waters of the strait, splash a farewell with his tail and swim back to his waiting place in the sound to meet the next incoming ship.

Pelorus Jack remained at his strange post day and night, year in and year out; on only two occasions was this remarkable record broken.

The first time was when the *Penguin*, a ship that came often through the straits and seemed a special favorite of the dolphin's, foundered one wild, dark night while Pelorus Jack was

Scientists think that dolphins are among the most intelligent of all animals. These two, at the Miami Seaquarium, were very quick to learn the game of basketball, which they seem to enjoy. However, they make no attempt to keep score.

escorting it. It would be foolish, of course, to claim that the dolphin experienced grief at the loss of the ship, but it is a matter of record that Pelorus Jack was not seen for many days after the tragic sinking.

The second disappearance of Pelorus Jack took place some time later when a malevolent drunk, riding as supercargo on a freighter, seized a rifle and, before he could be disarmed by the outraged seamen, fired a shot that wounded the faithful animal. Trailing blood, the startled Jack sounded and streaked away. Days later, having forgiven man for his senseless cruelty, Pelorus Jack returned and resumed his old duties as sportive pilot.

Out of this incident, however, at the demand of a shocked public, an Act of Council was passed at Wellington, New Zealand, on Sept. 26, 1904, which made it a penal offense to "interfere with, hurt, harass or annoy" this phenomenal animal. The law was needed, it has been said, to protect Pelorus Jack from the "annoyance of the unthinking, and against the loving attentions of the ichthyologic investigators who hunger to analyze Pelorus Jack's brain and shut his skeleton into a museum."

Whatever the reason, by this official act, Pelorus Jack became the only dolphin in history to swim the seas protected by a law enacted solely for his benefit.

Under the mantle of the law, Pelorus Jack lived an untroubled life; the years grew long, and his fame spread. Then, in 1912, Pelorus Jack disappeared for the third and last time. For months, every sailor aboard every ship that entered the sound scanned the rolling waters for sight of the familiar dolphin but he was never seen again. The greatest of all dolphins was dead.

In a spectacular performance at Sea World, two friendly dolphins swim in perfect tandem to provide a pair of living skis for this marine sportsman.

Predictions

JULES VERNE'S PREDICTIONS

Foretelling the future is becoming a popular—and highly paid—business. But few soothsayers will ever be able to equal the record of Jules Verne in predicting what's ahead for the world.

First and foremost among all science-fiction writers, Verne reached the peak of his writing career before the start of the 20th century. In his books, he prophesied atomic submarines, the military tank, skyscrapers, aircraft, television, earth-moving machines, talking pictures, and a host of other modern inventions. And not only did he predict them, he explained how they would work.

But Verne's most uncanny forecast of things to come was his detailed description of a voyage to the moon. Verne described a moon rocket long before anyone dreamed of such a thing, and even told of a dog that would be sent up first—as the Russians did—to test the projectile.

Most amazing of all, however, in his book *Around the Moon*, this fantastic man actually described the place from which a moon rocket would take off. These are his words:

"Everyone in America made it his duty to study the geography of Florida. As a point of departure for the moon rocket, they had chosen an area situated 27 degrees North Latitude and 5 degrees West Longitude."

That location is only 80 miles from Cape Kennedy.

THE KENTUCKY DERBY

The famous Kentucky Derby has been run every year for almost a century, ever since the first winner, "Aristides," came thundering in to take a purse of $2,850 in 1875.

Year after year, records are made and broken at Churchill Downs . . . horses run faster, purses grow larger, jockeys get richer and smaller. Sometimes, they even turn out to be "fillies."

One of the most amazing records ever made in connection with the Derby took place in 1949.

The well-known sportswriter, Bill Corum, not only named the winner of the Derby that year, but he called the first four horses in the race. And he called them in the exact order in which they came in.

The day before the Derby, in his daily sports column, Corum named "Ponder" as the winner of the race . . . "Capot" for second place . . . "Palestinian" for show . . . and then added "Old Rockport" as the number four horse at the finish line.

It was the greatest racing prediction ever made, a horseplayer's dream come true. But when Corum was asked later how much he had bet on his amazing hunch, he said, "Not a dime."

OAK RIDGE PROPHECY

At the beginning of the 20th century, the inhabitants of a little Tennessee village were startled by the behavior of one of their neighbors, John Hendricks.

Hendricks, a deeply religious man, announced that God had spoken to him in a dream and told him to go into the woods for 40 days and 40 nights. If he did this, he would see a fantastic vision of the future.

Everyone tried to persuade Hendricks against heeding the dream, but he refused to listen and disappeared into the woods.

When the 40 days were up, Hendricks returned. His appearance was wilder than ever, and his eyes blazed like a prophet's. He had seen a vision of the future, he said.

As the villagers listened, Hendricks told them that in their unknown valley would someday be a humming city.

The oak-covered hills would disappear, and giant, complex buildings would rise in their places. People would flock to the valley from all corners of the earth, and the city that would one day rise in their wilderness would change the destiny of the world.

Hendricks spoke with such passionate conviction that the villagers believed him. But when he died a few years later, in 1903, and nothing had changed in the valley, they forgot him.

Then, in 1943, Hendricks' vision came to pass. Almost overnight, in that lonely valley, a fantastic city rose ... the awesome city which came to be known as Oak Ridge, birthplace of the first atomic bomb. As Hendricks had predicted, this changed the destiny of the world.

Presidents

TWO PRESIDENTS IN BATTLE

One of the most amazing stories that came out of the Civil War took place in 1862 at the Battle of Antietam in Maryland.

One day, when the fighting at Antietam was hottest, a Union commander named Colonel Hayes ordered his weary men back into the firing line before sunrise and without breakfast.

A young mess sergeant, known as Billy, took pity on the hungry men and, without consulting his superior officers, he rounded up all the available beef and bread, made thick sandwiches, and then passed them out to the hungry soldiers as they stood at their gun posts.

The surprised soldiers, grateful for the food, sent up a loud cheer for Billy and then turned back to the fight with new strength.

When the colonel learned what Billy had done for his men, he immediately promoted the sergeant to the rank of lieutenant right on the field.

The colonel who promoted Billy was Rutherford B. Hayes, who became the 19th President of the United States . . . and Billy, the mess sergeant, was William McKinley, who became the 25th President.

Jaspar before.

Raccoons

A SHORT TAIL

Animals have often been the subject of legal claims, but there is only one record of a raccoon ever appearing as a plaintiff.

The name of the raccoon was Jaspar, and he lived happily with his master, Jack Wilkinson, at the latter's hunting lodge on Cedar Lake in Ontario.

Jaspar had no complaints. He spent most of the year hunting with Wilkinson, climbing trees and gorging on fish and leftover chicken bones. When the winter set in, he would disappear beneath the lodge and, bearlike, snooze the frigid months away, worn out with the joys of his strenuous "dolce vita."

One day in early winter, 1953, shortly before Jaspar was to start his hibernation, he took a stroll down to the Canadian National Railway tracks which cut through the nearby woods.

Thinking the snow seemed whiter on the other side Jaspar started to cross over. It was a short trip, but a disastrous one for the little raccoon. A transcontinental express, highballing from Montreal to Vancouver, charged down on the startled animal. Jaspar made a desperate leap for safety but didn't quite complete it, and the spinning wheels of the train lopped off his beautiful Davy Crockett tail.

Jaspar, left with only a 2-inch nub where his bushy glory had once waved, streaked back to his master, who gave him sympathy and first aid, and immediately decided to do something about this undignified injury to his pet.

Shortly after the accident Jaspar and his master made their historic claim for damages, a claim bolstered with evidence, witnesses and before-and-after pictures. The petition asked compensation for the loss of Jaspar's tail, an appendage needed by a raccoon to survive the harsh northern winter, during which time he uses his furry tail as a blanket, curling it around his body to keep him warm.

Jaspar after.

But in the end Jaspar lost. The railroad could not be held responsible for a raccoon's safety along its right of way, and was not, therefore, liable for Jaspar's mishap.

The railroad, however, took a warm, unofficial interest in Jaspar's welfare, and was glad to learn he survived the loss of his tail. For some time thereafter the truncated raccoon slept in the kitchen of the lodge, in a box fitted out with a hot water bottle. Then, to everyone's surprise, Jaspar went back to his old custom of hibernating and, seeking out his former nesting place beneath the lodge, he trotted off carrying some leaves, twigs and the empty hot water bottle.

Poon Lim, seaman.

Rafts

<u>133 DAYS ALONE AT SEA</u>

A quiet, muscular little seaman experienced—and survived—
the greatest ordeal ever recorded in all the annals of the sea.

The man's name is Poon Lim and he was born in Hainan,
China, but he left his ancestral home while still a young boy to
follow the sea.

Poon Lim worked hard and by 1942, during World War II,
he had risen to second steward aboard the British freighter *Ben
Lomond*, which was headed home, one dark November night,
from a voyage to Capetown, South Africa.

As was usual in wartime, the *Ben Lomond* rode blacked out
as a precaution against hostile submarines. His work in the
galley done, Poon Lim lay in his bunk—but sleep never came.

Instead, rushing out of the midnight darkness came a German torpedo—it tore the hull of the *Ben Lomond* wide open.

Thrown out of his bunk by the explosion, Poon Lim managed to grab a life jacket, scramble out onto the listing deck and plunge overboard into the sea. There had been no time to lower the boats, but a few life rafts had been released. He saw one floating past, swam to it and pulled himself aboard.

Stunned and exhausted, he lay down on the raft and slept.

The light of day awakened him to a bleak world. Around him was the Atlantic Ocean—and he and his raft were the only things moving on its vast surface. The raft was a little wooden job about 8 feet square, seaworthy but obviously not fitted out to sustain life for very long. The supplies lashed to the side by a piece of rope were meager—some tins of hard biscuits, a jug of water, a few flares, a flashlight. A man couldn't last long on those.

But Poon Lim was determined to stay alive. Moreover, he was a practical man and he laid his plans on a long-time basis. From the beginning he limited himself to one mouthful of water and two biscuits morning and night. That way, he figured, his supplies would last him a few weeks.

After that, his primary problem would be fresh water—he must devise some method for catching and storing rain. He tore open the seams of his life jacket, removed all the cork filler and then used the stiff canvas to make a crude catch-basin.

When there was no rain in the canvas, he drank an occasional mouthful of sea water. In very small quantities, he knew, sea water can be drunk without harm.

As his supply of biscuits dwindled, he set about making plans for catching fish. The raft carried neither hook nor line. But the flashlight, he figured, was expendable. He pulled out the heavy wire spring at the base and made himself a fine fish-hook, using the water jug to pound it into shape. He made a line by pulling strands of hemp from the small piece of rope and braiding these together. It was tedious work and it took days.

Poon Lim caught his first fish with a piece of biscuit. He fashioned a primitive cutting tool from an empty biscuit tin,

Poon Lim re-enacts his life on the raft.

opened the fish and took out the liver, which he ate immediately. The castaway had little scientific knowledge, but he knew that the liver of any animal is one of the best of foods. From then on he caught and ate fish pretty regularly, using part of each previous catch as bait.

Hot sun beat down on him during the day, and cold winds swept over the sea at night, but he forced himself to keep in good physical condition with brief, suspense-laden swims in the shark-infested water.

Poon often heard sharks scrape along under the raft's planks. What an excellent meal the liver of a shark would make! He decided to catch one of the gray monsters; he would use a freshly killed gull as the lure.

To supplement his diet of fish, Poon Lim already had caught one gull. He had collected seaweed and barnacles from under the raft and had made a little nest, in which he placed a few pieces of rotting fish. When a gull swooped down and started pecking at the dead fish, Poon grabbed it. The meat was tough, but the liver proved edible.

Now, however, he would catch a gull and earn a far better prize—a bigger, richer liver, the liver of a shark. So another gull was caught and killed, the hook baited and the line tossed into the green Atlantic. A small shark, a few feet long, scented the blood in the water and in a quick swipe gulped down both the carcass and the hook. A strike!

Poon Lim had been wise to keep his muscles strong by daily swims. The shark fought wildly for its freedom but Poon gave no quarter; he was determined to get the big fish. Slowly, the man won out and, inch by painful inch, the thrashing monster was pulled onto the raft where Poon Lim, using the heavy water jug like a hammer, slugged it to death. Later, using his homemade knife, he hacked open the tough body and feasted on the liver.

Despite the dangers that surrounded him, Poon Lim experienced fear only once—when a Nazi submarine suddenly surfaced near the raft. Men spilled out of the conning tower and onto the sunny deck. The castaway was close enough to see that they were preparing for a gunnery drill.

He was certain they saw him and he expected to find a shell lobbed his way to finish him off. But nothing happened; the men went through the drill—even seemed to look right at him—without spotting him, and submerged again in a boiling froth.

On the 133rd day of his unbelievable voyage, Poon Lim sighted a small sailboat and, standing up on the raft, made frantic signs for help. The boat, a fishing vessel, came alongside and took him aboard.

So Poon Lim's astonishing odyssey came to an end. He had drifted clear across the Atlantic ocean from the coast of Africa to the coast of Brazil. Most amazing of all, he was strong enough at the end to walk ashore under his own power.

The men who rescued Poon Lim took him to the hospital at Belem, the nearest city, where he was found to be in good physical condition, having lost only 10 pounds.

For his courage, endurance and ingenuity, Poon Lim received many honors, including the British Empire Medal from King George VI. And because he later wrote a handbook on survival for Allied seamen, the United States honored him in 1949 by passing a special bill which waived all immigration laws and admitted him as a permanent resident.

And how did Poon Lim find the courage to accomplish his amazing feat of endurance? His answer: "I didn't worry. I knew the devil didn't want me."

Riding

THE GIRL WHO OUTRODE PAUL REVERE

The 16-year-old girl was named Sybil Ludington. She lived on a farm near New York with her father who was a captain in the militia.

On the night of April 27, 1777, a messenger arrived with urgent news for Sybil's father. The British, in a surprise attack from Long Island Sound, had burned the city of Danbury, Connecticut, and were advancing on the countryside. Every farmer must be called out immediately.

Because her father was captain of the militia, Sybil volunteered for the job of calling the farmers to fight.

Grabbing a big stick, the girl leaped on her horse and galloped off in the darkness. All night long she rode, pausing only at each farmhouse to crash her stick against the door and shout a warning: "The British are coming, fall out and fight."

Sybil Ludington far outdid Paul Revere's famous ride. Revere had traveled only about 10 miles when he was captured by the British at Lexington. Sybil covered a staggering 40 miles of hard riding. What's more, she mustered out enough men to send the British back to their boats in defeat.

This life-sized statue of Sybil Ludington stands near her birthplace in Putnam County, New York State.

Roofs

TOWN OF "FOOLISH" HOUSES

The Italians refer to the town of Alberobello as *trulli,* or "fool's head," because of the curious roofs there that resemble a dunce's cap.

Royalty

AUCTION OF AN EMPIRE

The great modern auction houses have had some strange items come under the hammer but nothing as strange as that which went on the block in Rome in 193 A.D. The bids taken at that auction were for possession of the Roman Empire, an area then covering several million square miles.

On March 28th of that year, the Emperor Pertinax was killed by his Praetorian Guards. These guards had originally been formed as a small, elite group of soldiers whose duty it was to protect the emperor. But in time the Praetorians grew so powerful that no one dared challenge their authority. Casually, they made and unmade the rulers of Rome.

Pertinax had signed his own death warrant by attempting to reform the corrupt guards. Three months after he became emperor, he was assassinated by the Praetorians who then cynically put the throne of Rome up for auction.

Didius Julianus, a consul under Pertinax, offered the highest bid and was immediately elevated to the throne.

But Didius did not last long as emperor either. Within a few months, the man who had bought an empire at auction was also assassinated, and his place on the uncertain throne of Rome was taken by a new emperor, Septimius Severus, who paved the way for the acceptance of Christianity.

THE WOMAN KING

One of the names that leaps from the pages of Egyptian history is that of Hatshepsut, who ruled from 1501 to 1479 B.C.

There's a difference between Hatshepsut and her predecessors, however. Hatshepsut was a woman.

Sacred tradition in ancient Egypt required that every ruler must be a son of the great god Amon. Thus, at least in theory, Hatshepsut could not rule Egypt. And, even for someone as capable and strong-willed as this daughter of Thutmose I, first king of the Eighteenth Dynasty, this was a tradition that could not be ignored.

The Empire, as the period of dynasties eighteen through twenty has been labeled, was one of those periods of powerful rule that lifted Egypt to greater wealth, power and glory than ever before. Much of the credit for those accomplishments may be laid at the feet of the queen who refused to acknowledge her sex.

Hatshepsut was raised to partnership on the throne of Egypt by her father, Thutmose I, as he neared the end of his 30-year reign. But because tradition decreed she could not succeed him, when he died, Hatshepsut's half-brother, who was also her husband, became King, Thutmose II.

In turn, when he died, he named Thutmose III, an obscure son of Thutmose I, whose mother had been a concubine. That move was too much for Hatshepsut to swallow, and she promptly seized the throne for herself.

To justify her move, she invented a biography which, to her satisfaction at least, solved the problem of her sex.

In the biography, Hatshepsut wrote that Amon had descended from his heaven and impregnated her mother, Ahmasi. As he departed, he announced that the fruit of the union would be a girl, but that all of his strength and valor would flow through her to the Egyptian people.

Then, as if in further justification, when she appeared in public, Hatshepsut dressed in male clothing and sported a false beard. In later years, she had herself represented on the many monuments she raised as a bearded, breastless warrior.

Pointless as the masquerade may have been, it satisfied both Hatshepsut and her subjects and kept Thutmose III from the throne for almost 22 years.

And, they were 22 years of glory for Egypt. She maintained her empire in peace and order and extended Egypt's markets throughout Africa, bringing prosperity to the nation's merchants and new luxuries to her people. Hatshepsut worked hard to beautify her capital, building new temples and repairing others that had been allowed to deteriorate.

There even are latter-day historians who claim to have found proof that it was Hatshepsut who rescued Moses from the bulrushes while she was still a princess. When she assumed the throne, the story goes, she raised him as a court favorite. But, when Thutmose III reassumed the crown Hatshepsut had seized from him, Moses fled to assume the position of leadership attributed to him in the Old Testament.

Be that as it may, Hatshepsut left her mark on Egypt. Before her death, she built for herself a secret and ornate tomb on the western side of the Nile, across from the then-capital of Thebes. In succeeding generations, more than 60 of the rulers who followed her would build royal sepulchers in Hatshepsut's city of the dead. Eventually, the collection became known as "The Valley of the Kings' Tombs."

THE WHITE RAJAH

Not all monarchs are descended directly from kings; some come to their high stations by the curious workings of chance. Like the rajah and ranee of Sarawak, rulers of that once-upon-a-time kingdom on the island of Borneo, in the South Pacific. The first white rajah of Sarawak was James Brooke, a bold and handsome young Englishman who was employed by the East India Company. Brooke's work for the mammoth trading company required extensive travel in the South Pacific, especially among the islands of the Indies, an area of the world Brooke considered to be the nearest thing to paradise. He loved the lush beauty of the islands, liked and understood the people who inhabited them and decided early on that he would live nowhere else.

One fateful day in 1839, Brooke arrived on the vast tropical island of Borneo just as the kingdom of Sarawak, on the island's northwest coast, erupted in a savage civil war. The uprising was directed against the sultan of Brunei, the absentee sovereign of Sarawak, and it threatened to destroy the country.

The sultan had previously heard of Brooke, and had been told that he was a clever and daring man in addition to being a superb trader who knew the island people well. These recommendations seemed to qualify Brooke as a leader, so the worried sultan asked the Englishman to try his hand at cooling the rebellion.

With the help of a small band of English mercenaries, Brooke was able to halt the uprising speedily. This act pleased the sultan so much that he gave Brooke a fine residence in Sarawak and a license to trade among the natives without any limitations.

Brooke soon proved that he was an astute businessman, and an excellent diplomat as well. In a short time he was charging up the economy of the backward island kingdom and charming the wildness out of the headhunting Dyaks and the cutlass-wielding Malays, the two opposing factions who lived on the island in a continuous state of combat.

Brooke's qualities as peacemaker and leader so impressed

The ranee of Sarawak on her first visit to the United States in 1946, when she met the author. Born Sylvia Brett, she was the daughter of the second Viscount Esher. She became ranee in 1917 when her husband, Sir Charles Vyner Brooke, inherited the title of rajah. He was the third in his family to become the absolute monarch of the island nation.

the sultan that he next made the Englishman governor of Sarawak. This conferred on him the title of rajah, the "white" being popularly added as a nod to Brooke's exotic color, which was highly visible in a brown-skinned population.

A few years later, the native sovereign suddenly turned over the entire kingdom of Sarawak to Brooke. He deeded the whole area—larger than the state of Texas—in perpetuity to the Englishman and his heirs. This made Brooke ruler over a quarter of a million Borneo natives.

James Brooke died on the island in 1868. The strange dynasty created by him continued unbroken for more than a century and spanned three lifetimes. It came to an end finally in July 1946, when the last white rajah of Sarawak officially ceded his hereditary kingdom to Britain.

A few years later, Sarawak again won its independence and it is now part of Malaysia.

THE HIGHWAYMAN

The reign of King James the First was marked by great political unrest in England and Scotland, and many of the king's subjects were arrested for treason and imprisoned.

One such prisoner was Sir John Cochrane of Edinburgh. He had been sentenced to death for treason, and was now in Tolbooth Prison waiting to be hanged.

One day, while Sir John's wife and his beloved daughter, Gizelle, were visiting him, they were told that he would be hanged the following morning. The warden explained, however, that they couldn't execute Sir John without a warrant signed by the king, but that the death warrant was now on its way by courier and the execution would be carried out as soon as it arrived.

The warrant never arrived. Late that night, the courier carrying the warrant was held up by a masked highwayman and robbed of all his official papers.

A wide search was made for the daring robber, but he was never found. No one ever suspected that the bold highwayman had been a girl—Sir John's own daughter, Gizelle. Posing as a highwayman, she had risked her life in a desperate attempt to save her father, knowing that he could not be hanged if the death warrant signed by King James did not arrive.

This delay did save Sir John; it gave his family the time needed to successfully negotiate with the king for Sir John's life.

MME. DE MAINTENON

In 1644, the crew of a French ship, bound for the West Indies, prepared for a burial at sea.

Such burials were common then, but this one affected even the most hardened seaman. Death had come for one of the children aboard, a bright and pretty little girl named Françoise who, with her parents, was bound for the French island of Martinique to begin a new life. Françoise had died suddenly, after a short illness.

Wrapped in canvas, the little form lay unmoving on the deck as a priest intoned the prayers for those who are buried at sea.

Suddenly, there was a faint mewling sound and a quiver of movement within the canvas. Quickly, the covering was ripped open. And out jumped a little kitten.

The mourning mother explained that it had belonged to her daughter and had been her constant companion.

Then, said the captain, your child must be alive, as all sailors believe no animal will stay near a dead body.

The child *was* alive. And she grew up to make history. She was the famous Madame de Maintenon who married King Louis XIV in 1683 and ruled France with him until his death 31 years later.

THE RISE AND FALL OF THE HOUSE OF OTTO

The breeze off the Adriatic came in the window crisp and cool, whipping in another bracing Albanian morning. But all color had drained from the prime minister's usually ruddy cheeks. He stared at the telegram in his hand in utter disbelief.

His secretary looked at him nervously. "Anything wrong, Your Excellency?"

"Merciful Allah," the prime minister croaked. "A national catastrophe. I must see the king."

The year was 1913, and the date was the fifth day of the fabulous reign of Otto the First, King of Albania.

Italy, which lies across the Adriatic from Albania, and wished to dominate its seaports, had supported the little country's declaration of independence from the dying Ottoman Empire in 1912. But, the country needed a nominal ruler.

So the Albanians chose, as their "Protector," a Turkish prince named Helim Eddine. The choice wasn't difficult, because Eddine was a Moslem, and most Albanians are Moslems.

While mountain tribes were indifferent to their ruler, the more cosmopolitan people of the seaports were not. The population of the port city of Durazzo was especially enthusiastic, for it had been named the capital.

Durazzo declared a day of celebration for the coming of the prince. Crowds gathered in the streets for Eddine's arrival, while flags flew and bands played.

The prince arrived by carriage and the crowd was treated to a display that made it worth all the hours they had stood waiting.

First, a man well over 7 feet tall stepped out. He wore a military uniform that glowed with braid and decorations, topped with a huge Turkish fez. The crowd gasped as he drew his great, curved sword and brandished it.

"Stand back!" came a booming voice out of a bristling beard. "Make way for Helim Eddine, Prince of Turkey, Protector of Albania!"

A second man appeared. He, too, was a huge man, but in a different way. He wore the standard Turkish peasant's blouse and baggy trousers, but he was almost as wide as the first man was high with enormous shoulders that stretched what should have been a loose-fitting garment. His turbaned head turned slowly on a thick neck as he eyed the crowd, then, apparently satisfied, he turned and made a *salaam.*

Then the prince appeared. There was no mistaking him. Tall, commanding, in a magnificent white uniform and be-jeweled Oriental headdress, he was every inch a nobleman. He did not glare at the people; a gracious smile played over his lips as he descended the steps, nodding and waving an open-palmed hand in the traditional gesture of friendship. The crowd cheered.

Soon the prince spoke in ringing tones that carried beyond a little group of officials to the crowds behind the barriers. "I, Helim Eddine, greet the people of Albania, whom I have sworn to protect. And I thank them for this splendid greeting. I wish my people to know also that I come not merely as a Pro-tector, but as a leader against those who are Albania's enemies."

He drew his glittering sword with a flourish and held it aloft. "As my first official decree, in the presence of my people, I hereby declare myself to be a citizen of Albania." The crowd began to cheer again, but he silenced them by lifting a regal hand. "Also, I declare a week of holiday and celebration, and amnesty for all those in prison." The crowd roared. Here was the hero they had dreamed about. Not since the legendary Scanderbeg had led them against the Turkish oppressor in the 15th century had Albanians had a true national leader.

It was a glorious day. The prince, flanked by his two awe-some companions, marched through the streets of Durazzo to the town hall, greeting his people. Waving, smiling, he won all hearts.

Once there, the fever of excitement continued. After wine was served to all, the prince rose to address the assembled town councilors.

"You might be wondering," he said with a smile, "about my two traveling companions. The military gentleman on my left is Ahmed Nasir, the captain of my household troops—100 men, all over two meters in height. They will arrive on the next ship from Constantinople. And the muscular fellow on my right is Omar, my personal bodyguard."

The councilors smiled nervously at the two giants, who glared back at them.

"And now before the celebration begins," the prince went on, "I wish to tell you that what I have seen here has impressed me well. Your streets are clean, your people healthy. Since this is my capital, I see no reason why you, the councilors of Durazzo, should not be my cabinet." Hurrahs filled the room.

The feasting continued with even more gusto. Then suddenly curtains at the head of the hall were parted and in minced 25 veiled ladies. They were the pick of the mountain tribes, clear-eyed and high-breasted, sent as a harem for the new Moslem ruler of Albania.

The prince acknowledged the gift graciously, and as he sent the girls to his chambers, one of the new cabinet members murmured wistfully, "A harem fit for a king."

The remark was overheard by an Albanian general, who immediately sprang to his feet. "Members of the cabinet!" he shouted, and all fell silent. "I have a proclamation that requires your approval. I hereby move we declare Prince Helim Eddine to be King of Albania!"

From every throat came an instant roar of approval. The new king accepted and thanked his people. Cheers shook the rafters and cabinet members rushed outside, shouting, "Long live the king!"

When asked how he would be known, the brand-new king selected the name Otto the First. While this puzzled a few cabinet members, since no Moslem of their acquaintance had ever borne the name Otto, there was no objection.

They danced and celebrated until King Otto, his captain and his bodyguard retired to the royal chambers—with the 25 beautiful wives.

Then, on the fifth day of the glorious reign of Otto the First, the prime minister received that startling telegram. It read,

"Puzzled by reports that I am in Durazzo. Have never left Constantinople. Kindly explain. (Signed) Helim Eddine, Prince of Turkey."

When the panicky prime minister arrived at the royal chambers, King Otto the First had vanished—nor was he ever seen again in Albania.

After a long, embarrassed investigation the prime minister learned that the bogus "Prince Eddine" had been Otto Witte, a circus performer. As a "retinue," he had brought along the circus giant who masqueraded as the "Captain of the Guard," and the circus strong man, who posed as the "Personal Bodyguard" without whom no royal prince would travel.

Attempting to cover the scandal, local officials quashed all records of the affair, so it is not known whether Otto the First came to Albania to steal from the national treasury, carry off the harem—or just as an adventurer bent on a roaring good time.

The real Prince Eddine remained in Constantinople and may never actually have set foot in Albania. And so we might well wonder—would the bogus Otto have been such a poor leader for Albania? In his masquerade, Otto Witte did exhibit qualities of boldness, intelligence and leadership—as king for five days.

After Witte's royal role, he continued his acting career with other far-out parts. Height and all, he managed to become chief of a pigmy tribe . . . attempted to elope with the daughter of the Emperor of Ethiopia . . . formed a fiery political party called "The Party of Artisans, Cafe Keepers and Circus Performers" . . . was a candidate for the presidency of the German Republic.

But Otto's proudest memory, which he would have gladly carved in the annals of time, was recorded on an identity card when he died in 1958 in a small German village. It reads: "Otto Witte, One-time King of Albania."

Running

"IMPOSSIBLE" FEAT

In October, 1917, in a small farmhouse in Rolla, Kansas, a stove exploded and badly burned an 8-year-old boy. The doctor told his parents that the boy's legs were so badly burned that he would never walk again.

However, the boy thought otherwise; he made up his mind that he *would* walk again.

The boy spent many months in bed and then, when he did get up, he couldn't even stand. It took him more than two years just to straighten out his right leg but, finally, he did start to hobble around. Months later, he was actually walking again, although still troubled by severe pains. It was then he decided to start running, to loosen up the painful muscles of his legs. Daily, he chased cows and horses all over his farm, and after a few years his legs were strong again.

At college, he went out for track, and became a distance runner, concentrating on the mile.

The rest is sports history. For that boy who was told he'd never walk again was Glenn Cunningham, one of America's greatest all-time milers and once holder of five world track records.

MEET ME IN ST. LOUIS

To all who knew him, Felix Carvajal, the tiny Havana post-man had found his niche in life. He was a conscientious mail carrier, obviously destined to remain that to the end of his days. So, in 1904, when Felix Carvajal announced that he would represent Cuba in the Olympic Games in St. Louis, people simply shook their heads and decided the young man had gone *loco*.

But Felix was not mad. He had set his heart on a goal. And he achieved this goal in the most determined manner ever recorded in the annals of sports.

Exactly when Carvajal began thinking about entering the Olympics is not known. But early in the spring of 1904 he began telling friends and fellow workers that he intended to go to St. Louis and participate in the Olympic marathon there.

The marathon is the major long-distance event in that international contest. It honors the Greek runner who raced from the battlefield of Marathon to the city of Athens to announce his nation's victory over the Persians in 490 B.C. After delivering his message, the runner dropped dead.

Many of Carvajal's friends felt the same fate awaited Felix if he persisted in his determination to run the marathon in St. Louis.

But despite the fact that he had never before run a long-distance race, Carvajal sent in his entry and began to train regularly in the public squares of Havana. Each day he would beg for money to finance his trip to St. Louis. And donations began to flow in.

Finally, one night Carvajal counted his money and found he had enough to pay for his passage to the Olympics and his food and lodging along the way.

So Felix booked passage on a steamer from Havana to New Orleans. In Louisiana, he was so entranced by the Crescent City that he decided to go sightseeing before buying his railroad ticket to St. Louis.

His dream of running in the marathon nearly ended right

there. Carvajal fell into the hands of some of New Orleans' professional gamblers and was cheated out of all the money he had.

This would have defeated a lesser man, but Felix now decided he would run the rest of the way to get to the race he had entered.

It mattered not that St. Louis, the site of the Olympics, was more than 700 miles up the winding Mississippi. To a man who already had run hundreds of miles to raise his fare, this didn't seem like an insurmountable distance.

So, Felix set off to run to St. Louis. Dead broke, he begged food and shelter along the way. Finally, close to exhaustion, he staggered into the Olympic Stadium just minutes before the 30 other well-rested runners were ready to toe the mark.

Wearing heavy walking shoes, a long-sleeved shirt, and long trousers, Carvajal announced his arrival to officials and took his place beside the other runners.

Taking pity on the tiny Cuban, one of the runners asked the officials to hold up the start of the race for a few minutes. With a pair of scissors he cut off the sleeves of Felix's shirt and the legs of his pants. But running shoes to fit Carvajal's small feet could not be found.

When the starting gun sounded, there was Felix, racing away with the others. It was a broiling hot day, and the Missouri sun and humidity soon began taking their toll. One by one, the runners fell by the wayside. Felix plodded on.

Almost 3½ hours after the runners raced away from the starting line, the first of them staggered back into the stadium. This was Thomas J. Hicks, the United States representative, and the winner. Soon another and yet another appeared on the track.

Then, suddenly, a roar of greeting washed over the huge arena. There, his tattered shirt and cut-off trousers flapping in the breeze, was Carvajal.

Felix Carvajal finished fourth in that memorable race. What made his finish even more unbelievable was that only 13 other runners, all superbly trained, were able to complete it.

Although he had failed to win an Olympic medal, the tiny Cuban postman had written a chapter into the history of the Games.

SOLO CHAMPION

The popular Olympic Games have produced more than their share of unusual sports stories and political beefs, but maybe none so strange as the saga of Wyndham Halswell.

Halswell, one of England's premiere quarter-milers, won the 400-meter race in 1908 when the Games were staged in his native country. But he had to run the distance twice, and the second time he ran it alone.

Unlike today, when literally dozens of runners enter this popular event, there were only four men entered in the 400-meter race in 1908.

Three were Americans. The fourth was Halswell and he was far and away the favorite of the crowd. The members of the American trio were looked upon as intruders, hardly fit to set foot upon the same track as the popular Englishman.

But when the starting gun barked, the four men sprinted away almost as one. Into the first and second turns and down the back stretch they battled it out head to head.

Finally, the flying quartet rounded the final turn and headed toward the tape, almost shoulder to shoulder.

Suddenly, one of the American runners, a sprinter named Carpenter, a student from Cornell University, burst from the pack and charged into the lead.

Almost at the same instant, one of the officials gathered near the finish line leaped out onto the track, threw both hands above his head, and shouted "Foul!"

Seconds later, Carpenter breasted the tape, closely followed by a second American sprinter and then by Halswell, a disappointing third.

But as the participants returned to the finish line, the officials gathered in a tight little knot, discussing the actions of the judge. Before the group could disperse, Halswell shouldered his way close and lodged the complaint that he had been jostled coming out of the last turn.

While the spectators and runners waited for the officials' decision, a tense silence settled over the stadium. The discussion went on for several minutes, and then the four runners were called to the group of officials to hear the decision.

"We have decided to allow Mr. Halswell's protest," a spokesman said. "However, we have been unable to decide which runner was responsible for the foul. Therefore, we order the race rerun."

The three Americans shook their heads. Carpenter spoke up on their behalf.

"We cannot agree with your decision. We feel that if a foul was committed, the guilty runner alone should be punished, and the rest of the results should stand. If you insist upon running the race over, we will not participate."

But the judges' minds were not to be changed. They ordered the runners to return to the starting line, and set a time limit for their appearance.

When that time limit had expired, only Halswell stood at the starting line. Then, with the stunned spectators looking on, the formality of an official start was carried out and Halswell sped around the track, rerunning the 400-meter race all by himself.

He was declared the official winner of the event for the 1908 Olympic Games, the only time in history a one-man race determined a gold medal.

Ironically, Halswell posted a time of 50 seconds flat. Never since and only once before in the history of that event has any man ever won the 400-meter race in slower time than that. His achievement still ranks as one of the strangest in the long history of the modern Olympic Games.

Russia

ROYAL BORSCHT

In 1645, Czar Alexis, second ruler of the famed House of Romanov, became the ruler of Russia at the age of 16.

Alexis was a quiet person, more interested in family life than in affairs of state and, despite his youth, he made immediate plans to marry.

His first choice was a wealthy young lady, daughter of one of Russia's most prominent royal families by the name of Eudoxia. But, before the wedding could be blessed, it was necessary that she appear before the court in her royal robes for approval.

Eudoxia's ladies-in-waiting were determined that this appearance would be one that the members of the court would never forget and, to make certain, they took great pains with her dress and appearance.

The problem was they planned too well. In braiding the hoped-to-be-czarina's hair, they wound it so tightly that the pressure caused her to faint as she bowed before her husband-to-be. Members of the royal court were outraged, and persuaded the royal doctors to declare her an epileptic.

Cancel one royal wedding.

Alexis began the search for a more acceptable bride. This time, he chose Marya Miloslavski, and married her.

Unlike Alexis's first choice, Marya really was a sickly girl. Over the years, however, she managed to survive long enough to bear 13 children. Only 2 of them survived, and Marya herself died when the last of this clan was born.

But Marya had brought more than 13 children to the royal house. She also had brought one of Russia's most renowned chefs, and that gentleman's specialty was borscht—a commoner's ragout or soup made usually of left-over meat, colored red with beet juice—which became the Czar's favorite dish.

With Marya's death, the chef resigned. Alexis was crushed. Not only had he lost his wife, but he now also was without the chef who had prepared his favorite dish.

It was an affair of state that required an immediate solution. Unfortunately, it also was a problem that Alexis's chief advisers were unable to solve. Beyond advising that the Czar remarry, they offered no solution to the kitchen problem.

In desperation, Alexis sent for his most trusted servant. "I want you," he said, "to search the city of Moscow and find the person who makes the finest borscht in the city. Bring him to me. I will make him the royal chef, and his future will be assured."

It was the sort of royal command that could not be ignored. Potkin, the servant, was loyal if nothing else. For days, he plodded the streets of Moscow, sniffing the air and sneezing as he went, for he was allergic to the smell. Finally, his search brought him to the door of the Naryshkin household. The delicate aroma wafting out on the breeze bordered on the superb, despite the problem that it was causing Potkin.

His search, he felt, was at an end. In a great state of excitement, he rushed back to the palace and informed his master of his find.

Together, they returned to the home. The royal nose twitched in excitement. Tossing dignity aside, Alexis knocked on the door of the household and waited impatiently for an answer. Finally, the door was opened by a beautiful, shy young lady.

"May I help you?" she inquired.

Alexis identified himself and, before the flustered young lady could apologize for her lack of recognition of the royal person, the Czar continued. "The aroma of that borscht is superb. I must have your chef for the royal kitchens."

Still unable to speak, the young lady was relieved to see her father approaching down the long hall.

"Father," she stammered, "this is the Czar."

Her father, a minor official in Alexis's government, immediately bowed the ruler into his home and asked what he could do to please His Majesty.

"Your chef. I must have your chef as my own." Alexis insisted. "The aroma of his borscht is heavenly. I must have him cook for me."

A smile played around the corners of Artamon Naryshkin's mouth before he answered. "Your Majesty, I have but a lowly station in life. I have no chef. The borscht you smell was prepared by my daughter, Natalia," he continued, indicating the young girl who stood by his side.

The Czar hesitated only for a moment. Then, breaking into a huge smile, he quickly recovered. "But that is perfect," he shouted. "If I were to marry your daughter, I would not only gain a wife but someone who could cook the perfect borscht for me for the rest of my life."

"I doubt that that is possible, Your Majesty," Naryshkin answered. "The royal advisers would never allow the Czar to marry someone from a family as lowly as ours."

"That is no problem," the Czar said. "As of now, Naryshkin, you are chief of the section in the Ministry of Foreign Affairs."

Stunned into silence, Artamon bowed deeply. The Czar prepared to depart, determined to seek immediate approval from the members of his court for a new marriage.

But, despite Naryshkin's new status in life, the court advisers refused to sanction the marriage.

"What must I do to convince you?" the Czar pleaded.

"If Naryshkin were something more than a chief of section, we might approve," the spokesman minister answered.

"So be it," Alexis nodded. "I name Artamon Naryshkin Minister of Foreign Affairs."

And so Natalia brought her borscht and her charm to the royal palace. Alexis married the lovely young woman, and a year later the happy couple's first child was born—a big, healthy boy.

In 1696, that son of Alexis and Natalia at the age of 24 came to absolute power as Czar of all the Russians. He was already a giant of a man physically and he was determined to make medieval Russia a modern nation no matter what the cost.

To shape his backward country to the form of progressive Europe, the young Czar immediately decreed drastic changes in the social and political life of Russia. He created a modern army and navy, reformed his country's ancient currency, introduced universal taxation, organized a civil service system

The son of Alexis and the girl borscht-maker, who became Czar in 1696, and was so famous that a new capital of Russia was built and named for him.

and, most startling of all, issued laws raising the status of women.

Because Russia's old wooden cities regularly burned to the ground, the new Czar decreed that future houses were to be build of stone. To further protect these, he ordered that fire departments be formed and operated at public expense.

Under his direction schools were built, the cumbersome Russian alphabet simplified and the calendar modernized. Public hospitals were opened for the first time and an excellent medical school was founded, staffed with the best available doctors from Europe.

To make his subjects aware of the progressive course upon which he had set the nation, the Czar decreed that the loose, Eastern-looking garments of old Russia were to be replaced with European clothes. He also demanded that all men shave off their traditional beards. These, he felt, were symbolic of Russia's backwardness. When some of his noblemen refused to obey his order, the Czar had them dragged before him and he personally cut off the offending growth.

Russian trade and industry expanded and flourished under the forward-looking Czar. And guided by his aggressive military genius, his large nation grew even larger with territory gained in successive wars.

But the Czar really set the seal to his progressive reign when he moved his capital from shabby, log-cabined Moscow to the glittering, stone-and-glass city of newly built St. Petersburg, on the Baltic Sea.

He had created the new capital, said the Czar, to be a "window on the West," an ultra-modern city that turned its back on the ancient Eastern culture of Russia and faced westward toward sophisticated, scientific Europe. Today, the city (now called Leningrad) stands unchanged, still one of the world's most classically beautiful cities of all time—and the Czar's most enduring monument.

Although the Czar was a man of gross appetites and cruelty and although his all-powerful reign was often marked by injustice and violence, no other Russian ruler has ever done more for his nation.

Despite his many flaws, the son who was born to Alexis and the pretty girl borscht-maker deserves the name that history has given him—Peter the Great of Russia.

St. Bernards

BARRY, THE GREAT

The most famous of all St. Bernards was "Barry," who between the years 1800 and 1814 saved the lives of more than 40 people—a record for even these brave dogs.

Many stories surround Barry, who had not only to fight the hazards of snow and ice, but sometimes the very men he tried to save. Once, a dazed and half-frozen soldier, waking up briefly as Barry was digging him out of what would have been an icy grave, thought in his delirium that his rescuer was a monster and, rousing himself in mad strength, almost killed the faithful dog.

Undoubtedly, the St. Bernard is the most famous and admired of all dogs. Its ancestry is a mystery, but it is believed that the breed descended from a cross between a female Great Dane and a Mastiff. Whatever its antecedents, this rugged dog was first heard of more than three centuries ago at the ancient monastery of St. Bernard. This monastery, founded in 980 by

St. Bernard de Menthon, was on the north-south Alpine route and was built at the fearsome Great St. Bernard Pass so that monks of that order might help travelers in their struggle to cross the Alps.

The dogs were probably first used only to guard the monks. Later, when their fantastic sense of direction was noticed, they were put to rescue work. The St. Bernard never loses its sense of direction, no matter how far from its base or how stormy the weather. It can sense the position of a buried victim 300 yards away; then it goes unerringly to the exact spot and starts digging.

The famous rescue dogs of the monastery of St. Bernard in the Swiss Alps have a fantastic sense of direction, are able to predict avalanches, and can locate mountain climbers in the snow from as far away as 300 yards.

"Avalanche Dog" is another name for the St. Bernard, because of its uncanny ability to sense the changes of weather which bring snow slides; the monks can tell what is brewing by noting the animal's increasing restlessness. Outdoors, the dog can anticipate an avalanche, and guide its master safely around it. Science cannot explain this acuteness, or why it degenerates when the dog is removed from its natural environment.

One of the common misconceptions concerning the true St. Bernard rescue dog is that it has a long, silky, luxuriant coat. This is not so. The big, shaggy-haired St. Bernard—generally portrayed carrying a small keg of brandy—is a recent development, dating back only to about 1830, when the original dog was cross-bred with the long-haired Newfoundland. It was bred purely to make a gentle, handsome, intelligent pet. The long, heavy hair and out-sized furry paws would be the death of such a dog in the Alpine snows. Its fur would soon collect a heavy mantle of ice, and its heavily-furred feet would become useless, frozen balls; it would bog down and perish. The true rescue dog has a short, coarse coat, very little hair on its paws, and is somewhat smaller in stature than is generally thought.

This amiable mountain of a dog answers to the name of Sonya and lives with the Longfellow family in Largo, Florida. She patiently accepted the role of mother figure to tiny Basketball Jones, an orphaned infant monkey who found Sonya's warm bulk a comforting haven in a hostile world. The big St. Bernard provided her adopted "baby" with affection, protection and a great means of getting around.

Roadway leading through the mountain of salt into the cathedral. Cars leaving use another tunnel through the mine.

Salt

CATHEDRAL IN SALT

Many years ago, a village priest in the little town of Zipaquira, Colombia, South America, dreamed of some day having a beautiful church for his little flock, all of whom were poor workers in the local salt mine. It is the largest active salt mine in the world, and it supports the entire town.

The priest's dream came true. But the church grew into a cathedral—and it is made entirely of salt!

The cathedral, called "Our Lady of the Rosary," is constructed entirely within a towering mountain of salt, 800 feet beneath the summit.

Everything within the cathedral is carved and shaped from the hard, glistening white salt . . . the towering pillars, the great vaulted dome, the stations of the cross, the side chapels, the statuary, the magnificent central altar. And all the work of construction, of carving and shaping, was done by the devout miners.

The cathedral took 6 years to build, and can seat 5,000 worshippers. The great nave is 400 feet long and 73 feet high, and is supported by columns of solid salt 33 feet square. Workmen used pneumatic drills in constructing it.

"Our Lady of the Rosary" is reached by way of deep tunnels, each a mile long and wide enough for the passage of a

Miners work and pray in the salt cathedral of Zipaquirá, located in the largest active salt mine in the world. There is enough salt here to keep the mine in full production for 500 years, and the mine has already been worked for over 600 years. Here you see salt being refined by mixing it with iodide of potassium in boiling pots.

single car; one tunnel leads in, the other winds out. Just outside the gates to this strange house of worship is a vast underground parking lot for over 200 cars.

(Above) One of the three main corridors in the mammoth salt cathedral. (Below) One of the altars.

A HARVEST OF SALT

On the northern coast of Colombia more than 2,000 Guajira Indians and their families take part in the annual salt harvest. Each year these Indians leave their cattle and sheep ranches and come to harvest the salt that has been evaporating for 10 months under a hot tropical sun. Thousands of little mounds of salt are piled up in the salt beds, brought to shore, put into bags and carried away for domestic and commercial use. Each family builds up a mound of salt of about 1,800 pounds. The women carry it to shore in 100-pound bags, receiving about $10 for every 100 bags they carry.

Workers handle the salt as if it were sand.

Seahorses

THE FATHER HAS THE BABIES

Looking like a carved chessman and propelling himself forward in an upright position by means of a fanlike dorsal fin is the short-nosed, 6-inch-long seahorse.

Not content with his singular appearance and swimming style, the male seahorse further compounds his strangeness by actually giving birth to his offspring, a procedure considered highly unorthodox for any father, in or out of the water.

A few weeks before the seahorse gives birth, the sea mare has a rendezvous with Papa and carefully deposits her eggs in a kangaroo-like pouch in his abdomen. (The female is pouchless.) Within this protecting pouch the eggs are fertilized and incubated.

When his tiny, squirming progeny are finally ready to be hatched, the pangs of birth seize the parent. With delivery near, the seahorse fastens himself securely by his strong, prehensile tail to some convenient underwater plant and waits for his little quarter-inch babies—the image of Daddy, of course—to leap violently out of his distended brood pouch.

From the time the little sea colts emerge, they can swim and move completely on their own. For a moment, the little ones swarm over the body of the parent and then off they go, striking out bravely to meet the hazards of the dangerous, watery world into which they have been so strangely brought forth.

A pregnant father. When the time approaches for the babies to be born, the father seahorse curls his tail around a piece of seaweed. Soon the little sea colts begin to emerge. From the moment the babies are born they are on their own, for when the father has discharged the last infant, he swims away without a backward glance.

Security

THE UNSEEN SENTINEL

The man Londoners never see: he stands in the shadow of the
Quadriga on top of Wellington Arch surveying the rear approaches to Buckingham Palace. Even if visitors crane their
necks they cannot see this watchman.

Sextuplets

AMERICA'S FIRST

Large multiple births are almost commonplace in the news today, thanks to fertility pills that sometimes outperform their purpose. Of course, many such infants do not survive this competitive crowding at the gateway to life, but those that do are given star-quality publicity.

The Rosenkowitz youngsters of South Africa are a good example. Bright and bouncy, these six little brothers and sisters were born in 1974 and are the world's only known instance of surviving sextuplets.

Their remarkable birth was a worldwide public event, and we were regularly informed of the progress of this unique sibling six-pack. But such openness was not always the case, and the birth of the first sextuplets on the North American continent was kept secret for a long time.

The children were born in Chicago on September 8, 1866; their parents were James and Jennie Bushnell. Jennie Bushnell's physician was Dr. James Edwards, and because there had been a history of multiple births in his patient's family, he was prepared for something unusual at the time of delivery. So when he was called out that night to attend Jennie, the doctor brought along with him midwife-nurse Prissilla Bancroft to assist him.

The doctor was right in his assumption. By the time the astonished man had finished with the delivery there were six tiny, living babies in the room. But these did not bring joy to Jennie. She was utterly humiliated at having had so many children at one time; it seemed to her a degrading and unnatural performance. It was, she said, "like giving birth the way an animal does."

So she pleaded with the doctor and the nurse to keep the births a secret. To quiet the distraught mother they agreed to her request; they would make no public disclosure of the night's events.

However, by law, Edwards had to make out a birth certificate. He held it back a week but on September 15 he completed the official notice and quietly filed it without comment. He also gave a copy to the parents who promptly hid it away.

Of course, the births could not be kept entirely secret; you cannot, after all, successfully hide six babies. So a few relatives and close friends shared knowledge of Jennie's strange delivery, but out of affection for the young mother they followed her wishes and said nothing.

The secret was made easier to keep when two of the babies died during their first year. From then on, it was given out that the four surviving children were quadruplets and the youngsters themselves grew up believing this to be so.

Fifteen years later, however, when Jennie lay dying, she felt that the time had come to tell the children the truth about their birth. She called them to her, kissed each one farewell and then told them that they were sextuplets.

How this announcement affected the children I learned firsthand many, many years later when I interviewed two of the Bushnell sextuplets on my NBC radio program. At that time, they were close to 80 and three of them still survived. Of these, I interviewed Alberto Bushnell of Albion, N.Y. and his sister Alinca Parker of Silver Lake, N.Y. A third sister, Alice Hughes, lived in Flagstaff, Ariz.

"Mother kept the births secret so that people wouldn't think of us as freaks," explained Alberto. "She was afraid that we'd be stared at, treated like curiosities and that this would hurt us. Of course, being quads was pretty attention-getting, too. She couldn't protect us from that."

I asked Alberto and Alinca how they felt about being sextuplets. They didn't mind at all. They had lived with the knowledge for a long time and now scarcely gave it a thought.

"But my sister Alice feels differently," said Alinca. "She feels the way our mother did, that it's like having a litter and very humiliating. That's why she wouldn't come and appear on this program. She just won't talk about it."

All the Bushnells are long dead now.

Sharks

KISS OF DEATH

Shark hunting is a game sport, and while *Jaws* may have scared off some impressionable hunters, it has spurred others on to greater effort. Every night, boats leave Florida and Caribbean ports loaded with fishermen, and baited for that saw-toothed predator.

Voracious eaters, sharks will grab at almost anything. When they do, they are caught, pulled in, and killed just like any other big fish. In the Fiji Islands, however, sharks are caught by a different method.

Twice a year, the natives of the Fijis stage what they call a "vara wai," an unusual fishing expedition into the inlets of the area. It is designed to gather ordinary fish, and also to rid the waters of the vicious sharks which lurk there.

Using bamboo, the natives weave a long fencelike net to be

The Fiji Islanders have surrounded some sharks in their corral-like bamboo fence.

Kissing a Fiji Island shark on its belly has the effect of immobilizing it, as we see here.

used as a trap. They anchor one end of this on the near shore and then move the other end out across the water.

Once they have reached the opposite shore, they work the free end back toward the anchored end in a large arc, thus trapping thousands of fish in the shallow water within the corral that is formed by the net.

Dinner is now just a step away, but there remain the sharks to be gotten rid of. For included in those teeming thousands of fish within the net are sometimes dozens of sharks.

Moreover, there's only one way to get them out of that corral, and that's to get in there with them.

Certain islanders—apparently trained just for that purpose—wade into that mass of trapped fish, searching for the sharks. When they find one, they lean over and catch him with their bare hands. Then, turning the shark on his back, they plant a solid kiss on his belly. This quiets him immediately.

Why sharks react as they do this strange treatment is a mystery. Whether the kiss conveys some kind of special power, or whether the place where the kiss is planted immobilizes the sharks, no one seems to know. But from the time they are kissed, the sharks show no further signs of life and they are then disposed of easily.

Catching sharks Fiji-style probably won't become popular elsewhere. All sharks are not necessarily man-eaters, but to deliberately get into the water with one, turn it over, and plant a kiss on its belly is not the most logical way to deal with them.

But it certainly is sporting.

CAESARIAN OPERATION

A Caesarian operation was performed on a dying mother shark at Marine Studios in Florida. This sand tiger shark was known to be pregnant when it was captured, and it was hoped it would bear its pups (baby sharks) in captivity. Sand tigers normally bear a litter of two, but this premature birth produced only one—the other was found dead inside the mother shark. The living pup was placed into an incubator-type aquarium.

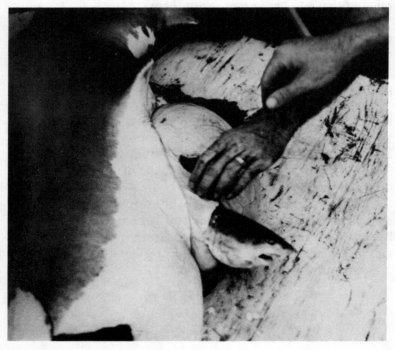

The shark pup about to be born after the operation.

THE SHARK PAPERS

Many strange objects have come to light in the opened belly of a captured shark.

Although most of the internal cargo found in these man-eaters is of the expected grisly sort—like the completely intact skeleton of a human foot, which is exhibited in the museum at Dakar—sharks have also been found to carry other mementoes of human owners, ranging from bits of clothing and jewelry to musical instruments, such as flutes and small drums.

But the strangest cache ever carried by a shark, and one that had far-reaching effects, came to light inside one of these monsters caught in the Caribbean almost two centuries ago.

On the 3rd of July, 1799, the American brig *Nancy* cleared from Baltimore for Curaçao, in the Dutch West Indies. Presumably, she was bent on a simple coffee-buying voyage.

At that time, however, Britain was at war with France, Spain and the Netherlands, and the Royal Navy was active in preventing neutrals from trading in contraband goods and weapons with these enemy countries, or with their colonies. Since Curaçao, in those troubled days, was one of the main Caribbean ports used for clearing contraband cargo to prohibited destinations, the mission of the *Nancy* was suspect from the start.

On the 28th of August, 1799, while proceeding to Port-au-Prince, Haiti, to refit a broken mast, the *Nancy* was captured by the British Navy cutter *Sparrow* and taken to Port Royal as a prize of war.

The following month, on the 9th of September, a "libel," or suit, was brought against the captain and owners of the *Nancy* in the Vice-Admiralty Court at Kingston, Jamaica. It was claimed that the brig had traded unlawfully with the enemies of Britain, and therefore the ship should be condemned and confiscated as a war prize.

The *Nancy*'s captain, James Briggs, loudly protested his innocence and argued that the suit should be dismissed with costs on the ground that the ship was owned by citizens of the

United States, and that no wrongdoing had been proved, or could be proved.

Actually, the captain was right. The Crown had little evidence to go on, and its case was limping along badly when suddenly a new element was introduced into the proceedings. A young British naval lieutenant, Michael Fitton by name, burst unceremoniously into court one day and, asking leave to be heard at once, produced papers which he had found in the stomach of a shark caught by his crew shortly before, off the coast of Haiti.

Upon examination by the court, it was found that these papers belonged to the brig *Nancy* and proved she had indeed been trading with the enemy. Previously, under oath, her captain had sworn that nothing aboard his vessel had been "burnt, thrown overboard, destroyed, cancelled, concealed or attempted so to be." Now his lie was revealed; because of their incriminating nature, he had jettisoned his papers at the time his ship was captured.

With this new evidence, found so astonishingly in a dead shark, the court had no difficulty in finding the captain guilty of trading with the enemy, and on November 25, 1799, the English took over the *Nancy* as a prize of war. No record exists of the captain's eventual fate, but for such a wartime crime the mandatory punishment was death by hanging.

The jaws of that historic shark were sent to the Royal Service Museum in London. The actual "shark papers," along with Lieutenant Fitton's sworn affidavit to the court, are still in Jamaica.

These incriminating papers, found in the belly of a shark by Lieutenant Michael Fitton of the British Navy, were produced in Admiralty Court and used to convict the skipper of the American brig *Nancy* of trading with the enemy in 1799. Holding up the papers to the camera is author-explorer Doug Storer.

BATTLING SHARKS
IN THE CARIBBEAN

Off the coast of the Domincan Republic a native makes a living by battling sharks for tourists.

Singapore

FESTIVAL OF THAIPUSAN

Religious fervor marks this Hindu celebration in Singapore. This man, pierced with dozens of steel rods through his body and little silver arrows through his cheeks and tongue, shows no signs of physical discomfort. No blood is surfacing as he walks along.

Skull

HOLE IN THE HEAD

Not long ago, a man was shot in the head and didn't know that the bullet had gone in on one side and come out the other until a friend told him. How come? Well, the bullet had traveled just under the skin of his forehead, from temple to temple, and had barely grazed the skull in its passage.

That's pretty weird, but it doesn't compare to the incredible head injury suffered by 25-year-old Phineas Gage, a native of Vermont and once a foreman on the Rutland-Burlington Railroad.

On Sept. 13, 1848, Gage was working with his line crew blasting holes for new installations. To compress the charge, he used a tamping-iron, a heavy metal rod 3 feet 7 inches long and 1¼ inch in diameter. Suddenly, one of the charges went off prematurely and blasted the iron rod straight up into Gage's face. It entered slightly above the left side of his upper jaw and exited through the top of his skull, just behind his forehead. The iron hit with such force that after passing through Gage's head it sailed through the air and landed many yards away from its shattered victim.

Gage was an appalling sight, of course, but he did not lose consciousness and spoke rationally to his crewmen who ran to help him. With some assistance from them, he was even able to mount an ox cart which took him into town, to the small hotel where he had a room on the second floor. Incredibly, he climbed the stairs on his own, made it to his room and laid down to await the doctor.

Dr. John Harlow arrived two hours later and found Gage still rational. But the doctor had never seen such a frightful wound and not for a moment did he think Gage would survive. He had lost an enormous amount of blood, along with bone and brain tissue. However, the doctor completed what repairs were possible, cleaned and dressed the wound, did what he could to make Gage comfortable and left. He never expected to see his doomed patient again.

But Harlow did see his patient again—many times—because

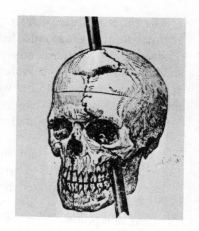

The actual skull of Phineas Gage's head shows how the tamping rod was blasted up through his jaw and exited through his cranium. It is on exhibit at Harvard Medical School, along with a cast of his head.

Gage lived. It wasn't easy, though; his recovery was long and painful and there were many setbacks along the way. Twice severe infection set in, and once he suffered repeated convulsions and dementia. He was racked with head pains and lost his left eye. But his wound healed.

Four months after his accident, Gage was strong and active again. He carried a facial scar and there was a deep depression in his skull, but he was free of pain. His only complaint was that sometimes he "felt queer in the head." He did exhibit some personality changes, however. His friends noticed that he was restless, easily irritated and often used profanity, something he'd never done before.

Gage did not go back to railroading. Instead, he traveled around the country with his destructive tamping-iron (later mistakenly called a crowbar) and gave exhibits at town halls and country fairs, wherever he could drum up an audience.

Eventually, this means of support grew thin and he hired out as a stableman. He was very good at handling horses, and in 1852 he sailed down to Chile where he drove a six-horse stagecoach for a number of years.

Gage did well in Chile, but in 1859 he began to have health problems. So he returned to the States and accepted a job offer from some friends who had moved west and bought a farm near San Francisco.

The quiet routine of farm work and the California climate seemed to suit Gage and his health improved considerably. Then one day, without any warning, while he was plowing a field, he was seized by a violent convulsion. He recovered from that fit and returned to his work. But others quickly followed and he died in a convulsion on May 20, 1861. That was 13 years after an injury which, by all natural laws, should have killed him on the spot.

Gage's bizarre accident made medical history throughout the world and it is still the only one of its kind on record.

Doctors were fascinated by Gage's survival of such a "killing" injury and they kept in touch with him all during his lifetime. At one point, Gage visited a Dr. Bigelow who examined the healed wound and then made a fine cast of Gage's head. Bigelow wrote a paper on the subject, as did Harlow. Others have written about it since then.

After Gage died, his skull and the tamping-iron which had blown through it were recovered from his family for further medical study.

All three of these—the head cast, the skull and the iron—may now be seen in the Warren Anatomical Museum at Harvard Medical School, all exhibits in what is often called in medical circles the "American Crowbar Case."

Slavery

SIMÓN BOLÍVAR

In 1824, Peru finally won its freedom from Spain. Soon after, Simón Bolívar, the general who had led the liberating forces, called a convention for the purpose of drafting a constitution for the new country.

After the convention, a delegation approached Bolívar and asked him to become their first president. Bolívar declined, saying that he felt someone else deserved the honor more than he did.

But the people still wanted to do something special for Bolívar to show their appreciation for all he had done for them, so they offered him a gift of a million pesos, a very large fortune in those days.

Bolívar accepted the gift and then asked how many slaves there were in Peru. He was told there were about 3,000.

And how much does a slave sell for, he wanted to know? About 350 pesos for an able-bodied man, was the answer.

Then, said Bolívar, I will add whatever is necessary to this million pesos you have given me and I will buy all the slaves in Peru and set them free. It makes no sense to free a nation, unless all its citizens enjoy freedom as well.

Snakes

KING OF THE SNAKES

At Silver Spring, Florida, Tom Allen captures a giant anaconda in a long underwater struggle.

Of all the snakes, the mightiest is the anaconda, a non-venomous, constricting giant from South America that sometimes reaches a fearsome length of 40 feet or more—a muscular monster that can weigh in at more than 300 pounds.

A true aquatic snake, the anaconda is at home in any sluggish river or deep swamp. It can move well on land and even climbs trees to sunbathe, but it prefers its watery habitat. Generally it takes to the land at night, moving silently and so close to the ground that it seems almost flat.

The anaconda, like the somewhat smaller boa constrictor, has often been accused of eating humans, and there are records of small children being found inside captured reptiles.

It is unlikely, however, than an anaconda could eat a man. Unless the snake was a true monster in size, the broad shoulders of a man would be just too big for the snake's mouth, elastic as it is.

But there is no doubt that the anaconda can kill a man, especially if the encounter takes place in water. The snake doesn't have to eat the man; it can simply drown him. There are several reported cases of anacondas pulling unwary swimmers to their deaths.

The secret of capturing an anaconda, according to professional reptile hunters, is to take the snake by surprise with a viselike grip on its neck and jaws. With its jaws clamped shut and out of operation, the anaconda loses its best defense. It cannot use the enormous strength of its coiled body to overcome its attacker because to do this it must first fasten its jaws firmly on some object. This provides it with an anchorage; only then is it able to constrict its body into powerful coils and squeeze its prey in a deadly embrace. The victim finally suffocates on his passage into the reptile's stomach.

However, if the man attacking the snake were to misjudge his timing and find his hand not firmly around the snake's jaws but in its huge mouth instead, he would be in desperate trouble. There is virtually no escape from an anaconda once it has fastened onto its prey.

An aquatic reptile, the anaconda feeds mostly under water. To make certain that the snake won't lose its freshly caught dinner by having it washed away if it should open its mouth, nature has arranged the anaconda's teeth like those of a trap. Not only are they numerous and sharp, but also they all slant back toward its gullet. Any attempt to escape from these cruel raking teeth by pulling backward only causes them to dig in that much deeper.

Once the anaconda has securely latched onto its victim, it often whirls it furiously around in the water, either to kill or dismember it. Fortunately, for those who professionally hunt the anaconda, man is too big an animal for this pinwheel treatment.

SNAKE SITTING

Rudolf Schmid smashes his way out of a glass case in which he spent a year and six days keeping company with several rattlesnakes. He lost 66 pounds and toured 100 European cities.

LIVING WITH SNAKES

It's hard to live with snakes. But a South African man has set a record for living with adders, cobras and other poisonous companions. After 50 days, he quit this dangerous domestic arrangement and is free to enjoy the pleasure of being immortalized in this book. That is, as soon as his nerves stop quivering.

In Barranquilla, Colombia, I once saw a man who had already completed 18 days of cramped living among an assortment of vipers. To make his life even more miserable, he lay on a bed of nails and was fasting. He was kept under guard in a glass case secured by a number of padlocks, the keys to which were held by local officials. He was on exhibit in a public building and could, for a fee, be viewed at any time.

For the privacy he occasionally needed, the glass enclosure was equipped with draw curtains, and there was a small pass-through at one end of the case to provide him with air and to give him water as he asked for it.

There is one discomfort attendant on this freakish endeavor that is seldom mentioned. It is that snakes smell bad. The air in that room in Barranquilla was eye-watering foul, strong enough to kill scorpions.

However, this hero under glass managed somehow to survive all this for 30 days. He emerged from his voluntary ordeal in very bad shape but, like all seekers of the grail, was already making plans for another live-in with more snakes and for a longer period.

Why any man would want to curl up with snakes is a mystery. The serpent has been viewed with fear and revulsion ever since it made its destructive appearance in Eden, and there's good reason for this. Even today, despite the spread of civilization and the use of antivenin, more than 30,000 deaths from snakebite occur each year. More than half of these take place in India, home of the deadly cobra and the evil krait.

Not all snakebite deaths are accidental; many are listed as murders and suicides. Using a snake to self-destruct was an old custom long before Cleopatra made her exit by means of an asp. And this ancient method is still used, even in the United States.

A California man sought to end his oppressive life by leaping into a pit of rattlesnakes. He suffered 85 bites and died almost immediately.

A Florida scientist killed himself with an injection of venom, which was readily available in the laboratory where he worked.

After extraction, venom is frozen and dried into a fine powder which is easily stored, and it remains toxic for many years. One researcher found venom still potent after almost 40 years in storage.

The snake has long been used as a murder weapon, too, especially in Asia. Old laws noted this and provided special punishment for those found guilty of planting snakes in the victim's bed, clothes or house.

In 17th-century India, snakes were used as a means of execution for those convicted of particularly brutal murders. The condemned was brought to a public execution place, stripped naked and forced to stand upright as two serpents were wound round his legs and thighs. Their deadly bites soon brought on death.

Several years ago, a California man tried to kill his wife by having a rattlesnake bite her. But the wound was not fatal and the man finally dispatched the unfortunate woman by drowning her. The job, botched from the beginning, ended in his speedy arrest.

As this man discovered, snakebite is a chancy means for murder. The lethal effect of a bite is not readily predictable. A snake may have only a small amount of venom stored in its glands at the time of the incision; or it may decide to emit little or no venom at that particular time. It's up to the snake.

In addition to these factors, the reaction to a poisonous bite varies with the individual victim, some of us being less susceptible to the venom than others. In one instance, this may have changed history.

St. Paul, on one of his many missionary journeys to spread the gospel, was shipwrecked on an island whose inhabitants were so suspicious and hostile that they considered killing him.

But before they could do so, he was bitten by a viper which struck at him and buried its deadly fangs deep in his hand. Unperturbed, the future saint walked over to a fire and shook the snake into the flames.

This display of coolness and courage amazed the natives and later, when Paul showed no effects from the venom, they decided that he was a god and he was able to leave the island unharmed.

So the bite of a poisonous snake actually saved the life of St. Paul, the most powerful figure in the early history of Christianity.

Solomon Islands

CANNIBAL CHIEFS

Martin Johnson, the famous explorer, visited an island in the
Solomons where the natives were known to be cannibals and
particularly hostile to white men, who had been kidnaping
members of their tribe and selling them into slavery. When
Johnson arrived, he was surrounded by natives who closed in
on him menacingly. Just as the cannibals were about to rush
him, a ship's whistle blew and into the bay steamed a British
patrol boat. Johnson snapped this shot of Chief Nagapate,
bowed politely, and bolted for the shore and safety.

Songs

"DEAR FRIENDS AND GENTLE HEARTS"

Everyone has heard about the notorious Bowery of New York, that sad, hopeless hideaway that is "home" to thousands of derelict men.

One winter's night in 1864, the landlady of a shabby Bowery rooming house heard a heavy crash overhead. Investigating, she found lying unconscious on the floor a sickly young man to whom she had just rented a room for 25 cents a night. Blood was streaming from a gash in his throat, and the frightened woman immediately sent for the nearest doctor.

There was very little the doctor could do. However, he sewed up the young man's throat with a piece of black thread that the landlady gave him and then got a police wagon to take the man to Bellevue Hospital.

The landlady could give no information about the man who, in addition to the serious wound, was also suffering from starvation.

Three days later the man died. No one was too concerned, for men die violently on the Bowery every day. The police made a routine check of his effects, but all they found were 38 cents and the title of a song that the young man had planned to write.

The title of that song was "Dear Friends and Gentle Hearts," and the man who died on the Bowery, so very far from any friends, was Stephen Foster, America's greatest folk-song composer.

Francis Scott Key watches the "Banner."

THE ROCKETS' RED GLARE

Without an Englishman named Congreve, the United States would not have had its national anthem.

The rockets which inspired Francis Scott Key as he watched the bombardment of Fort McHenry on that historic night during the War of 1812 were the invention of Sir William Congreve, royal firemaster to the king. They were also the first rockets ever seen in America.

Made of narrow wooden tubes filled with gunpowder and tipped with iron warheads, the rockets were guided by simple, polelike rudders and launched from rows of tilted frames in a series of giant assaults. With a range of 2 miles, they were designed to explode on impact, scattering deadly shrapnel over a wide area.

Streaking across the sky, tails hissing and blazing, these new missiles were a terrifying sight. But they did not win the war for England. Instead, Congreve's rockets are remembered today only because their brilliant "red glare" gave America—the enemy—the great "Star-Spangled Banner."

Payne and the first cover of his sheet music.

"HOME SWEET HOME"

John Howard Payne—who wrote "Home Sweet Home"—never had a home of his own.

Payne was born in New York City in 1791. His father was an unsuccessful schoolmaster who kept his family on the move.

Payne was living alone in a New York boarding house when, at the age of only 14, he startled the theatrical world by publishing a magazine on show business. Although he alone made up the entire staff, the magazine was an instant success.

While still in his teens, Payne won fame as an actor and a playwright. Then, in 1813, he went to London to try his luck there.

In 1820, after a theatrical failure, Payne was sent to London's infamous Fleet Street Prison for debt. Friends helped him escape and he fled to Paris.

Still homeless and broke, he wandered the streets of Paris thinking of suicide. Finally, he found a job writing the words for a new operetta called *Clari*. One of the songs he wrote for this was "Home Sweet Home."

Although the song was a worldwide hit, Payne never made any money from it. He was always broke, always on the move.

Finally, through friends, he was made the United States counsul in Tunisia—then a very bleak hardship post. He died there, still alone, in 1852, his grave marked only by a pepper tree.

Years later, Payne's body was brought back to the U.S. and buried with honors in Washington's Oak Hill cemetery.

The homeless man who had written the most popular song of his century had come home at last.

The Soongs

FAMOUS FAMILY OF CHINA

In 1876, a little Chinese boy who had been brought to Boston by his uncle, a successful silk merchant, decided to run away. He hated working in the shop, so he stowed away on a coastwise steamer and was not discovered until the vessel was well out to sea.

The ship's captain, Charley Jones, gave the lad a job as cabin boy. Then, pleased by the youngster's intelligence, Jones started to teach him English. So rapidly did the boy progress, that Jones decided he deserved a good education.

One day, when the boat was in Wilmington, North Carolina, Jones interested a friend, a Methodist minister, in bringing the boy up in his household and educating him.

The youngster, who eventually took the name of Charley Jones in honor of his original benefactor, proved a brilliant student. He forged ahead rapidly, and, in time, graduated from college with honors.

After graduation, the boy decided to return to China in order to marry and raise a family.

This he did. And the family he founded became the most powerful in modern China. This one-time stowaway was the famous Charley Jones Soong, the father of T. V. Soong, once premier of China; of Madame Sun Yat Sen, wife of China's liberator; and of Madame Chiang Kai-shek, who is today the mother of the president of Nationalist China (Taiwan).

South Africa

FAITH TO ENDURE PAIN

These South Africans perform astonishing feats with their ability to endure forms of pain. The sharp sword shown above actually sinks into the man's tongue and neck, and the long needles shown below are inserted deep into the man's cheeks.

No pain!

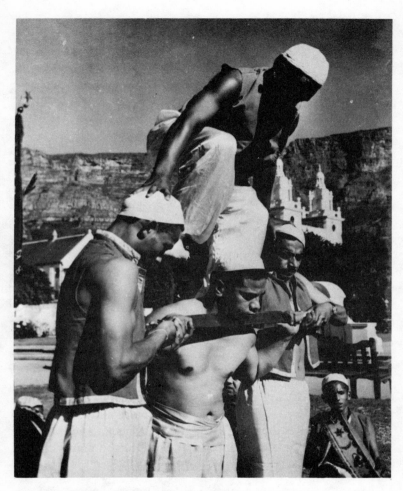

The man's head is actually pressed against the blade of the sword by the weight above, yet he is not cut or bleeding.

Incredibly, the men say they feel no pain and, more surprisingly, no blood is drawn from what normally would be deep wounds. Their faith and training to endure pain, they explain, make these feats possible.

Squirrel

THE SKIING SQUIRREL

With furry tail awash in the wake, Twiggy is off and skiing. Raised by Chuck Best, Jr., a Sanford (Florida) roller-rink operator, the gray squirrel performs on styrofoam water skis towed at 12 miles per hour behind a remote-controlled model boat. Best trained her in about a month, using peanut butter rewards. When she tires, she paddles over to Best and climbs on his shoulder to rest.

"I now take Twiggy quite often to the river," Best told the author, "but most often I let her practice in the small pond next to my rink!"

Stairs

THE MIRACULOUS STAIRCASE

In the charming chapel of Our Lady of Light in Santa Fe, New Mexico, there is a narrow staircase which winds up to the choir loft.

It is called "miraculous" because its thirty-three small steps spiral upward without visible means of support, as if carved out of a single piece of polished mahogany. It appears to be made without nails or braces, and it is a masterpiece of the carpenter's art.

In 1878, when the little chapel was just completed, the choir loft was left stairless. The nuns of Loretto, for whom the chapel was built, had run out of funds.

Shortly afterward, a wandering carpenter appeared, asking for food and shelter. The nuns responded generously and the stranger offered to build them a stairway to the choir loft.

He shut himself up in the chapel and, working furiously, soon had the little circular stairway finished. Then, as the nuns stood lost in admiration at his craftsmanship, the man left without a word, never to be seen again.

All that the nuns of Loretto were ever to know about him was that he was a carpenter and his name was Joseph, and that this mysterious stranger had left for them a "miraculous staircase."

Long a tourist attraction, this staircase in Santa Fe, New Mexico, has spiraling steps with no visible means of support.

Stamps

THE "CANAL" STAMP

In 1882, the French secured the right to build a canal across Panama. When the project failed, a young French engineer named Bunau-Varilla tried to interest the United States.

The Americans were interested in a canal, but not across Panama. They wanted it to go across Nicaragua. Rejecting Bunau-Varilla's plea, Congress decided to vote funds for the Nicaraguan Canal.

But they reckoned without the resourceful Frenchman. Racing against time, Varilla wrote a letter to every Congressman. And in each letter he enclosed a very interesting stamp. The stamp was from Nicaragua, and it showed one of that country's small volcanos in full eruption.

As Varilla had suspected, the message came through loud and clear. The Congressmen read the letters, took a long look at the stamp—and then promptly reversed themselves. It was obvious that the United States could not build a canal through a country of active volcanos.

In 1904, the United States bought the canal rights from the French. After years of incredible hardships the great engineering project was finally completed. On August 15, 1914, the first ship made its historic passage through the Panama Canal.

And the reason it crossed the Isthmus at Panama instead of at Nicaragua was due to the picture of a volcano on an obscure stamp.

THE POSTAL SYSTEM

The postal system used today started because an English poet was shocked by an old woman's trickery.

The poet was Samuel Coleridge, author of "The Ancient Mariner," and the woman was a farmer's widow he met one day while taking a country walk.

Coleridge found the woman arguing with a postman about accepting delivery of a letter. At that time, all payments for postal services were based on distance, and the fee could be paid at either end. In this case, it was the woman who had to pay, but she had no money. Then, said the postman, you can't have the letter.

Touched by the woman's poverty, Coleridge paid the postage.

Instead of thanking him, however, the woman said he'd put out his money needlessly. The letter, she said, was from her son in the south of England. Every week he mailed her a blank piece of paper, and every week she refused to accept the mail. Her son had worked out this little trick so that his mother might know he was well without paying the high postage fee.

Coleridge was shocked. It seemed to him that something was wrong with a system that made poor people resort to such trickery.

So Coleridge went to his friend Rowland Hill, then the postmaster general of England, and told him that the system must be reformed.

Hill agreed, and in 1839 the Penny Post Act became law. This Act allowed an ordinary letter—prepaid by the first adhesive postage stamp every used—to be sent anywhere in England for the same penny rate.This was the beginning of the world's modern postal system.

THE CHARNLEY FIND

A number of years ago, a junk dealer was called into a Philadelphia bank and asked to make an offer on a heap of old letters that the bank wanted to get rid of.

The junk dealer offered $15 to cart the paper away. The bank accepted and gave the junkman a receipt.

Later, while putting the paper into bundles, the junkman discovered a small batch of old letters which had been mailed to the bank in 1845 and 1846. Thinking that these old, stamped envelopes might be of interest to someone, he took them to a stamp dealer.

The dealer gasped when he saw the envelopes and offered the junkman $75,000 for the lot! For these old envelopes were a rare collector's item. They bore the famous "Bear" stamp which had been issued by the postmaster of St. Louis before the United States had federal postage stamps.

When news of this amazing transaction was published, the bank brought suit to recover ownership of the envelopes. The junk dealer, however, with his $15 receipt as evidence, won his case and kept his fortune. Today, a single "Bear" stamp is worth $18,500.

THE FOUR CHAPLAINS

One icy night in January, 1943, an old troop carrier, the *U.S.S. Dorchester,* silently left Boston Harbor and headed out into the Atlantic. Aboard were four young chaplains of three faiths: Rabbi Alexander D. Goode, Father John P. Washington, and two Protestant ministers, George L. Fox and Clark V. Poling.

They had been strangers to each other before sailing, but their duties on the ship soon made them close friends.

On the night of February 3, the *Dorchester* was sighted by an enemy sub. The sub's first torpedo scored a direct hit, entering below the waterline and blowing up the engine room. In a few minutes, the *Dorchester* started sinking, her decks ablaze.

The four chaplains worked heroically, rescuing men trapped below decks, getting others into life rafts, comforting the dying. Then, as the doomed ship settled into the sea for her final plunge, the four men of God, acting as one, took off their life jackets and gave them to save the lives of four men who had none.

The last ever seen of the young chaplains was as they stood on the deck of the sinking ship with their arms linked in friendship, each quietly intoning his own prayers for the dead.

THE LOVE STAMP

It happened in 1918, when the Swedish post office once ran short of stamps. The government authorized the overprinting of old 25-ore issues to make them valid for 12-ore local postage. During the overprinting, a single sheet of 30 old stamps went into the press upside down, thus making the overprint appear inverted in relation to the basic stamps.

When this error was revealed, collectors immediately tried to buy up the 30 "rare" stamps only to find that the entire sheet had been bought by a young lumberjack who had gone to the north of Sweden on a job.

The lumberjack was finally traced through a paper company but, when found, he no longer had any of the stamps left. He had used them all on the daily letters he sent to his sweetheart far to the south.

The collectors then rushed to find the girl. An affectionate and tidy young woman, she had not only kept the love letters but the envelopes as well.

All 30 of the rare stamps were recovered and the young couple, made prosperous by a large payment of 6,000 kroner for the stamps, were able to marry at once and buy a home with their unexpected riches (6,000 kroner was equal to three years' wages).

Because of this, the stamps that made their happiness possible are called "love stamps" by collectors.

Stanley

WHO WAS STANLEY?

In 1841, a young Welsh woman gave birth to a son whom she named John Rowlands. Two years later the boy's father died and the mother had to place the child in a poorhouse.

While still a boy, Rowlands went to work, first in a shop and then for a butcher. But he was not happy, and decided to go to the United States.

He worked his way over as a cabin boy and finally arrived in New Orleans. But to his disappointment, life for young Rowlands was no more successful in the New World than it had been in the Old, and again he went from one job to another.

When the Civil War broke out, he served first with the Confederate forces. Then, after being captured by the Union Army, he secured his freedom by serving on their side.

After the war, still restless, Rowlands found work as a reporter and wound up on the *New York Herald* which, in 1874, sent him out of the country on a special assignment.

Today, the story of that assignment is known throughout the world. For John Rowlands was none other than Henry Morton Stanley, the great explorer who found the source of the Congo River, and whose famous words: "Dr. Livingstone, I presume" are known to every schoolboy. And the reason Rowlands used the name "Stanley" instead of his own was in honor of a man who once befriended him.

Statues

THE WRONG STATUE

About a century ago, the citizens of Cuzco, in Peru, decided to erect a statue honoring Atahualpa, the last king of the Incas, who was executed by the Spanish in 1533.

The statue was to be of bronze, and a foundry in Philadelphia got the job.

When the finished monument finally arrived in Peru, however, an unhappy discovery was made. The statue bore little resemblance to the famous Inca king. Furthermore, it was wearing buckskins, something never worn by a South American Indian.

Then it was discovered that the Philadelphia foundry had made a mistake. At the time the order was received from Peru, the foundry had also been working on a statue of Chief Powhatan, father of Pocahontas. Somehow this statue, the wrong one, had reached Peru.

But the people of Cuzco could not afford to return the costly bronze of Powhatan, so it was erected in the town square where it still stands today, on top of a high marble column, in memory of the great King Atahualpa.

Powhatan is the figure on this statue in Cuzco, but the Peruvians think it is Atahualpa.

The statue in Curaçao, Dutch Antilles, of Peter Stuyvesant, showing his peg-leg. Governor of the island before he became Governor of colonial New York, Stuyvesant lost his leg in battle and the leg was given a separate military funeral.

PETER STUYVESANT'S LEG

Old Peter ("Peg-Leg") Stuyvesant, last Dutch governor of colonial New York, got that name because he had only one leg. He lost the other one in 1644 when he stopped a Spanish cannonball during a battle in the Caribbean.

Stuyvesant was then governor of Curaçao, and he was brought back to that little Dutch-held island for amputation of his shattered leg.

But after the leg was successfully separated from Stuyvesant's body, it was not treated like any ordinary remainder of a surgical operation.

In those days, it was the custom that when a man lost a leg or an arm, the severed member was then given a formal "Christian burial." In Stuyvesant's case, however, his important rank as governor and military leader of Curaçao called for even more deference to be shown in disposing of his amputated limb.

So the governor's leg was given a full military funeral.

With a guard of honor, Stuyvesant's leg was carried in a small coffin to the little graveyard which lay just outside the protecting stone walls of the Dutch fort. Here, with regimental banners waving and drums beating a mournful tattoo, the leg was laid to rest in an impressive ceremony.

Twenty-eight years later, the owner of the leg died and was buried in New York with far less ceremony.

However, a statue to Stuyvesant was erected in Curaçao, and a college there was named for him.

STATUE OF SHOES TO A POET

A beloved poet of Colombia, Luis Lopez, wrote a sonnet describing his affection for his native city of Cartagena. The historic Spanish city created this memorial for him because he loved his city as deeply as some people do an old pair of shoes.

LARGEST BRONZE STATUE IN THE WORLD

The Diabutsu is a bronze Buddha of colossal dimensions. This religious image is the largest bronze statue in the world, weighing 651 tons and standing 71 feet tall. The Hall of the Daibutsu is also the largest wooden structure in the world, measuring 160 feet high, 187 feet long and 166 feet wide. The statue and the hall are located in the Todaiji Temple at Nara, Japan.

THE GILDED BUDDHA

Chih Hang was a devout Buddhist monk who lived on the island of Taiwan. Shortly after World War II, as Chih Hang lay dying, he called his followers together and promised that he would protect them even after death.

But, he warned, they were on no account to bury him. Instead, they were to place his body in an urn, sitting cross-legged in the Buddhist position of devotion. The urn was then to be sealed and kept in a niche in the temple where he had served as a monk for so long.

At the end of three years, Chih Hang continued, the urn was to be opened. If his body showed no sign of corruption, then his followers would know that, through him, Buddha continued to smile upon them and bless them.

Chih Hang's last wishes were faithfully carried out.

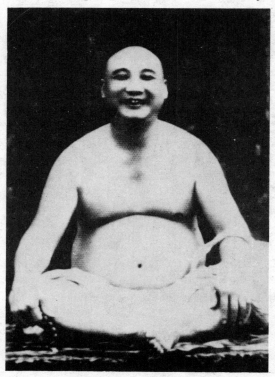

Chih Hang as he appeared when alive.

Chih Hang, sitting cross-legged, has been covered in gold after death, and his body has been preserved.

Gilded, the body of the monk is being enshrined in a monastery near Taipei, Taiwan.

At the end of three years, the urn was opened and the witnesses gasped in astonishment. Chih Hang's body was found to be miraculously preserved and still sitting upright.

In homage to their dead monk, his followers had Chih Hang's body gilded in pure gold and set on an altar in the hillside Temple of Tranquil Devotion, near Keelung, where it may be seen today.

OLIVER CROMWELL'S TURBAN

In 1660, King Charles II returned to the throne of England from the exile imposed on him during the rule of Oliver Cromwell.

King Charles proved to be a well-liked monarch, and one of his subjects, Sir Robert Vynor, decided to erect a monument in the king's honor.

Vynor commissioned a London sculptor to execute a statue of the king on horseback. It so happened that this sculptor had just made a statue commemorating a Polish victory over the Turks; it showed the king of Poland on horseback, trampling a Turkish soldier. But the Polish monument had not been accepted, so the sculptor decided to use this same statue for the King Charles monument. By making some changes, he converted the Polish king and the Turk into the English king and his enemy, Oliver Cromwell.

Everyone was delighted with the statue when it was unveiled in London. King Charles himself attended the ceremony.

It was not until later that a curious thing was noticed about the statue. The Englishman Cromwell was wearing a fine Turkish turban. In converting the figure of the Turk into that of Cromwell, the sculptor had neglected to remove the Turk's headgear.

Storms

THE TEMPEST

In 1609, an English ship, *The Sea Venture,* under the command of Sir George Somers, set out on a voyage to the New World.

Caught in a violent storm, the little vessel was wrecked on the coast of Bermuda. The crew managed to make shore safely. Then, from the wrecked timbers of their ship they made two small boats and sailed across the water to Virginia, where they decided to settle.

But the hard, primitive life on the Virginia coast disappointed these early settlers, and they decided to return to Bermuda.

Shortly after their return, Sir George Somers died. His son buried his father's heart in Bermuda and then sailed back to England with the body.

The romantic story of the storm, the shipwreck, and the death of Somers proved a sensation in London, and a popular writer decided to do a play about the adventure.

The play became one of the most famous and enduring of all time, for the writer was young Will Shakespeare and the play was "The Tempest."

Submarines

A PROPHETIC DREAM

In September, 1920, Captain Edward Johnson was despondent because his ship, the *Alanthus*, was docked in Boston harbor, unchartered and idle. The company which normally chartered the ship had decided to place the vessel in retirement. Johnson, a devoutly religious person, had been a seafarer all his life. He often experienced dreams that prophesied future events. In every instance his dreams came true, and whenever he experienced one there was nothing that could stop him from seeing that his presentiments were fulfilled.

Weeks before he learned that the *Alanthus* was not to be chartered he experienced a series of dreams that were as explicit as any he had ever had. The voice of his dead father told him that he must sail on his ship because he would save the crew of a sunken submarine. The voice told him that he must charter the ship himself if he was to save the men. Johnson told everyone of his dream. He phoned the Maritime Office in Washington and told officials there. They all laughed at him. Undaunted, Johnson managed to charter the ship himself. His dream-voice persisted, telling him that he must sail by 3:00 P.M. on September 12 if he was to save the crew.

Unknown to Johnson, the U.S. submarine S-5 had left its mooring in Boston harbor on September 11 and glided down the channel toward the sea. It was the largest submarine the U.S. Navy had ever built, measuring 231 feet in length. Its skipper, Lieutenant Commander Charles M. Cooke, had orders to proceed on a training and recruiting cruise. His crew consisted of 38 officers and men.

Johnson, on board the *Alanthus*, was involved in a noisy dispute with his crew, who wanted higher wages. Johnson refused and they walked off the ship. That night he rounded up two friends to substitute for his normal deck crew of eight, and sailed the next day at 3:00 P.M. for Norfolk. In his haste Johnson left behind his radio operator. Nothing was going to stop him from saving a crew from a sunken submarine.

The 231-foot submarine S-5 on its way to sea.

Meanwhile, the S-5 was going through its paces some 50 miles off the Atlantic coast. During a crash dive the main induction valve was not shut properly, flooding the main ventilating system and causing the sub to sink. The S-5's bow stuck in the soft floor of the sea 170 feet below the surface at an angle of 60 degrees. Cooke feared the stern was below the surface.

A picture of the S-5's stern protruding from 170 feet of water at a 60-degree angle. Johnson came upon this sight as he was cruising south on the *Alanthus* toward Norfolk.

Submarines 361

Captain Johnson has drawn an arrow in this photograph, to indicate his position on the submarine. The *Alanthus* has fastened its bow next to the S-5's stern with cables. For many hours the two ships were in this position until all crew members from the sunken submarine were saved.

Increasing gas pressure made the crew's situation precarious. The temperature reached 135 degrees, and chlorine fumes escaped into the crew's compartment, burning their eyes and throats. A crew member managed to pierce a 6x5-inch hole in the sub's stern with a hand drill. The stern was above water. It was night.

Johnson on the *Alanthus* was cruising south. His dreams recurred, compelling him to scan the horizon at every opportunity. The men on the S-5 had been suffering in the infernal heat and chlorine atmosphere for nearly 25 hours when Johnson, having altered course, spotted its stern sticking above water about 6 miles off the port bow of the *Alanthus*. Johnson closed in on the S-5 and secured it with cables so it would sink no farther. Water and air were pumped to the men of the S-5. Johnson then put up distress signals.

The next day a cargo ship, the *General Goethals*, sighted the signals and steamed within hailing distance. The *General Goethals* notified the Navy of the situation. Tugs and destroyers raced to the scene. In the meantime, Chief Engineer Grace of the *Goethals* and his men worked furiously to make a hole large enough to pull the crew of the S-5 out of their trap. All men were saved. Thanks to Johnson's abiding faith in his dreams and his heroic efforts, a major disaster had been avoided. It was the one and only time in history that an American submarine went down and all hands were saved.

This picture taken from a Navy destroyer shows the *Alanthus* steaming away after her heroic rescue work was completed.

Clara Barton, the renowned founder of the American Red Cross, was the first woman to go down into a submarine. The submarine first graced by a lady's presence was the U.S.S. *Holland,* the first submarine commissioned by the United States.

James P. Holland himself emerges from the hatch of the first U.S. Government submarine. It was named for him, as he had designed this type of so-called "torpedo boat" in 1901. Submarines had been designed from the time of Alexander the Great, but it was not until World War I that they came into practical military use.

Off they go on designer Holland's submarine.

THE S.S. "TANG"

One dark night in October of 1944, the U.S. submarine *Tang,* which had just completed a series of successful raids, suddenly picked up a Japanese convoy on her radar.

The call to battle stations was sounded at once and, because it was night, the *Tang* rose to the surface.

The convoy was very large. The *Tang,* which had 8 torpedoes left, decided that every one must count.

The first torpedo was a hit, and a Japanese ship went down. By luck and careful aim, 6 of the remaining torpedoes found their targets also.

Then the last torpedo was launched. As soon as it left the tube it was noticed that it wasn't steering properly. Then it went completely off course, and began turning around and around in crazy circles. Suddenly, it straightened out ... but now it was heading right back at the *Tang.* The emergency alarm to submerge rang out, but it was too late. A minute later, the *Tang* received a direct hit and sank almost immediately.

Nine men survived the explosion. They lived to tell of how the courageous *Tang* was destroyed by her own last torpedo!

THE FRIENDLY TORPEDO

There is one instance where a torpedo proved a friend. During World War II, Seaman Roy Dikkers of Minnesota was on a tanker that was attacked by a German sub in the Caribbean near Cuba. The attack came early in the morning, before daybreak, and the first torpedo welded shut the cabin door and trapped Dikkers inside the stricken ship. A second torpedo hit soon afterward and jarred the door open. Dikkers reached the upper deck only to find the water around him an inferno of blazing oil. Again he seemed hopelessly trapped—he could go down with the ship or go overboard and burn to death. But Dikkers never had to make that decision. A third torpedo hit and blew Dikkers up into the air and far out to sea, beyond the burning oil. He landed near a floating raft, pulled himself aboard and then sweated out three long days before he was rescued by a Norwegian freighter.

Suicide

LEMMINGS

Suicide is not practiced by man only; many creatures destroy themselves at times. The robihorcado, a Guatemalan bird, kills itself by strangulation in the fork of a tree when it cannot find food. And only a few years ago, a whole school of small whales committed suicide on a Florida beach, despite the persistent efforts of a team of rescuers to save the whales from their own death wish.

But the most amazing suicides in the animal kingdom are the little lemmings, who have an inborn urge to self-destruction which asserts itself at regular intervals.

Cold-climate rodents, the lemmings live in vast numbers on the lonely tundra and mountain ranges of the Scandinavian Peninsula. They live well and are not unduly molested by predators, but every 4 or 5 years they start a fantastic race westward to the sea.

Swarming over the frigid land by the millions, in a flight so vast and awesome that even the elks get out of their path, the little animals travel for hundreds of miles without stopping, over towering peaks and icy lakes, until they reach the ocean. Then, without a moment's hesitation, these mouse-like hordes plunge into the waves and commence to swim frantically to nowhere! On and on they swim out into the sea until finally, overcome by exhaustion and cold, they sink beneath the waves and disappear forever.

Just why the lemmings regularly destroy themselves is not fully known, but it is known that they are the captives of a natural cycle. Every few years they reach a fantastic peak in population; then, as if by a signal, they head by the millions for the sea and death, eating voraciously as they go and devastating wide areas.

This wholesale self-destruction then causes a sharp decline in the lemming ranks, and for a while they seem almost to disappear entirely. But the cycle holds true, and eventually the lemming population starts to burgeon once more, growing to fantastic proportions, and then another decimating march to the sea takes place.

One of the most recent theories advanced for the migration of the lemmings is that they are seeking a drastic answer to the problems of overcrowding. The lemmings, with an abundant food supply (they are the only small vegetarians on the tundra), few natural enemies, and the extremely high birth rate characteristic of all cold-clmiate animals, soon suffer from overcrowding, which in turn leads to such stress that the animals resort to frantic efforts to thin out their ranks. It is believed that their mass suicide, intended or not, is the answer to their own population explosion. Another theory is that every few years certain food elements necessary to their well-being disappear mysteriously from the vegetation on which they subsist.

But whatever the reason, the lemmings' death at sea is a fantastic phenomenon. They sometimes cover the surface of the water in such vast numbers that a ship sailing along the coast of Norway once reported that it took 15 minutes to pass through a single huge swarm of tightly packed lemmings swimming in the opposite direction.

SUICIDE FISH

Off Marathon Shores, Florida, a school of blackfish, resembling small whales, made a dash for the beach, in a mass suicide attempt. Conservation workers tried to tow the fishes back out to deep waters, but they came back again. The suicide school included 50 blackfish, members of the porpoise family.

Towing the "suicide fish" out to sea failed to achieve the objective of saving their lives. The fish swam back again.

Swimming into shallow water and beaching themselves, these Florida blackfish obviously had suicide in mind.

Ski Torzewski shows how he plunges the sword down his throat.

Swords

THE SWORD SWALLOWER

Ski Torzewski really does swallow that sword. This X-ray picture was taken to prove it.

Torzewski, a member of the Ringling Bros./Barnum & Bailey Circus World, had X-rays taken to convince doctors attending the recent International Conference on Gastroenterology that his startling feat was not a trick; it could be done.

He showed them and they believed him, but they still went away amazed, for Torzewski can swallow a bayonet 15 inches long and draw it out again without a drop of blood showing on the gleaming steel.

"It's a matter of controlling the throat muscles," he explains. "If you're not lined up just right, you can get badly hurt."

Of course, there are certain other fine technical points that must be known before a sword can be swallowed without doing lethal damage. But these are closely-guarded professional secrets known only to other sword-swallowers. They are passed on from one generation to the next as older performers train the young ones who will replace them.

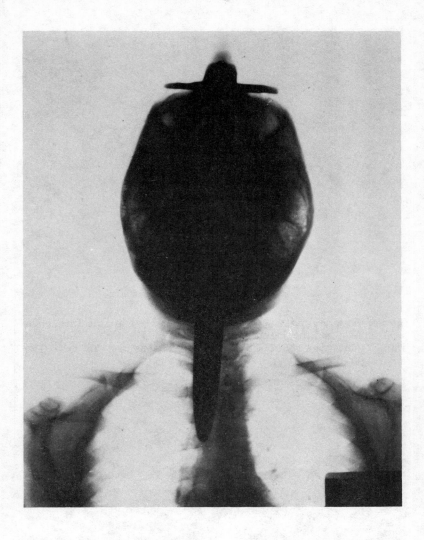

The steel bayonet used by Torzewski is kept both sharp and clean. Grit on the blade, he says, can scratch his esophagus as the bayonet goes down this narrow passageway.

The length of the sword a swallower can handle depends on his height. The deepest sword-swallowing ever done by Torzewski was when he used a 17-inch blade that actually reached into his stomach.

Two of the rarest and most vicious animals on earth are the Tasmanian wolf (above) and the Tasmanian devil (below). The wolf was declared extinct some years ago, but a few wild specimens may still exist. The devil is rapidly dying out.

Tasmania

THE WOLF AND THE DEVIL

Three centuries ago, when the Dutch navigator, Abel Tasman, sailed the Indian Ocean and discovered what is now called Tasmania, the two strange animals pictured here abounded in the wild forests and mountains of that remote, primeval island that is a state of Australia.

The striped Tasmanian wolf is now one of the world's rarest animals. Officially declared to be extinct in the wild years ago, with o ly one or two living specimens remaining in Australian zoos a that time, it is now believed that a few Tasmanian wolves have managed to survive and are living—or hiding—in a distant, almost inaccessible, mountainous region of the island.

Sharing the island with the striped wolf, and also found nowhere else in the world, is a little black and white, bearlike animal, no larger than a fox, called the Tasmanian devil and bearing an evil reputation.

Ounce for ounce, the Tasmanian devil is one of the fiercest animals alive and a merciless predator. Bad-tempered and utterly untameable, the devil is on the way to becoming extinct.

In addition to being both rare and native only to Tasmania, these two animals also share an amazing relationship. Although their appearance would seem to belie it, they are related to each other and to the kangaroo as well for the Tasmanian wolf and the devil are marsupials and carry their young in fleshy pouches on the undersides of their bodies.

Temple

INDIAN TEMPLE BUILT DOWNWARDS

The Kailas Temple in India was built down from the surface of the ground. First all the rock at the proposed site was excavated. The next step was carving the outside of the temple; then the interior was excavated and carved throughout. The entire construction job took 100 years to complete.

Tenrecs

THE LITTER-BEARER

During the 1770's, a Frenchman named Sonnerat, a spice-trader who was also an amateur naturalist, discovered three strange new animals never before seen by Europeans. All were found only on the remote island of Madagascar in the Indian Ocean.

Sonnerat named two of his finds after words he heard the natives use at the time he first spotted the animals. He thought, of course, that these words were the Malagasy names for the two.

Unfortunately, Sonnerat did not understand the local dialect, and so his finds wound up with very odd names. One—the largest living lemur—he named "indri," which simply means "Look there" in Malagasy. The second animal he called the "aye-aye," which turned out to be nothing more than a native exclamation of surprise.

Both these very unscientific names have, however, stuck and

This little tenrec mother with her record brood has too few feeding stations!

so we now have two monkey-like creatures with the unlikely names of "Look there" and the Malagasy equivalent of "Wow!"

The third animal discovered by Sonnerat fared better with his name than the lemurs did. He was called "tenrec," which is a French corruption of the native word for the animal.

The tenrec is one of the least known of animals. It looks something like a hedgehog, sporting a bristle-like brown coat mixed with spines and striped irregularly with yellow. It has a long snout for digging up insects, makes its home in mountain brush and is found only on the island of Madagascar, except for a few now kept in zoos.

In 1970, a pair of rare tailless tenrecs was sent from Madagascar to the Wassenaar Zoo in Holland. They were placed in a glass enclosure and immediately set up housekeeping, building a nest from leaves supplied by the zoo.

The little tenrecs soon seemed to make a friend of their keeper, though when alarmed they would show anger by bristling "their thin manes of guard hairs, emitting shrill squeaks . . . and opening the mouth very wide, about 140 degrees."

Although insect-eaters, the tenrecs thrived at the Wassenaar Zoo on a diet mainly of minced meat, raw eggs, cottage cheese, day-old chicks and mealworms.

The tenrecs are among the most prolific of mammals, often bearing litters of 16 to 18 young after a gestation period of about 8 weeks. But at the Wassenaar Zoo, the rare little mother from Madagascar outdid herself. In 1972, she astonished her keeper with a litter of 31 tiny tenrecs—an amazing achievement even for this prodigious baby-producer.

More amazing still for wild animals born in captivity, 30 of the infants survived despite the shortage of feeding stations. But nature has its own compensations. Although the tenrecs are born blind and remain so for about 6 days, the little animals were observed at the end of the third day licking chewed food from the lips of their fond and busy parents.

The strange nests of Australia's "magnetic ants." The mounds always line up north to south.

Termites

THE SKYSCRAPER BUILDERS

At first sight they look like the worn stones in a giant's grave-yard, or the ruins of some pagan temple. But they are neither. They are the skyscraper nests of Australian termites. If an army of men were to build a comparable structure, in proportion to their size, they would have one as tall as Mount McKinley.

The termitaria, as the mound or nest is called, is a narrow, tomb-like wall about 12 feet high.

Because the narrow ends of the walls always point directly north and south, the termites are also known as "magnetic ants."

The reason for this directional architecture is that an even interior temperature is needed in the mound if the complex termite community is to function well. At noon, when the day is hottest, only the narrow edge of the nest is exposed to the intense rays of the sun. In the cooler mornings and afternoons, the sun's rays fall on the flat east and west walls.

Inside the mound, the temperature is further kept termite-right by a complex air-conditioning system which the insects invented long before man appeared on the earth.

Just under the mound's surface, numerous narrow ventilating shafts run from top to bottom. Some of these carry the stale air up to the top level of the mound where it is rerouted downward through other shafts to be cooled. On its way down, the used air releases its carbon dioxide and picks up fresh oxygen through pinpoint holes in the mound's outer walls.

These walls are very hard. They are made of subsurface soil which blind "bricklayer" termites haul up to each rising level of construction. There the soil is mixed with a hardening secretion from the termites' mouths and used immediately as building material. This quickly dries into a cement-like substance.

The blind bricklayers get no rest until the mound is completed, and termite "policemen" stand by to see that there is no shirking on the job. If a worker falters, he is killed.

Tibet

MULTIPLE MARRIAGE

Multiple, simultaneous marriages were permitted for years in Tibet. This Tibetan beauty kept her first husband and married Tibet's Foreign Minister *and his son*, thus becoming the wife of three men. The boy is by her first husband. Men have also been allowed to have more than one wife at a time.

Tower balanced in the wind.

Towers

TOWER SEVERED IN TWO

A 1957 earthquake in Turkey severed the top of this tower. The loosened section, which has been completely sheared off, sways precariously in the wind.

THE LEANING TOWERS OF BOLOGNA

Pisa is not the only Italian town with a leaning tower. These old towers lean in opposite directions.

Trees

THE DIVI-DIVI

On the island of Aruba in the Netherlands West Indies, the trade winds blow from the same direction all year long, day and night. This accounts for the strange leanings of the divi-divi trees, which flourish here and in a few other parts of tropical America. The curiously twisted pods are astringent, containing large amounts of tannic and gallic acid.

Turkey

<u>PALACE OF TURKISH EMPERORS</u>

The old palace of Turkish emperors, the Topkapi in Istanbul, contains 12 mosques, 12 baths, 2 hospitals, 2 pharmacies, 5 schools, 17 libraries, 22 fountains, 353 bedrooms and parlors, 5 dormitories and 21 kiosks. It can be visited by tourists today.

(Above) Around midnight, the turtles come out of the river to lay their eggs. (Left) Egg laying completed, a turtle tries to return to the river before a hunter catches him.

Turtles

TURTLE MIGRATION

During the spring months along the banks of the Orinoco River at Paraguaza, Venezuela, the annual turtle migration takes place. Hunters and merchants are always on the scene for the daily permissible catch of 800 turtles. Thousands of turtles move inland around midnight to begin their egg laying (60 to 120 eggs each), which continues until dawn. Then the turtles start their return to the Orinoco River. On their return the white flag of the Ministry of Agriculture drops and the hunters rush out to the beach and catch them, turning them over on their backs to make them helpless.

These turtles have been caught and turned on their backs. They are now on their way to the soup bowl.

Volcanoes

ONE MAN SURVIVES

On May 8, 1902, on the island of Martinique in the Caribbean, the volcano known as Mount Pelée erupted in a thunderous horror of flame, lava, and suffocating gas. In the catastrophe, the city of St. Pierre was immediately destroyed.

Days later, when rescuers were able to start searching the still-burning ruins, they found nothing but death beneath a pall of smoke and ash. All the inhabitants of the town of St. Pierre, more than 30,000 people, had been killed.

Then, suddenly, as the search continued, they heard faint cries coming from beneath the earth. The rescuers investigated ... and found that one man was still alive.

The name of the lone survivor was Auguste Ciparis and the reason he was alive was because Ciparis was a criminal and had been serving his term in the deepest dungeon of the old French prison.

So well did the massive stone walls protect him that he did not even know that Mount Pelée had erupted.

The city of St. Pierre, Martinique, was completely destroyed in 1902—or was it? One man, deep in a dungeon, didn't even know Mount Pelée had erupted.

An underwater volcano near the tip of Fayal Island in the Azores is sending up steam to announce it is about ready to erupt.

BIRTH OF A VOLCANIC ISLAND

Off Fayal Island in the Azores an underwater volcano began to disturb the waters. Shortly the sea was boiling and fuming with activity that resulted in the birth of an island. In this series of photographs you can see the progress of this phenomenon from beginning to end. The new land attached itself to the tip of Fayal Island, thereby adding new territory to Portugal—but only briefly, because a few months later another volcanic disturbance caused the newborn island to disappear.

Solid land is beginning to emerge from beneath the ocean.

(Above) As the steam and smoke begin to clear, you can see the new island taking shape.

Thrusting high above sea level, the newborn island seemed destined to stay—but it was not to be—only a few months later the volcano acted again and the island sank into the undersea crater and died.

(Opposite page) The sea has receded, leaving beach between the new island and Fayal.

Volcanoes

THE DEVIL'S BOTTLE—
VESUVIUS AND POMPEII

Several years ago, while I was in Naples, I drove out to Vesuvius and, with a guide, descended to the floor of that still-steaming crater, which the local people call "The Devil's Bottle." It is indeed an apt name for this brooding old volcano, because when this "bottle" explodes it does the devil's own work throughout the entire countryside, sending its lethal ash, steam, and lava down to the very edge of the beautiful Bay of Naples.

When I came up from the depths of Vesuvius, I went on to nearby Pompeii, where I was the guest of the late Amedeo Maiuri, the great archaeologist responsible for the modern excavation of that famous Roman city that was so tragically destroyed by the savage eruption of Vesuvius in 79 A.D.

That historic explosion buried all of Pompeii under a hot, suffocating blanket of ash and pumice 32 feet deep and claimed the lives of more than 20,000 inhabitants. So quickly did the disaster take place that only a few had time to escape. Most victims died suddenly in their homes and shops or as they fled toward the safety of the nearby bay.

As we picked our way through the ruins of Pompeii, Dr. Maiuri explained to me the strange technique that he had created for making lifelike casts of the bodies found by the excavators as they dug through the buried city.

The solid blanket of hot pumice and ash that had killed the inhabitants of Pompeii, said the doctor, had in a macabre way also perpetuated them. As the deadly sediment cooled, it had hardened around its victims, forming natural and perfect molds of their bodies. Over the centuries, these bodies had gradually turned to dust, but the hard molds that outlined the once-living contours remained intact.

Now, almost 2,000 years later, workmen digging carefully down through the hard ash to unearth the ancient city would hear their tools tap on a hollow place. This sound would tell

The author starts climbing down into steaming Mt. Vesuvius' "Devil's Bottle." The coat is protection against the heat.

them that the body mold of a Pompeiian killed by Vesuvius in 79 A.D. lay beneath.

Upon this discovery, a hole would be carefully bored into

One of the lifelike body-molds of people who died instantly at Pompeii in 79 A.D.

the top of the mold, and through this opening would be poured enough plaster of Paris to fill the empty space within. When the plaster hardened, the ancient covering of ash would be broken away and an absolutely lifelike cast of one of Vesuvius's long-dead victims would be found.

That day Maiuri showed me three such figures that had recently been cast and were being readied for public exhibition. The figures were of two men and a boy, one lying prone and the other two on their sides. The doctor pointed out that, judging by their positions, they had all been running toward the water when they fell and died, overcome by the noxious fumes of the volcano.

These victims of Pompeii in 79 A.D.—two men and a young boy—were preserved by the layers of dust.

Walking

SHANKS' MARE

Walking is the easiest and cheapest form of athletics.

Track and field records list some prodigious walkers. Edward Watson, in 1909, at the age of 70, walked from New York City to San Francisco in 105 days. He covered just under 4,000 miles, and all of these over the rough roads of that time.

In 1912, a vigorous lady named Beach made it from New York to Chicago over a measured distance of 1,007 miles. It took her 42 days. Fifteen years later a New Yorker named William Reinhold trotted over the same track and cut the lady's time down considerably. He made it in 17½ days.

The greatest walker of all, however, was an Englishman named James Hocking who settled in Teaneck, New Jersey, in the early 1900's.

In his youth, Hocking had already made a name for himself in his native country by walking from the southern tip of England to the northern tip of Scotland, and back again. That was a total walking distance of 1,800 miles, and it took him just 17 days. That's footing it at an average of better than 100 miles a day, more than double what the Army expects of a soldier on a forced march with a light pack.

In the United States, Walter Hocking continued to pursue his favorite sport, easily breaking all existing records for walking, time and distance. If he ever suffered the painful disabilities of burning bunions, caved-in arches, or shin splints, these never slowed him up. He kept right on walking for 75 long years, a record in itself.

Hocking took his longest walk in 1932 when, at the age of 68, he made it all the way from New York's Coney Island on the edge of the Atlantic, to Seal Rock, San Francisco, on the edge of the Pacific. This transcontinental hike stretched out for 3,750 miles, and Hocking put this mileage behind him in just 75 walking days. If it hadn't been for all the uphill work over two mountain ranges, he'd have done even better.

At the age of 95, not long before he died, Hocking was still hard at it. He celebrated his birthday that year by taking an 11-hour stroll from Teaneck, New Jersey, to the village of Suffern in New York. Hocking admitted at the time that he seemed to be slowing up; at the age of 92 he had made the same walk in only 9 hours.

Hocking and all the other great long-steppers have inscribed their names indelibly on the Shanks' Mare Roll of Honor. They were all superb one-foot-before-the-other endurance walkers, and they merit every bit of their posthumous fame.

But there is another long-distance walker who deserves not to be forgotten. He was a man with a different idea of what a walkathon should be, and he set a record which has never been duplicated—or even challenged.

He had the curious name of Plennie Wingo, and, in 1931, he found himself with very little cash in hand. He'd owned a restaurant but it had gone bust; the Great Depression had just started.

There weren't too many ways to make a living in those black days, so Wingo hit on the idea of doing something that had never been done before. He'd walk around the world, and he'd do it the hard way—backward. That should bring him fame, fortune, and maybe even a new restaurant.

It's not easy to walk backward. Anyone who's ever retreated in the presence of royalty, or eased away from a junkyard dog, knows how difficult it is. But that didn't daunt Wingo. Instead, he set himself to practice this awkward form of locomotion daily for several months, until he could step out (or back) with ease. A mirror, hooked up to a halterlike frame around his neck, showed him where he was going. This kept him from bumping into things, tumbling into holes, and stepping off piers. And he carried a cane.

Wingo started on his backward journey from his home in Fort Worth, Texas, on April 16, 1931. His official starting time was duly observed and notarized by a Western Union clerk, and a crowd of doubting well-wishers was present to see him off. As he necessarily walked away facing his friends, the farewell waves kept up for a long time.

Wingo crossed the United States in good shape and made it to Boston, where he walked backwards up the gangplank of a freighter bound for France.

In Europe, he continued his strange backward junket. He walked without hindrance through the western countries, then through the eastern countries of Czechoslovakia, Hungary, Rumania, and Bulgaria. Finally he backed into Turkey, the gateway to Asia.

In Istanbul, where he took time out to admire the handsome Blue Mosque, Wingo received word from the American Embassy that he could go no further. Asia, he was told, was boiling with unrest. The area he wanted to travel through was dangerous enough for a forward-looking native; for a backward-looking foreigner it could be a disaster.

So, with nowhere else to go, Wingo did what most of us would do in that situation; he returned home.

Wingo didn't get clear around the world, as he had planned. But what he did do has never been done by anyone else. He walked backward for a year and a half, and in that time covered a distance of more than 8,000 miles. During his walk he wore out dozens of pairs of shoes, had hundreds of adventures, met thousands of people, and lost 35 pounds.

The only mishap suffered by Wingo throughout his amazing odyssey occurred when he backed into a ditch in Ohio and injured his ankle.

And what happened to Plennie Wingo eventually? Well, he became a bank guard, a job that requires a vigilant eyes-front posture at all times.

In 1977, he celebrated the 45th anniversary of his walk by walking the 452 miles from Santa Monica to San Francisco—backwards, of course, in 85 days, although aged 81.

Walrus

THE WHALE-HORSE

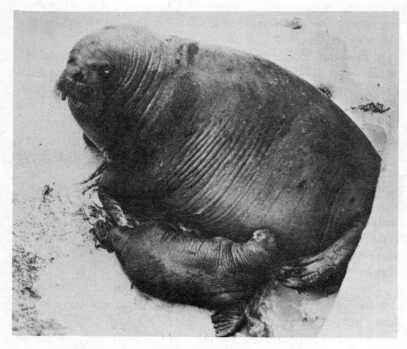

This is Petula, a 3,000-pound walrus, as she is nursing her pup. Petula and her mate, Farouk, are the only walrus couple in captivity ever to bear a living pup.

This large bristle-snouted walrus, born in the Bering Sea is shown here at the Marineland of the Pacific.

No walrus has ever been born, and few have ever survived, in captivity. Therefore, this healthy young baby living south of the Polar region, and in captivity, is the object of considerable affectionate concern.

The ancestors of the good-natured, blubbery youngster once lived in vast, close-packed communities among the Arctic floes. Today, the walrus is found in only a few diminishing herds, preyed on by hunters who have valued their tusks and hides since the time of the sea-roving Norsemen who gave them their name of "whale-horse" (valross).

The walrus is a gregarious animal and likes to talk things over with another walrus in a series of bellows, snuffles and barks, often with such verve that he tumbles into the water.

To protect him against the frigid Arctic Ocean, the walrus has a leathery hide so padded out with fat that his body will remain afloat for almost a day after he dies. Clumsy on land, he's a fine swimmer and diver, often reaching a depth of 300 feet.

This 300-pound baby gained weight rapidly on a daily diet of whole clams supplemented liberally with a blend of whipped cream, minced clams, yeast and vitamins. He weighed more than a ton at maturity, and required 60 pounds of clams and mussels a day to still the pangs of hunger. He grew heavy tusks almost 2 feet long, a murderous set of weapons which would discourage any enemy from attacking him head-on.

War

THE BLACK ROSE

In 1913, a wealthy Austrian nobleman invited a Dutch horticulturist to stay at his palace for the purpose of growing a black rose.

Now a black rose was a great floral oddity, but the people of Vienna wanted no part of it. They said that whenever a black rose had been produced before, disaster had always followed.

The people begged the nobleman to abandon his project and send the scientist home to Holland. But the nobleman ignored their pleas as being pure superstition and continued his experiments. These finally met with success, and a beautiful black rose was produced.

Shortly afterward, the nobleman and his wife left Austria on a state visit to a neighboring country. Their tour was a great triumph and they were greeted by happy, cheering crowds wherever they went.

Then one day, as they bowed and smiled from their open carriage, they passed a man whose heart was filled with hate. Suddenly the man raised his arm—and two deadly shots split the air. The proud owner of the black rose fell forward in his carriage, dead! His wife fell beside him.

Those two murdered aristocrats were the Duchess Sophie and the Archduke Franz Ferdinand, heir to the throne of the Austro-Hungarian Empire. The place was Sarajevo, Serbia. The time was June 28, 1914. And those two fatal shots signaled the start of World War I.

WARTIME JUSTICE

Early in 1945, Baron Von Schlavrendorff was brought before a Nazi court charged with an attempt on Hitler's life.

After a short trial, the baron was found guilty of high treason and sentenced to death.

Because it was wartime, the execution was ordered to take place at once.

Suddenly, as the baron was being led away from the court room, the terrifying sound of an Allied air-raid was heard.

Before anyone could run to safety, a giant bomb scored a direct hit on the court and demolished it into a pile of rubble. All of those connected with the trial were killed instantly by the blast. All, that is, but one man.

By some incredible miracle, the explosion which killed everyone else in the courtroom spared the life of the baron, the very man who had just been doomed to die before a firing squad.

With no one to hold him, the baron escaped from the shattered building and found his way to freedom.

NAME-PLATED SHRAPNEL

During World War II, two young American GIs, stationed in Australia, were driving along in a jeep on their way to an anti-aircraft station when a Japanese squadron came over, intent on bombing the airfield and everything around it. The young airmen heard the planes coming, jumped out of their jeep, and dove into a roadside ditch. They took cover just in time. One of the planes, on a low run, dropped a bomb that hit the jeep and completely destroyed it.

After the attack was over, the two men got out of the ditch, shaken but unharmed and walked over to see the damage. Poking around, they found a large piece of shrapnel from the bomb wedged into the seat where the driver had been sitting. Picking it up, they saw clearly stenciled on the metal the name of "Ray Ewing." The GI who had been driving the jeep gave a hoot of astonishment. His name was Curtis Ewing, and his father's name was Ray.

And how did that piece of shrapnel get there?

Well, before the war, Ray Ewing had sold his old Plymouth for junk; previously, he had stenciled his name on the engine block. The car, like other steel and iron junk discarded by Americans, found its way to Japan, the major market for old metal at that time. Later, all this metal went into weapons.

That piece of metal from a father's car, years later and on the other side of the world, almost killed his son.

THE CHAPLAIN AND THE GASOLINE

During World War II, a bomber carrying a chaplain ran out of gas over the Pacific and was forced down on a Japanese-held island. Without gas to get away, the crew knew they would be captured and resigned themselves to this fate.

But the chaplain did not. A firm believer, he prayed for deliverance. The crew respected his faith but did not share his hope.

But the next day they changed their minds.

Early that morning, just before dawn, one of the crew was awakened suddenly with—as he said later—a strong feeling that he should go down and walk on the beach.

He did. And there he found, bobbing on the incoming tide, a huge drum of aviation gasoline.

With a shout, the astonished airman awakened the rest of the crew who rushed down to the water, pulled the big drum ashore, and transferred the miraculous gift of gas to the stranded plane.

Then they were off, safely airborne to their not-too-distant base.

Later, the facts concerning the gasoline came to light. The drum had been part of a cargo of fuel that had been jettisoned from its barge following a Japanese attack. All the other drums had been lost, but this one had floated almost 1,000 miles, past 25 other islands, to finally wash up at the very feet of the men who desperately needed the gasoline to save their lives.

A GOOD LAUGH

In 1798, Napoleon Bonaparte dreamed of extending his empire to India and landed his troops in Egypt as the first stop on his eastern campaign. He brought with him not only soldiers but scientists as well, so that they might study these ancient countries as the campaign progressed.

In Egypt, part of his army, under the command of General Friant, marched into the desert accompanied by scientists and the mules which bore their equipment.

The troops had not gone far when they were suddenly attacked by a howling horde of armed Arab horsemen. The attack was a complete surprise to the Frenchmen and they were caught off guard. For a moment all was confusion, and then there was a loud command from General Friant. "Form a square," shouted the general. "Put the donkeys and scientists in the middle."

This strange command caught the humor of the French soldiers and one by one they started to shout with laughter.

The great roar of their laughter was heard by the Arabs who were so amazed at men who could laugh during a battle that they paused in their attack. This pause gave the French time to rally their forces and eventually to beat off the Arabs.

RARE BLOOD IN THE PACIFIC

During World War II, a young marine lay badly wounded in a military hospital on a South Pacific island. Shrapnel had ripped through his chest, and unless he received a series of blood transfusions at once the boy was doomed to die.

But the type of blood required turned out to be very rare. No donors were immediately available, and hope for saving the marine was given up.

Then a medic discovered a supply of the rare blood in a recent shipment from the United States. The transfusion was given, and the marine lived.

When he recovered, the grateful young man asked about the donor. She turned out to be a Boston woman and he wrote to thank her for the gift of her life-saving blood.

Then the marine wrote to his father, in Kentucky, about his miraculous experience. His father recognized the donor's name. She was his long-lost sister and the marine's own aunt.

The wounded man had never known his aunt, but her donation of rare blood, which matched his, saved his life in the faraway Pacific.

Washington

WASHINGTON AND HOWE'S DOG

Washington's sense of honor and courtesy was a byword even during his lifetime, but no incident demonstrates these characteristics more than one which took place late in 1777 while Washington was holding a council of war with his officers in an old mill in Pennsylvania.

The subject under discussion was, as usual, the British forces and their commander-in-chief, Sir William Howe, who was then living comfortably in nearby Philadelphia and toasting his "victory" over Washington's little army of citizen soldiers.

Suddenly, out of the night, appeared a dog, obviously lost and hungry. Washington, realizing that the animal was a fine hunting dog, examined its collar to find the owner's name. By one of those rare ironies, the name on the collar showed that the dog belonged to Sir William Howe, the enemy general.

A lesser man might have kept the animal as a gratifying prize of war, but not Washington.

Understanding, from his own experience, how a man feels about a good dog, Washington gave immediate orders to have the animal fed, groomed, and then, under a flag of truce, returned to its enemy owner.

With the dog went a note, dated October 6, which read: "General Washington's compliments to General Howe—does himself the pleasure to return him a dog which accidentally fell into his hands and, by the inscription on the collar, appears to belong to General Howe."

This courtly gesture on the part of Washington greatly impressed Howe and he acknowledged the return of his dog with a warm note of thanks. The exchange, however, made no difference in the pursuit of the war.

THE COUNTERFEITERS

Almost as soon as the American Revolution had gotten under way, the British decided to use counterfeiting as a psychological weapon to beat the rebellious colonies back into submission.

The fledgling American government had already started to issue its own "Congress money," and the English planned to discredit this by a flood of counterfeit currency, most of it to be printed and distributed in New York, which was then a hotbed of intrigue and Royalist sympathy.

Among the first to see the danger posed by counterfeit money was George Washington, already named commander in chief of the Revolutionary army.

Washington did what he could to combat the threat of false currency, sending out his spies wherever counterfeit bills turned up in quantity. It was in the spring of 1776 that Washington received his first solid information about a spy ring operating in New York.

The source of Washington's information was a Long Island button-maker named Charles Friend, a patriot who had grown suspicious of some activities carried on in the house of the Youngs, a family living in Cold Spring Harbor. There were three Youngs brothers, and all of them were known to be hardcore Royalists, still faithful to King George. Not long before, said Friend, a stranger had come to live at the house of one of the brothers. The newcomer, Henry Dawkins, was an engraver, and it was this fact, coupled with some mysterious nighttime excursions and a display of currency, that had led Friend to believe that the Youngs and Dawkins were engaged in counterfeiting "Congress money."

On this news, Washington acted immediately, sending his aid, Captain Jeremiah Wool, with a small detachment of soldiers, to make a surprise raid on the Long Island farmhouse of the Youngs. The military party sailed across the Sound and reached the house early in the morning, a few hours before dawn. Pounding hard on the door, Captain Wool awakened the startled Youngs and then demanded to see Dawkins and to search the house.

"Dawkins ain't here," one of the Youngs said sullenly. "And by what right do you search?"

"By order of General Washington," answered Wool curtly, and then proceeded to go over the house carefully, paying special attention to the bedroom occupied by the absent Dawkins.

Finding nothing of an incriminating nature, the Captain was preparing to leave the room when a sharp-eyed soldier turned for a last look. Struck by something he thought unusual on the wall behind Dawkins' bed, he spoke up:

"Captain, sir, there's something a mite odd about that wall. That little crack, it's too even, sir."

Indeed it was! A bayonet, inserted into the narrow chink, pried open the edge of a small, hidden door behind which was a steep stairway. The searchers mounted the stairs and found themselves in a dark attic containing a rolling press, engraving tools and a bundle of bills, all excellent reproductions of "Congress money."

With the evidence before them, the Youngs stopped protesting their innocence and, along with Dawkins who was picked up at a nearby tavern, the counterfeiters were taken to New York. Under questioning, they all confessed, and that summer they stood trial.

The trial disclosed that Dawkins was a brilliant engraver, and one of the first in this country to work on copperplate. He had come from England as a young man and had settled in Philadelphia where he had eventually opened a printing shop. Although good at his trade, he was a poor businessman, had soon run heavily into debt and then sought financial aid in New York. It was at this time that he met the Youngs who, serving the Royalist cause, were on the watch for a good engraver to make counterfeit money, money which would eventually "injure the new Congress."

The Youngs paid all his debts, and Dawkins set up shop in the Cold Spring attic and started on his now treasonable trade.

So successful was the distribution of this false currency that in a few years "Congress money" had become valueless, and the expression "not worth a continental" became entrenched in our language.

The British occupation also resulted in a small irony about which it is probable George Washington never learned. Dawkins was freed when the British captured New York, disappeared for a few years, then turned up in a curiously reversed role. Old documents show that in 1780, Henry Dawkins presented a bill to the young Federal Treasury Department for $1500 to cover his services that year as an expert engraver of genuine Federal currency. The master counterfeiter had turned legitimate!

Wealthy Eccentrics

A STRANGE LEGACY

New York's famed Hospital for Special Surgery once received a strange legacy. The bequest was left to the hospital many years ago when, as a small pioneering institution, it was known as the Hospital for the Ruptured and Crippled and was located in mid-Manhattan.

The incident which led to the legacy occurred one winter night early in the 20th century and concerned Dr. Virgil Gibney, the brilliant young surgeon who was then director of the hospital. Dr. Gibney happened to be at the Hospital when a call came from the home of some wealthy people who lived on Fifth Avenue requesting that a physician be sent immediately to treat someone who had been injured.

Dr. Gibney at once put on his hat and coat, and went to this old house which was surrounded by a high brick wall. He was admitted, and on asking to see the patient, was informed that the pet dog belonging to one of the ladies had broken its leg.

Instead of being perturbed and leaving in disgust, Dr. Gibney set the fracture and splinted the limb. During the next month or so he saw his "patient" frequently.

The house to which Dr. Gibney had been summoned that night was a huge shuttered greystone mansion on the corner of 39th Street and Fifth Avenue. Built before the Civil War and still lit by gas and candles, the old house sheltered eccentric, domineering John Wendel and his seven spinster sisters.

The Wendel wealth had been made in booming New York City real estate, but the family had few friends, and its members rarely left the old house hidden behind its high brick wall. The sisters, fearing fortune-hunters, had no suitors, and Brother John's curious behavior repelled everyone. He believed that dye was harmful to the health and had all the cloth for his old-fashioned suits woven from the wool of pure black sheep. And he was so terrified of disease that he had inch-thick soles put on his shoes to protect him from the unseen germs that swarmed over the pavement.

In such a household, it was not strange that the lonely, childless women centered all their human affection on a succession of pet dogs, mostly poodles. The dogs slept in specially made four-poster beds, ate broiled lamb chops at the table, and had a grassy runway maintained just for their use on property valued even then at more than a million dollars. Naturally, too, when such a pampered pet is injured, only the best medical counsel is called.

Years later, in 1931, the last surviving member of the eccentric family died. She was Ella Wendel, and she left a fortune of more than one hundred million dollars. Almost all of this was left to charity, including a multi-million-dollar bequest to "young Dr. Gibney's" hospital. This large legacy went far toward helping build the hospital's present handsome home on New York's fashionable East Side.

It was a very nice "remembrance" for setting a little dog's broken leg.

Ella Wendel and her poodle, Tobey. This is one of the rare pictures taken of the wealthy recluse.

Weddings

<u>IN THE JAWS OF A WHALE</u>

MIDGET MARRIES 400-POUND WOMAN

The midget: Jack Glicken. The lady: Mildred Monte.

416   Wells

Wells

WELL DEDICATED TO A SAINT

In Orvieto, Italy, there is a centuries-old well dedicated to Saint Patrick. Constructed 300 feet downward into the earth, it is an amazing feat of engineering. Its builders devised a unique labor-saving device: a winding, twisting staircase placed flush against the sides of the well. The stairway is wide enough so that men and burros can walk down to the well's bottom, collect water in sacks on the burros' back and lead them back up to the surface.

Whales

THE RELUCTANT BENEFACTOR

Everything on the whale is useful.

From the very first, the rich blubber of the whale's body supplied the oil which helped to light up the dark, superstition-ridden nights of the Middle Ages. And it served its purpose so well that whale oil continued to light the lamps of Europe and the New World right up to the advent of petroleum in the last century. Today, whale oil is widely used in making soap and glycerine, for dressing leather and as a lubricant. When highly refined, it is even made into edible fats.

Blubber, from which the oil is rendered, is the chief product sought in the whale. (That this is abundant is shown by the recorded capture of a 95-foot, 150-ton whale which carried so much blubber that it yielded up more than 110 barrels of oil.)

The thick, strong hide of the whale is used for making sturdy luggage and leather goods, and the flesh of the watery mammoth is eaten in place of beefsteak which it closely resembles in texture and taste, being only a little darker in color and somewhat less succulent. In no way does it resemble the flesh of fish, although it was once considered so and eaten with sinless satisfaction in many Catholic countries on meatless Fridays. In 16th-century France, the tongue of a whale was considered the peak of gourmet delight.

In the head of the big sperm whale—the most valuable of all whales—is a huge cavity filled with a pale, odorless substance called spermaceti, which is used in the manufacture of soothing medical ointments and fine cosmetics, as well as in making high-grade candles.

Ambergris, another substance from the whale, but thick, yellow and evil-smelling, is still used as a fixative in the blending of luxury perfumes. It is generally found floating on the surface of the sea after being cast up from the stomach of a sick whale.

The baleen—the strands of bony fringe from 2 to 12 feet long which hang down from the upper jaws of most whales and

Bucking like a wild bronco, Shamu, the 2-ton killer whale, takes his trainer for a bone-jarring ride at Orlando's Sea World.

act as strainers when the animals eat—has been used for centuries in many diverse ways. Its use has varied from indestructible plumes adorning the helmets of medieval knights to the long ribs of utilitarian umbrellas ... from the wigs worn by English barristers, to the rigid "whalebone" corset stay, that relentless guardian once used to confine a lady's runaway midriff.

Even the teeth and enormous jawbones of the great whales are used. The first, from the sperm whale and called "ivory of the sea," are carved into art objects. The jaws, often seen in Norway, are used as towering, ornamental gateposts before the homes of whalers.

Finally, after the dead whale has been completely flenched—stripped of skin, blubber, baleen, spermaceti, everything—and there is nothing left but the great skeleton, then this is dried and pulverized into bone meal and, along with guano, is sold for high-grade fertilizer.

Wills

CHANGE OF NAME

In the little town of Woodleigh, England, Annie Grey grew up knowing she would one day marry Will Coltart, the boy who lived next door. And Coltart knew he would marry Annie.

But Coltart decided to seek his fortune before settling down, and off he went to Australia. When Annie did not hear from him for several years, she concluded that Will's ardor had cooled and she married Jonathon Tong, a very rich merchant.

Soon after this, Coltart returned. He was disappointed to find his Annie married, but he settled down in Woodleigh just to be near her.

Then Jonathon died, and Coltart felt that now he could marry Annie. But when Jonathon's will was read, it stated clearly that Annie was to be cut off without a penny if she married Coltart. Obviously, Tong was not a husband to brook a rival.

But Jonathon Tong's spiteful will proved useless. Unknown to the dead man, Coltart had legally changed his name to "John Temple" during the time that he lived in far-off Australia.

Jonathon's will went into litigation, but the English court finally decided that Annie could marry "John Temple" and still keep her inheritance, despite her jealous husband's attempt to disinherit her if she married her childhood sweetheart.

KISS REWARD

Early in this century, a young man named Michael O'Connor was brought before a Melbourne, Australia, court on the complaint of a Miss Hazel Moore, a spinster. She charged that the defendant, a shopkeeper, had suddenly hugged and kissed her when she entered his store to make a purchase.

O'Connor pleaded guilty but defended his action by saying that it had been a lovely spring day, he had been reading "Don Juan," and that he'd also had a few beers for lunch.

The judge found O'Connor guilty of a breach of the peace and sentenced the overly affectionate young man to a few months in the workhouse.

Ten years passed. Then one day, without warning, an attorney walked into O'Connor's shop and told the surprised man that he had just come into a fortune of ¡20,000.

Miss Moore, the lawyer explained, had recently died and had left this legacy to O'Connor in memory of the only kiss she had ever received from a man in her long spinster's life.

Women in Sports

FABULOUS FANNY

Francina Elsje Blankers-Koen—commonly known as Fanny Blankers-Koen—had accepted defeat in her initial venture into the sports world but, before her story was completed, she became one of the most famous women athletes ever to vie in international competition.

The future star was born in the Netherlands in 1918, just before World War I slogged its way to a bloody climax. She grew up in an atmosphere plagued by postwar problems.

But as she grew into her teens, she discovered that she was blessed with more than average athletic ability, and she turned to competititve swimming to test the extent of those talents.

Unfortunately, her success might best be labeled "always a bridesmaid but never a bride." The young Francina Elsje was good enough to compete at the national level but never good enough to win a championship.

Then, in neighboring Germany in 1936, Adolf Hitler and his Nazis played host to the eleventh Summer Olympic Games and an event occurred which changed Francina's entire life.

A young American black man stunned the sports world (and Hitler) by winning four events, all track and field, in Berlin's Olympic Stadium. Jesse Owens swept to two victories in dashes, captured the long jump, and anchored the United States 400-meter relay team to victory.

With such a performance as inspiration, the Dutch teenager shook off the water of the competitive pool and turned her talents to track. Before many months had passed, she also had shaken the agony of her swimming losses and began piling up track victories in droves.

Then World War II erupted and international competition moved from the cinder path to the battlefield.

For a lesser athlete, the long years of fighting and recovery might have spelled the end of ambition. Twelve years elapsed between the games in Berlin and the next Olympiad, which was staged in London in 1948.

The most talked-about woman athlete in 1948 was "Fabulous Fanny." She won four gold medals in the Olympics of that year.

But when the opening parade of the nations was staged, there was Francina, now a 30-year-old housewife and mother of two, marching proudly as a representative of the Netherlands. Thirty, of course, borders on the ancient for Olympic athletes, but that over-the-hill age did not discourage the blonde heroine.

In quick succession, Fanny Blankers-Koen won the 100-meter dash in 11.5 seconds; the 200-meter in 24.4 seconds; the 80-meter hurdles in 11.2 seconds. Then she ran the anchor leg in the 400-meter relay, which the Netherlands also won.

Thus, Fabulous Fanny became the second person in athletic history to garner four gold medals in a single Olympiad, and the first woman to accomplish this remarkable feat.

Owens' records were tied—though not in track—by Don Schollander during the 1964 Games in Tokyo, and were shattered—again not in track—by Mark Spitz's seven victories in Munich in 1972.

But the amazing accomplishment of Fanny Blankers-Koen never has been equalled. And the fact that she set that standard at the age of 30, when almost everyone conceded that she was past her peak, makes the record of the "Hurryin' *Hausfrau*" one of the most incredible in track-and-field history.

Women's Lib

THE ORIGINAL WOMEN'S LIBBER

Ladies on their own aren't anything new. Ever since Eve tried that apple, "Les girls" have long been doing their own thing. The only difference is that now they are organized.

One of fiction's most daring heroines was actually taken from life. She was a gal who went all out for liberation way back in the 1600's; Gautier used her in his novel "Mademoiselle Maupin." Actually, her name was Julie Aubigny and she was the spoiled daughter of a French nobleman.

A spirited beauty, Julie insisted on an education equal to a man's. An achiever in intellectual pursuits, she also became an expert rider and swordsman.

She cut off her hair, wore men's clothing, rampaged through the dark streets at night, fought several successful duels, and was notorious for her love affairs.

At the age of 16, she married an old, rich count and then promptly left him to become the first French contralto ever to perform publicly.

As the darling of the newly founded Paris Opera, Julie continued her independent and unconventional life. She was a free soul and the toast of the town.

Then, for the first time, love came along and turned Julie completely around. Now it was nice Julie, good Julie.

But virtue didn't work for Julie. Her lover suddenly left her and married another. Shattered, the rejected woman entered a convent and remained there until she died at the age of 37.

Worms

WORM OF MANY TURNS

What looks like a thick rope is actually a part of the world's longest earthworm, found only in a small corner of Australia where it thrives mightily in the moist, dark soil along the river banks of Southern Gippsland, in the State of Victoria.

These fantastic crawlers, the dream of every live-bait fisherman, often reach the well-nigh incredible length of 12 feet.

Without organs of sight or hearing, these giants in the earth are harmless and require no food other than decaying vegetation.

It is fortunate for this worm that it lives in Australia, where the inhabitants view it only as a natural wonder and not as an item of diet, for worms are still eaten with gusto in many parts of the world.

For instance, the head-hunting Jivaro Indians of Ecuador do not share the feelings of the English poet Cowper, who called no man friend "who needlessly set foot upon a worm." One of their greatest gastronomic delights is a juicy worm about 4 inches long, which they find beneath the bark of dying chonta palm trees.

The worms get inside the dying tree and proceed to munch away at top speed. Their greed is their own undoing. They make so much noise while devouring the tree that they are heard from the outside by the alert Jivaros. The Indians, greedy for a treat in their turn, chop down the tree, capture the worms, and have a feast. The worms are eaten alive, starting with the head.

The most amazing story about the value of worms as food, however, was told by John Muir, the famous American naturalist of the last century.

The Mono Indians, who once lived on Mono Lake, in California, were very poor and very hungry. The lake was salt-laden and contained no fish, and there was little game nearby. Once upon a time the Monos had hunted the birds that nested on the islands of the lake, but they abandoned this pursuit after a violent storm caused many of the Indians to drown while returning from a bird hunt. Superstitiously, they regarded the storm as a warning and did not venture out on the lake again.

One of the items that became most prized in the Monos' diet was a little worm found in quantity along the margin of the lake. It was a great delicacy and, writes Muir, "when the worms are ripe, and the waves have collected them and drawn them up on the beach in rich, oily windrows, then old and young make haste to (collect) the curious harvest . . . ."

The worms were then stored and dried for the winter, and used as a "delicious dressing for other kinds of food—acorn mush, clover salad and grass-seed pudding."

So important did these worms become to the Indians that fierce tribal wars erupted over them. To stop the killing and keep the peace, a treaty was finally made between the warring factions, and boundaries for worm-gathering were marked out.

A few of the weaker tribes were ignored by the treaty and allowed no access to the beach at all. These Indians were then forced to procure their worm supply through barter with their stronger, worm-rich neighbors. Some Indians would actually trade their horses for a basket of little wet worms!

This Australian lad may be too young to fish, but he knows where to find an earthworm 4 feet long. Some Australian worms have been said to attain the near-fantastic length of 12 feet.

Wrestling

WEIGHTED DOWN

Tales of those whose greed has led them into disasters are not unusual, and athletes also figure in them. For instance, consider this case of the athlete who was carried to his death because of his love for gold.

Youssouf, the Terrible Turk, a professional wrestler, was so intent upon keeping the fortune he had made that it cost him his life. He was a huge, ugly man who weighed more than 300 pounds. He traded upon his unusual appearance to become one of Turkey's leading professional wrestlers.

Like most athletes from relatively poor countries, Youssouf recognized early in his career that he could not expect to make much money plying his muscular trade in his native country. To grow rich, he must seek the land of opportunity—the United States.

Therefore, once he had saved enough money to pay for his passage to America, Youssouf packed his meager wardrobe and took a cheap berth on a cattle boat. He was determined to return to Turkey with enough money to live like the proverbial king.

Once Youssouf landed in the new country, he had no trouble convincing wrestling promoters that his huge body and scowling face would make him an immediate drawing card with enthusiastic mat fans.

He was right. Soon arrangements for matches were flooding in and Youssouf was appearing night after night before capacity crowds.

However, the Terrible Turk was different from most of the wrestlers with which the promoters were accustomed to deal in setting up matches. For one thing, he had no manager since he refused to share his winnings. For another, Youssouf always demanded that he be paid in advance for his appearances, and that payment be made in gold. The scowling Turk refused to stir from his dressing room for a match until he had that gold in his hands. Then, behind locked doors, he would stuff it safely into an old, worn money belt that he constantly wore,

Turkish wrestlers oil their bodies before a match, and they often wrestle to the music of flutes.

even in the ring. Only after that would he lumber forth and go about his chore for the evening.

Despite his "crazy" demands, as most promoters labeled them, Youssouf was a big hit with the fans. Wherever and whenever he appeared, thousands turned out to watch him, and the demand for his name on wrestling cards continued to grow.

Then suddenly, at the height of his popularity, the Terrible Turk announced that he was quitting the ring forever and returning to his native land. No amount of arguing, no promises of more gold, could deter him. He had achieved his goal and now was heading home. He said farewell, booked passage on a tramp steamer, and left the United States.

Even on board ship, Youssouf continued to play his solitary role. He locked himself in his tiny cabin and came out only to take his meals. As soon as he had eaten his fill, he returned to his cabin and once more locked the door behind him.

This routine never varied. Then one night the ship steamed into a violent storm. The aging freighter pitched and tossed, wallowing in the heavy seas. Finally, its seams opened and water flooded its holds.

Within minutes the captain decided to abandon ship. He sent his junior officers to make the rounds of the cabins and warn passengers to prepare to take to the lifeboats. Soon, everyone was on deck. Everyone, that is, but the Terrible Turk.

Twice the captain sent stewards to warn Youssouf to hurry, but he did not appear. Finally, the ship's master had no choice but to order the lifeboats lowered, leaving the laggard wrestler still below decks.

Minutes after the last boat had cleared the ship, the huge form of the Turk appeared at the rail of the sinking ship. Occupants of the lifeboats spotted him and shouted for him to jump into the water. They would grab him and pull him to safety.

Still Youssouf hesitated. Then, at a shuddering lurch of the doomed ship, he made up his mind. He climbed on the rail and leaped into the stormy sea.

His rescuers headed toward him at once. But before any of the lifeboats could reach the floundering man, the weight of his bulging money belt, laden with gold, dragged him under. With his cries ringing in their ears, the horrified passengers watched Youssouf disappear beneath the angry waves.

The Terrible Turk had been pulled under by the weight of his closely guarded fortune.

Writers

ALICE LIDDELL'S FRIEND

In the winter of 1928, an old lady approached a London auctioneer and asked if he'd be interested in a manuscript which she wanted to sell. She needed money badly, and she'd been told old manuscripts brought good prices.

The man said that his company, Sotheby's, did accept manuscripts for auction but they had to be original and by famous authors.

This was an original manuscript, the old lady explained. It had been written and given to her when she was a very little girl. The man who wrote it was a friend of her family's. He had visited them one long-ago summer and, while their guest, had invented wonderful stories for her childish amusement.

The auctioneer took the manuscript and read the handwritten inscription: "A Christmas gift to a dear child . . . in memory of a summer's day."

The astonished austioneer read no further. He knew he held in his hand one of the great literary finds of all time . . . the manuscript of "Alice in Wonderland." It had been written by Lewis Carroll in 1865 for Alice Liddell, the little girl who was now an old woman.

Sotheby's did auction off that rare manuscript of "Alice in Wonderland." It was sold for a record $77,000.

Writers

O. HENRY

In 1882, a young teller working in an Austin, Texas, bank was charged with a shortage of funds. The man fled to Honduras but later returned to stand trial. He was convicted and sentenced to five years in prison for embezzlement.

The teller was troubled by a deep personal problem. He was a widower and the devoted father of an 8-year-old daughter named Margaret, and he did not want the child ever to know that he was a criminal.

The imprisoned man had left Margaret in the care of his dead wife's mother. He had prevailed upon the woman to tell the little girl that her father was away on a long, long business trip.

Then, to keep the child's memory of him alive during their long separation, the man began to send his little daughter a steady stream of letters containing fairy tales, bits of doggerel, and detailed plans of the journeys they would take when "business" allowed him to return home.

And so skillfully did that warmhearted father practice this touching deception that Margaret was a grown woman before she ever learned the truth of his imprisonment.

But by that time everyone knew his secret. For that man was William Sydney Porter, known the world over as the popular American author, O. Henry.

William Sydney Porter, known to the world as O. Henry.

THE BIRD OF PARADISE

In 1858, a daughter was born to a wealthy family in Sweden. But joy turned to sorrow a few years later when the little girl suffered a mysterious paralysis and could not walk.

The following summer, the family went to a resort on the Swedish coast and stayed at the home of a local sea captain. The captain was away, but his wife entertained the child with stories about her husband and his ship. What fascinated the little girl most was a description of a beautiful bird of paradise which was in the captain's cabin. The child grew to love the bird and eagerly awaited the return of the ship so that she might see it for herself.

The happy day finally arrived and the excited child was carried aboard the ship by her nurse, who placed the little girl on the deck and then went in search of the captain.

But the impatient child could not wait and, calling to a cabin boy, she asked to see the bird of paradise at once. The boy, not knowing she was crippled, offered to take her to the bird.

It was then that a miracle occurred. For so great was the desire of that paralyzed child to see the bird that she took the boy's hand and, slowly, walked to the cabin. From that day on, she was cured.

That child was Selma Lagerlof. She became Sweden's greatest writer and, in 1909, was the first woman ever to win the Nobel Prize for literature.

THE HANS BRINKER MONUMENT

In 1865, an American woman named Mary Mapes Dodge wrote a child's classic called "Hans Brinker or the Silver Skates." From this book, generations of Americans have grown up familiar with the story of the heroic little Dutch boy who, by putting his finger in the dike, saved his native city of Haarlem from being flooded.

Many of these Americans traveled to Holland to visit the ancient city on the North Sea and find the place where little Hans had held the dike. But in Haarlem they would be told the sad truth that Hans Brinker had lived only in the imagination of the author and that the Dutch had never even heard of him. He was purely an American legend.

But the legend persisted despite the facts. Americans would *not* let it die. They just kept turning up asking about Hans Brinker.

So the good people of Holland decided to do something about the matter.

Today, on the outskirts of Haarlem, you may see the delightful statue of a little boy holding his finger in a leaking dike. The statue bears the name and form of Hans Brinker, the mythical boy, but the Dutch have erected it to honor all the brave men and women who have worked—and died—to keep the dikes of Holland strong.

The Steamer trots smartly off in his first harness race.

Zebras

ZEBRA RACING

The only harness racing zebra in the world ran his first race at Pompano Park in Florida.

A 5-year-old gelding named The Stanleyville Steamer, the racing zebra hails from the man-made veldt at Busch Gardens, Tampa. His racing colors are the traditional stripes of black on white. Or are they white on black?

The Steamer was trained by veteran harness driver Jim Papon, who took up a friend's challenge that it couldn't be done, that it was impossible to train a zebra to do anything. So Papon went ahead and did the impossible. And he has the scars to prove it.

To get The Steamer broken to harness took lots of time, patience and agility to escape flying hooves. Zebras are not noted for their amiability and do not see themselves as friend or servant to man. The Steamer was no exception to the habits of his tribe and fought hard for his independence. Says a now-wiser Papon: "A zebra is the only animal I know who can kick all four legs at the same time and in different directions."

It took Papon two months to teach The Steamer to run at a trot. Another month and several broken carts later, he had the zebra harnessed and accustomed to the sulky rolling along behind him. Then followed three more months of intensive training, and The Steamer was finally ready for his first race.

The race was held as a special feature at Pompano Park's five-eighths-mile track. The Steamer was paired off against a standard-bred trotter named Cara Winn, a veteran harness horse who had been around so long that nothing could shake her. Not even the sight of the crazy in the striped pajamas unnerved her. The Steamer behaved himself, too.

The race turned out surprisingly well. With a little handicap to help him, and with trainer-driver Jim Papon in the sulky seat, The Steamer made a better-than-expected showing. He

The Stanleyville Steamer, the world's only racing zebra, with driver-trainer Jim Papon handling the sulky's reins.

was clocked at 1:42 as against Cara's winning 1:37, and he was faulted only once during the race. That was just before the wire when he made a stumble break. But he quickly regained his stride and came up to the finish at a fine regulation trotting gait.

That makes The Steamer the speediest of all harness racing zebras in the world—as well as, of course, the first and only one.

In the wild, the zebra's worst enemy is the lion—and, in this case, the lioness.

Index

443

444

446

Photographic Credits